ALSO BY OMAR SUTHERLAND

Musings of an Unlettered Faith
The Shaman of Second Avenue
Six Degrees of Saturation
When Shiva Laughed

RUSTLINGS
IN THE
DARK

Omar Sutherland

authorHOUSE®

AuthorHouse™
1663 Liberty Drive
Bloomington, IN 47403
www.authorhouse.com
Phone: 1 (800) 839-8640

Published by AuthorHouse 06/20/2018

ISBN: 978-1-5462-4333-5 (sc)
ISBN: 978-1-5462-4332-8 (e)

Library of Congress Control Number: 2018906053

Print information available on the last page.

This book is printed on acid-free paper.

For Kathye Bergin, Chet Frederick, and Mark Sanders.
I finally learned (most of) what you had to teach.

THE COMMISSION

By the time Timothy Lake died screaming, many of those who had counted him as a close friend for years would not willingly admit to ever having known him.

Even the psychiatric facility where he spent the last months of his life was an accomplice in the erasure of his existence. Within an hour of his death, his body had been removed from the facility and buried in an unknown grave, his file had been deleted from their system, and all handwritten notes taken on him had been burned. Every member of the staff was under strict orders to deny, under oath if necessary, that he had ever been a patient there. The other patients might speak of him, but their testimonies could be discounted easily enough.

These were all my explicit instructions, and I continue to believe I did what had to be done. I was the director of this facility at the time of Mr. Lake's confinement, but I resigned soon after. Nor do I believe I will ever return to the treatment of troubled minds. My own mind, I am certain, will never be untroubled again.

It is my fervent hope that the new director will continue to enforce the policy I implemented regarding Mr. Lake, but there is little hope of this. I know Dr. Salazar to be an eminently rational man, which ordinarily is indispensable in the practice of psychiatry. But in this particular case, it will doom him.

Given the choice, my emphatic preference would be to take the enigma of Timothy Lake to my own grave. But the fate of humanity requires I deny myself that choice. I signed off many times on the prescription of antipsychotic medications for patients who expressed similarly grandiose opinions of their own destinies, yet I insist there is no irony in my doing the same. For I *know* there are things that lurk at the threshold of this tiny reality, things that quietly work at the fragile minds and souls of humanity, seeking to unhinge them. When the door is unhinged, great and horrible *presences* may enter, and devour.

I know, too, that a form of insanity worse than any I have treated has gripped certain individuals, and that is why they search even now for Mr. Lake's last painting, and for the man—if man he was—who commissioned it. Neither must ever be found. That is why I must finally tell all I know of the matter. No doubt when you read this, you will call me mad, and worse. You will not offend me by doing so; quite the contrary. I was never a praying man before these events, but I have prayed long and earnestly to be allowed to lapse into the oblivion of madness.

We kept Mr. Lake medicated nearly to unconsciousness toward the end because for all our pretensions we did not know what else to do with him, yet I do not believe he was mad. Even when he raved and gibbered of elder gods, of a crawling chaos, of a goat with a thousand young...I believe he spoke, to the extent that he was capable, of the unspeakable—things he had seen that no one ought ever to see. He was unhinged, yes, but I know now that is not the same as insanity. He went looking for something, and it found him. It rent his mind asunder in order to make room for itself, and he screamed and howled and flailed day and night in a hopeless attempt to expunge it from him.

Almost to the very end, however, he retained moments of terrible lucidity. Therefore I have preserved a single copy of our interviews with him in order to distill them into this account, and when I have finished I will destroy them. Perhaps then I will destroy myself as well. I have spent my entire life in the eager pursuit of knowledge, only to discover there are some kinds of knowledge none may acquire and ever be right again.

Timothy Lake was an artist of local notoriety, who specialized (if that is the word) in grotesqueries. Sometimes he amused himself with depictions of satyrs, goblins, and other monsters from fable and myth, but what gave him the most pleasure was to take familiar scenes from Christian iconography and give them sacrilegious makeovers. Sabrina Lincoln, one of his college friends, owned a small gallery on Montrose Avenue in downtown Houston. She was the only one willing to display his portrait of the Virgin Mary as a white-furred gorilla with a look of beatific exaltation in its simian visage. Two days of vehement protests were not enough to convince her to remove it, but she capitulated after the city threatened her with severe penalties for violating its obscenity laws.

Unlike other artists known for controversial imagery, he did not pretend that he painted such pictures for any reason other than to spark outrage and vitriol. Indeed, he reveled in it. "At least they take me seriously enough to insult me" was a frequent boast of his.

A very few individuals expressed some measure of liking for his work, but none of them liked it enough to buy it, so he was obliged to eke out a living by doing "cheesework" as he called it—paintings of the sort that were mass-produced for postcards and motel rooms.

For a time his "real" work continued to attract sporadic attention, almost uniformly contemptuous, until the day it attracted a visitor to his studio.

Lake's studio was a shabby efficiency apartment in a complex frequented by prostitutes and drug dealers. So when he opened his door to a tall, silver-haired man who looked as if he could have posed in an advertisement for yachts or Rolexes, he made an excusable error and said, "Hey, man, if you're looking for one of your whores, there ain't nobody in here but me."

"I assure you, Mr. Lake," said the stranger, "I am not seeking the company of a woman. I have come to see you."

"Uh...thanks, guy, but I don't swing that way." He started to close the door, but the stranger shot out an arm and blocked it.

"I have come to commission a painting from you, Mr. Lake."

"Uh...yeah. Yeah. Sure." Lake stepped back from the door. "Uh, come in. Can I get you something to drink or—"

"My time is short, Mr. Lake. I wish to come straight to the point. The Nazarene once gave his followers a so-called Great Commission. I now give you a greater one. You shall paint a portrait of the Void, and of the Gate that opens upon it, through which the worthy may gaze upon ultimate knowledge. When you have completed this task to my satisfaction, I will pay you five thousand dollars."

The stranger's diction was precise, and he had a slight accent that was difficult to place. What Lake found equally difficult to place was his instinctive aversion to the man. Not only did his visitor look handsome enough to get any woman he wanted, but he carried himself in a way that implied wealth—enough to set up a struggling artist in their own gallery, if their work pleased him. Yet Lake felt a compelling need to keep him at a distance. He backed up several paces while considering the offer, and hoped the stranger would not notice.

He himself scarcely noticed he was doing this. Whatever it was about the stranger's appearance, his head was spinning from the stranger's words, especially his last three words.

"Okay, um...I mean, yeah, I can do something like that, no problem. But it sounds like you want something specific, so have you got a sketch I can work from, or maybe you can describe exactly what you have in mind?"

Lake had not noticed that the stranger carried a large book under his arm until he placed it on the floor in front of him and said, "This book will reveal to you all that you need to know. I will return in one week to collect the finished painting."

"One—hey, wait! Hang on a min—"

But the man walked out without looking back and shut the door behind him, leaving Lake to try to make sense of what had just happened.

One week, the man said. Lake had never worked on deadline before. But then, he had never been offered a commission before. And $5000 was more than enough to quiet his misgivings about accepting this one. As he expressed it, money from a weirdo was still money.

However, there was that peculiar remark about "the Nazarene." Obviously, it was a reference to Jesus Christ. But did it mean he was supposed to paint a religious picture? The stranger knew Lake's name, where he lived, and that he was a painter, so it followed that he knew what kinds of images he liked to paint. Perhaps, though, this did not bother him. Anyone who would casually say that his commission was greater than the Great Commission of the Gospels was unlikely to have religious sensibilities that were easily offended.

That book on the floor was supposed to tell him everything he needed to know. The stranger had left it there and walked out, as if he had shared Lake's distaste for close proximity. Lake was not sure why that should be, since he happened to have showered that day, but he supposed it was irrelevant.

Probably the book had a picture of what he was supposed to paint. He picked it up and opened it to a page at random, intending to rifle through it until he found something that looked promising, even if it was only a dog-eared page or an underlined passage.

The writing was like nothing he had ever seen. It vaguely resembled Hebrew or Arabic characters, but it somehow seemed far older than even those ancient languages. The entire book, in fact, reeked of great antiquity, which for some reason made him uneasy. He had been around old books before, and books he could not understand were nothing new, but this one…

Then something happened that made him fling the book against a wall and scutter away from it. But too late.

The inside air was still, yet the pages turned rapidly, as if caught in a strong wind or as if an invisible hand flipped through them. As each pair of pages was separated, the lettering on them—he swears this is exactly how it happened, and I am no longer inclined to argue— crawled off the pages and into his fingertips, and moved quickly up his hands and arms, toward his brain. This happened in a split-second, and the effect of it, what he felt, was something I had seen many times. One of the symptoms of cocaine intoxication is fomication, in which the addict believes insects are crawling and burrowing just under his skin. Lake's skin buzzed and tingled, and his brain began to burn. The police later found a peculiar grayish dust scattered on the floor of his apartment, and so I assumed at first that the story he related to his doctors was nothing more than the byproduct of experimentation with some powerful hallucinogenic drug or cocktail of drugs.

He regained consciousness an unknown time later, but he could see through his window that the sun was still up, and the light was not appreciably different. He sat up, trying to focus his eyes and his thoughts, and his gaze fell on the accursed book, still in the corner where he had thrown it. He scrambled to his feet and backed away from it, and started to look around for some implement with which he could get rid of it. Fireplace tongs would have been ideal, but fireplaces are not essential amenities in Houston apartments.

Suddenly, as he looked, he knew.

Not how to get rid of the book. The book had been driven from his mind, a circumstance unimaginable a moment earlier.

He now knew precisely—*precisely*—what the stranger wanted him to paint, and how to paint it. Had he known sooner, he would have been forced to admit that such a painting would have required vastly greater skill than his own. But now he had the skill. He knew it. Frantically he gathered his easel, canvas, brushes and paints, and set to work. It was necessary to employ a wholly unfamiliar technique of mixing the enamels, one he'd never tried or even heard of, but he did it without faltering.

When the paints were ready, he dipped his brushes and began. He did not stop for meals, and ignored the fatigue that encroached upon him as he worked feverishly through the night. Finally he simply could not stay awake any longer, and trudged to his pallet on the floor.

The dreams came at once. He was standing at the Gateway, staring into the Void, letting his mind range where his body could not. There were things that lived in the Void, inconceivably ancient and malignant things, but he did not fear them. He felt a strange kind of kinship with them and sought them out. They conversed with him of primordial secrets and forbidden knowledge, of a kind of enlightenment qualitatively different from any preached by the limited, prosaic religions of Earth.

When he awoke, he was not entirely surprised to find himself at his easel. He had resumed work while he was asleep, or believed himself to be asleep. His eyes were red and itchy, and he could not stop yawning, but neither could he stop painting.

He worked in a trance all that day. Again he did not eat, and he ignored the rumblings of his stomach as he ignored the occasional rings of his phone. The sun arced across the sky, unnoticed by him. Evening was well advanced when he was finished. He took a slice of takeout pizza from his refrigerator, ate it, and went to sleep. This time, if he had dreams, he did not remember them.

It was late in the morning when he woke up, bleary and exhausted but oddly exhilarated. He staggered out of bed and went to look at his painting, and could scarcely believe it was his work. It was orders of magnitude better than anything he had ever done, but whatever skill had bewitched him these last two days had vanished. He stared at his work, marveling at it, and he knew he could not paint another such picture, or one even half as good, if his life depended on it.

His canvas depicted a desert of rough, grayish sand under a sky that was the blue of twilight. Looming above the sand was a portal of crumbling stone. The portal was adorned with no ritualistic symbols of any kind, but the viewer could tell that it was a sacred thing, and also that it was old. Older than Stonehenge, older than the pyramids, older than the Lescaux cave paintings...older than the human race. Who constructed it, how long ago, and for what purpose, were questions not to be asked. All of this was conveyed in the strokes and mottlings Lake had used to depict the aperture.

The horizontal slab at the top was connected to the two vertical ones by shorter slabs that tilted at 45-degree angles. There was little in the foreground to convey a sense of scale, but in terms of simple physical size, the structure appeared to be a humble one. If it were not sunk into the ground, four men might have carried it over the ashen waste.

What lay beyond the portal was the clear focus of the painting. For it opened, not onto more desert, but onto interstellar space—a part of space no astronomer had ever seen or would ever wish to see.

Beginning at the entrance was a pathway consisting of densely packed stars, the analog of a lonely stretch of highway. This "road" led to an object that had the shape of a spiral galaxy, except that its arms snagged everything within reach as they turned. This arm drew filaments of plasma from a luminescent cloud; that one caught a lone planetoid in its gaseous embrace.

At the very center of this spiral monstrosity, the vanishing point of the stellar highway—and of everything else—lay a perfect circle of blackness. This was not merely empty space. This was the Void.

Lake shook his head, wondering how any brush wielded by his clumsy fingers could have produced this minutely detailed masterwork. Then, out of the corner of his eye, he noticed something else. Rather, he noticed the absence of something that ought to have been there.

The strange book was gone. In the corner where it had been was a small pile of dust. It was not the kind of dust that covered every flat surface in his apartment, but it resembled the dust of his landscape. Did this wasteland actually exist, and had he been drawn there in his sleep...?

No, he saw now what this dust was. It was the remains of the book. What instantly occurred to him was that it only needed to maintain its form until he completed the painting that it gave him the wherewithal to create. Perhaps it needed to keep an eye on him until he discharged his commission, and once its task was done, it disintegrated.

He was too tired and disoriented to wonder that he could entertain such thoughts about a book. What mattered now was that he had completed the task he was given. But the stranger would come back in five days for the painting. What if he didn't like it? Lake was unable to fathom why he would not, but he was also acutely aware that no artist is capable of being objective about his or her own work.

What he needed was a fresh pair of eyes, and he trusted Sabrina Lincoln's more than anyone else's. He called and told her that someone came to visit him with a commission, he finished the painting in a white heat, but he was too close to it to know if it was any good. She understood perfectly and told him she would be over within the hour.

She told him also that some of his friends were worried about him, since they had not been able to reach him. He dimly remembered his phone ringing at intermittent intervals while he'd been painting, but the sound had been an abstract thing, unworthy of response.

He opened the door to her knock. The painting was the first thing her eyes fell upon. She walked directly to it and stared at it, her mouth hanging open, for five full minutes.

Finally she tore her eyes from the canvas and fastened them on him. "*You* painted this?"

He had sense enough not to be insulted. She had seen too much of his other work.

"Wild, huh?" he agreed. "But yeah, I did. I just knew what to do."

"How?"

He had not mentioned the book over the phone. Now he told her everything, including his dreams on that first night.

"Wild, huh?" he said again.

Lincoln looked again at the painting. "That's not just wild. That's bad medicine. But bad medicine never stopped me from showing new work."

Lake had disclosed that she, too, was not unfamiliar with psychotropic substances. These would have dulled in her the apprehensions of the unknown that are instinctive to human beings.

"So you really think it's good?" He knew she did, but needed to hear her say it.

"Tim, this isn't just good. It's incredible. Probably one of the best new works in any form I've seen in years. I'm going to take it with me and display it front and center until that guy comes to pick it up. But I think we should keep it our little secret about who painted it."

Lake laughed. "No doubt. Nobody would believe it, and if they did, they'd picket your gallery on general principles."

"So he just told you to paint the void?"

"And the gateway that leads to it, yeah. Something about ultimate knowledge too, but I didn't process that part."

"The Void." She rolled the word on her tongue. "Well, I can't think of a better title for this, can you?"

"For $5000 and a five-day place-of-honor exhibition? You can call it 'Invasion of the Crouton People' for all I care."

"You know, that's not a bad idea. With a title that abstract, some grad student might decide to write their thesis on it. But now I'm wondering," she went on, her eyes still glued to the canvas, "what you could've come up with if you'd been offered *ten* thousand dollars."

"Nice thing to wonder," he said, "but I can't shake the feeling this'll be the last commission I ever do."

Lincoln gave him a puzzled look but did not pursue the subject.

By the following evening, the Montrose art community was buzzing about "The Void" and its anonymous painter. Lincoln was approached with offers to purchase the work. Some of these offers were higher than the amount Lake had been promised, but he remembered his impressions of the man who commissioned the painting, and he believed that to renege on their arrangement would be exceedingly unwise. The stranger knew where Lake lived, after all, and he probably knew about Lincoln's gallery; and if he had a book with letters that could flow off the page and possess someone, it did not bear considering what else he might have.

For the first time Lake regretted the scandalous reputation he had so gleefully cultivated. Because of it he was unable to attend his own opening. People would recognize him and assume he was only there to cause trouble, perhaps even to try to deface a painting that represented the kind of true ability a dabbler like him could only dream of having.

Therefore he had to wait until the gallery closed before he could come and listen to Lincoln's account of what a great success it was.

"One lady offered me twenty grand for it!" she exclaimed. "Can you imagine? Most people I hang with don't make that in a year! You know what? When that guy comes back to your place to get the painting, you should tell him it's here, and I've been exhibiting it. Tell him what kind of offers it's gotten, you know, bring him here to see it. Maybe we can get him to give you more money."

"Unlikely, Miss Lincoln."

They spun around. The stranger was right behind them. Until that moment, neither had had the slightest idea he was there. That would have been disconcerting enough.

"How...how did you get in here?" Lincoln asked. "The door was locked!"

The stranger smiled. "There are other kinds of doors, Miss Lincoln."

They did not know what he meant by that and decided not to ask. The stranger came forward to inspect the fruit of Lake's work. He walked by Lake, grabbed his arm in a talon like grip, and pulled him forward with him.

"Ow! Hey! That hurts!"

"Let him go, you jerk!" Lincoln moved to intervene. Without looking at her, the stranger made a curious motion with his other hand and she slumped insensate to the floor. Lake tried to break free and go to her, but the thin fingers held his arm with irresistible strength.

"Look at it. Look at it!" the stranger commanded, when Lake did not obey at once. He looked.

"What an amusing boy you are," he went on. "You use your feeble skill to create amateurish representations of long-dead people in the forms of beasts, and you think you know what it means to blaspheme your paltry religions."

He released Lake's arm and moved to stand behind him, but Lake was still unable to move. The painting and the stranger's words held him mesmerized.

"A true religion once held sway over all that is, Mr. Lake. The first and only true religion. And its time is again at hand. It chose you precisely because you are so unworthy to know it, yet see how it spoke through you! That is the smallest part of the measure of its greatness. You believe your puling Protestant god to be the sum and substance of creation. One of the names your holy book appends to him is the All. Very well. Let this god think himself thus, while he is able. But the real meaning of blasphemy—in which you take such conspicuous delight but of which you have so little understanding—is to reject the All. Before you can reject the All, you must know the All. Before you can know the All, you must know the Nothing!"

On the word *nothing*, he grabbed Lake's head between his hands and thrust it forward until his nose nearly brushed the canvas. He was looking directly at the blackness in the center, but he could still see some of the design around it.

And then he could not. Everything vanished—the painting, Lincoln, the gallery. All was darkness. All was the Nothing. But within this Nothing was everything. All that came before, all that would come again. The deathless knowledge of hideously remote epochs, things of which history's greatest mystics and madmen could do no more than hint in cryptic snatches of half-fabulous lore. Things that came to him in whispers in his dreams, the night after he began the greatest and last thing he would ever paint.

That knowledge was his now. His mind was of the Void. Infinite. Empty.

He had a vague memory of wanting to scream, but being able only to express the mockery of his existence in a long, piteous moan. The next thing he remembered after that was waking up in his apartment. It was day, but which day, he had no idea.

He lay on his pallet, awake but too terrified to move, for an indeterminate period. Then he remembered what had happened to

Lincoln and fumbled about for his phone. It was in his pocket, but his hand closed on something much bigger. He knew what it was before he pulled it out.

Enclosed in his trembling fingers was a thick sheaf of hundred-dollar bills. He did not need to count them to know this was the $5000 the stranger had promised for the painting. He threw it aside like the blood money—or worse—that it was, pulled out his phone, and called Lincoln six times in succession. Five of those times, he left messages imploring her to call back and tell him she was all right. After the sixth time, he lurched out the door and started for the gallery.

Along the way he passed a small crowd of people who had gathered to while away part of a Saturday morning listening to a street preacher. Normally Lake ignored these spectacles and would have done so this time, but he happened to pass by just as the minister quoted this verse of Scripture: "For he is all, and is in all."

That was when, according to his statements to the doctors and the police, he lost whatever grip he still retained on his sanity. It felt to him as if some alien agency entered and assumed control of his body, carried him through the crowd to the bewildered preacher, opened his mouth, and made him yell out: "Fool! Think you that you know whereof you speak? The creation of thy God is naught but a mote of dust that shall be swept away on the chill winds that ever blow from the domain of Chaos! Bear thou witness, foolish minion of Jehovah! The gods of Shadow and Nightmare come again, and all shall know the Void that is Their cloak! Iä! Shub-Niggurath! The Father of Serpents will spawn—"

He now had the minister by the collar and was screaming these words into his face. Two security guards wrestled him to the ground and took him away, to the displeasure of some of the spectators, who averred that his tirade was far more entertaining than the sermon it had so dramatically interrupted.

Reverend James Maynall testified that he'd had ten years frightened off his life, but the venerable man of the cloth refused to press charges. "You tell that boy me and my church'll be praying for him," he said to the judge. "We'll be doing all *kinds* of praying for him."

In an interview I conducted with Mr. Lake shortly after he was remanded to psychiatric custody, he explained that Shub-Niggurath is the name of one of the gods of the primal mythology that the painting, the strange book, and his erstwhile patron all somehow represented. What this deity's purported nature and role are, he could not be induced to say. One more happenstance not in his favor was the fact that Reverend Maynall is African-American, and the pronunciation of 'Niggurath' is similar to that of a certain racial epithet.

When I asked him whether "Iä", in this ancient belief system, was an affirmation, something like "Amen" as it is shouted in tent revival meetings, he gave me a smile I did not at all care for and said, "Yes. *Something* like that."

There the matter might have rested (though I doubt it), had professional curiosity not impelled me to do what he asked repeatedly to be allowed to do, which was to check on the well-being of Sabrina Lincoln. Taped to the front door of her gallery was a sign that read "Closed Until Further Notice", but I looked through the glass doors at the spot where the painting ought to have been. That section of the wall was blank, but I fancied that I saw a corner of the painting on the floor, where someone had attempted to hide it from the view of any curious passersby.

A few minutes with the captain of the local police precinct gained me Lincoln's home address, and it was there that she told me her story.

"I don't know what to do with it," she confessed in a terrified whisper. "I want to throw it away, but as beautiful as it is, if somebody saw it in the dumpster, they'd probably fish it out and take it home. It's got something in it—a demon, or whatever you want to call it, but it's something that wants to be seen by lots of people. That's why I didn't want to leave it up on the wall. I should just burn it, is what I should do, but I'm scared to touch it again. I know, I shouldn't say something that nutty to a shrink, but that's the long and short of it."

"Whatever it is about this painting," I said, "clearly it's had a deleterious effect on the mental stability of Mr. Lake, and on your own equilibrium. He is now in our charge, as you know, and he's dangerously ill. Setting aside for the moment this mysterious stranger, the book he supposedly had in his possession, and everything else related to this painting, I don't believe the painting itself is anything more than it appears to be, but it is at the center of his delusions. If there is a chance that news of its destruction will facilitate his recovery—"

"I'll swear to that, Doc," she said at once. "It'll sure be a load off my mind."

I nodded, in a way I hoped would make her believe I knew what I was doing. "Very well. Is it still in your gallery?"

"Yeah. I had to get it off the wall, but like I said, after that I didn't want to touch the thing again."

A few minutes later I stood with her in an unlighted hallway of her gallery, seeing the dreaded painting myself for the first time. I did feel a peculiar urge to look long and closely at the black circle at its center, but this I dismissed as a vestige of the shared hypnosis that had caused Miss Lincoln to share Lake's unreasoning terror of what he himself painted.

We had each brought a bottle of lighter fluid, and we poured them out liberally over the canvas. The walls and floor were bare concrete, and there was nothing anywhere near us that might ignite if touched by a floating spark.

I struck a match, dropped it onto the canvas, and watched as the lighter fluid burst into flame—*flame that did not harm the painting.* We saw it through the haze of fire and smoke, and saw that it would not burn. The colors remained clear and distinct.

"Whoa," she said, and bent down to peer at the impossible sight. She leaned over far enough that her long hair could easily have caught fire, but she was heedless of the danger.

I moved closer, to pull her clear...and something else moved.

Psychiatrists are trained to dispute, ignore, and rationalize the evidence of their eyes if that evidence contravenes every known law of physics, and I said nothing of what happened next in the official interviews I gave regarding Mr. Lake. But I remember to the last detail what I could not possibly have seen, yet saw all the same.

The tendrils of the spiroform entity surrounding the black space rose up from the surface of the painting, more and less substantial than wisps of smoke. They sought out Miss Lincoln, caressed her face and upper body in an obscene parody of affection, then swirled over her, pulled her down as if they had become lengths of cable...they pulled her down, I say, to the painting, and then *into* the painting. The manner of her absorption is impossible to describe, but I may say that it was similar to watching a swimmer vanish beneath the surface of a body of black water, opaque as tar, of small circumference but great depth.

The tendrils then resumed their painted forms, but rotated a moment longer around the black center, compelling me once more to look into that font of darkness. To look, and to *know*.

I clamped my eyes shut, lurched from that canvas of horrors, and scrambled out of the haunted gallery into the wholesome sunlight of the normal world. I would not open my eyes again until I was almost to the doors, and in my mad flight I knocked something over and heard it shatter, but I neither know nor care what it was. The gallery was shuttered, though it has since reopened under another name. Sabrina Lincoln was never seen or heard of again.

I need not tell you that Lake heard none of this from me, but there were news reports of the fire of suspicious origin that may or may not have claimed Lincoln's life but left no remains to identify and seemed to have burned out only minutes after it started. Anyone who may have seen me exit the gallery was apparently unable to provide an exact description of my appearance to the police. In any case— thank whatever benevolent gods there may be—I have not yet been questioned about the fire.

Some of the staff members, however, may have carelessly discussed some of the known particulars and frenetic speculation within Lake's hearing. Whatever the reason, afterward he became progressively more unmanageable until we were forced to keep him permanently confined in the Quiet Room for the safety of the staff and the other patients. It was there that, some weeks later, he shouted, "They come! The arms of Shub-Niggurath come to embrace me! Iä! Iä! The Void is all, and I am the Void!" He then gave a bloodcurdling scream and breathed his last.

When the police went to the gallery to investigate, they found no sign of the painting, nor have they ever located the man who commissioned it. What happened to Sabrina Lincoln and Timothy Lake in connection with the painting has been a subject of the wildest conjectures, and I can only hope this testament will convince the reader that certain mysteries ought never to be solved, though I am fully aware that for some it is likely to have the opposite effect.

I will leave these papers on my desk so they will be among the first things discovered by the authorities. Only in death shall I pass beyond the reach of the questing tendrils. By this knowledge I am comforted.

For the Void hungers, and can never be sated.

LONELY HEARTS CLUB

Before I get into how I ended up in this sticky situation (pardon the pun, which you'll understand later), I suppose I should tell you a little bit about myself. Not that you care—I certainly wouldn't—but it's always much more difficult to comprehend that which follows without at least making the acquaintance of that which came before. That was how my history professor put it, anyway, and I only remember that because it was one of the few things he ever said that I both understood and liked the sound of.

I won't bore you with the mundane details, like what my name is or where I grew up or what my sign is. If you've been watching the news, you know those things anyway, and if you haven't, good for you. Life's too short to waste listening to talking heads who get paid to make everybody else feel as stupid as they sound. I wasn't kidding about my sign being on the news. *20/20*, or one of those shows, interviewed an astrologer who swore she could work up a psychological profile on me based on my birthday. So I watched, and I found that maybe eighty-five percent of what she said was accurate. That sounds pretty impressive unless you watched the interview too, in which case you know that maybe seventy percent of what she said could describe just about everyone on the planet. This is what America thinks is news. And we wonder why the rest of the world thinks we're morons.

Sorry. I go off on rants sometimes. But my court-appointed therapist says that's healthy. She says it's my mind's way of assimilating my conflicting feelings and convoluted self-image as part of progressing toward a state of wholeness and awareness of being.

She says a lot of other hogwash too.

For a lot of reasons, none of them important, I am a confirmed bachelor. I've just never bought into the whole soulmate thing, that jazz about how there's someone for everyone. But there have always been people who have made fortunes off the saps who believe it, with all the dating websites now and the personal ads before those and the village matchmakers before those.

There is one thing I've come to understand, however. One overriding principle, without which "until death do us part" remains either a pipe dream or a relic from the days of arranged marriages. Before two people can have any hope of living together without driving each other wiggy, they each have to know how the other person thinks, to remember the likes and dislikes they know and be able to anticipate the ones they don't know. In other words, they each have to agree to get inside the other's head to some extent. (Not bad, huh? And I don't even watch Dr. Phil.)

But there's my problem, you see. Or at least it's what a lot of psychologists and social workers who ought to mind their own business tell me is my problem. Inside my head is not a place most people want to be.

Which is how I found myself in another place most people don't want to be.

In case you haven't yet cracked my ingenious code, yeah, I'm in jail. My lawyer has advised me not to say any more than that, but seeing as I'm in here, I've decided his advice really isn't worth following.

This is the inside story for anyone who might be interested, or at any rate, as much of it as I can remember. There were times when my brain got a little fevered. All the details of what I did are in there, it's just that some of them have kind of melted and run together like wax from burning candles. It's easier to remember the headlines that blared the same things over and over: dropped out of college two months before graduation, spent weeks living in an abandoned house, savagely butchered eighteen people, yada yada yada. If anything, this is an exercise to keep myself centered, to keep from believing my own publicity. And before I start this saga, let's be clear. I'm not doing this with any hope or expectation of changing anyone's mind about me. I'm not looking for pity or sympathy or understanding or redemption. Frankly, I don't even care if you believe that or not. The last-minute phone call from the governor is the stuff of late-night movies on the nostalgia channel anyway. I didn't even vote for the schmuck.

Flannery O'Connor said "I write so that I know what I'm thinking," and I guess that sums it up as well as anything. I always knew exactly what I was doing and why, but maybe if I have it all written down in front of me, I might be able to figure out why so many people think I'm crazy.

So, as God might have said when He spoke the universe into existence, here goes nothing.

I still remember what she looked like, right down to the birthmark on her neck that looked like a botched hickey. She was one of the bridesmaids at my cousin's wedding, the only one of them not making a mighty effort to get stinking drunk off the cheap champagne my uncle had to be badgered into buying. That alone made her worth talking to. Well, that and the fact that she didn't seem to have a date.

She was sitting far enough away that I could watch her without her knowing. Before long I picked up her pattern. She went to the buffet table, put a little food on her plate, took it back to her table, ate it, then went back for a little more. I assumed she did this so she wouldn't be in one place long enough for any of the cut-rate Casanovas roaming the banquet hall to zero in on her. In fact I knew that was why she did it, just as surely as if she had told me. Don't ask me to explain that. Just know it's the truth.

When she got up, I counted to five and stood up too. Luckily I was seated close to the buffet table and she was at the other end of the hall, so I "happened" to get there at the same time she did. I got right behind her and made my way down the table at a matching clip. The trick was to wait and start a conversation right before she left, so it would sound as natural and spontaneous as I could manage.

"So," I said, thinking a witty icebreaker was in order, "you're at my cousin's wedding. Did you lose a bet too?"

Her response wasn't a full-out guffaw or a politely forced chuckle. It was a perfectly audible laugh, which was the best I could have expected. No, she said, her roommate was a friend of the sister of the bride, or something like that. The roommate burst in one night and told her they were going to be bridesmaids, wasn't that cool, and she didn't have anything else to do and didn't have time to think of a good enough excuse, so here she was.

"My condolences," I said, and she smiled. Two for two. Might as well go for a triple.

"What's your name?" I asked.

"Gail," she said, transferring her plate to her left hand and jutting out her right. I pumped it twice, held the grip for another third of a second, give or take, and let go. I've calculated that as the formula for the handshake that maximizes sincerity and minimizes imposition. "And yours?"

"David. That looks like a good selection," I said, referring to the two slices of turkey, two deviled eggs, and three sprigs of broccoli she had put on her plate. Always the same things, only the quantities varied slightly from trip to trip. From this I got the vibe of her. She wasn't necessarily against trying new things, but once she found something that worked for her, she stuck with it until she had her fill of it. Predictable, though not to a fault. Probably not boring, but not impulsive either. Those kinds of things are always useful to know about a person.

"Oh, thanks," she said.

"Comfort food?" I asked.

She looked up. "How did you know?"

There. The hook had been baited and the fish snagged. When I was a child, my father spent a few Saturdays trying to interest me in fishing before he mercifully gave up. The one thing he said about it that I remember was that you couldn't reel a fish in too fast or it might slip off the hook. You had to finesse and tease it, bring it in little by little, so it doesn't know where it's going until it can't get back. I brought that lesson into play now. Instead of answering her question I said, "I'm sorry, I didn't mean to pry."

"No, no, it's okay," she said. "I mean, you weren't prying. You just surprised me, that's all."

"Would you like to talk about it?" I asked.

She gave me kind of a funny look. "Are you a psychiatrist?"

"No, psychiatrists are the fun doctors. They're the ones who can prescribe pills."

That made her laugh so hard she almost spilled her food. A few people glanced over to see what was so funny, saw us, decided it couldn't be anything they were interested in, and went back to their own idiotic conversations.

I couldn't speak for her, not then, but I've always been that kind of person. The one you don't notice when he's standing next to you in a crowded place, the one your eyes slide over if he's standing between you and something you're looking at, the one you work with, never talk to, don't know much about, and probably couldn't pick out of a police lineup. The kind of guy everybody knows and most people don't know they know, because their impressions aren't strong enough to leave any kind of afterimage. I've always been that kind of person. It's always come in handy.

"So you're the other one?" she asked, still smiling. "Psychologist?"

"I don't like to advertise. Unless I'm trolling for new patients."

This time she couldn't catch herself and it was food overboard. I bent down with her to pick it up and walked with her to the trash can. Her reaction was flattering, but it was a shame, too. Those were the last two deviled eggs, and I'd hoped to cadge one of them.

"You know what?" I said. "That was my fault, so I'll get you another plate." I was already starting back to the table.

"No, please," she said, laying a hand lightly on my forearm. Tactile stimulus is a woman's default medium, used to communicate interest, desire, empathy, or sorrow. Fortunately I was able to keep from flinching at the contact, and she didn't seem to notice I had stiffened slightly, because she was still talking. "Actually, you did me a favor. I think I've had enough to eat anyway."

That was my opening. I seized it. "Then would you like to sit and talk?"

"Sure," she said.

She walked with me back to my table, which was otherwise empty. I considered, not for the first time in my life, how fortunate it was that I was the kind of person nobody sat at a table with if they had a choice. In my surreptitious observations of her actions and interactions over the last hour or so, I had seen that she was both well-spoken and soft-spoken, unfailingly kind and gentle in rebuffing the advances of would-be suitors or dance partners no matter how drunken and loutish they were. So I had worked up in my head the beginnings of a psychological profile on her. She was a loner by circumstance rather than preference, but would neither actively seek out the attentions of a man nor accept the attentions of just any man. Both these actions signified desperation and lack of taste. Her chosen partner would pursue her without being obvious or hasty about it, because he prized civility and manners above all else in any kind of relationship.

From this assessment I deduced that she would appreciate a gentlemanly gesture, and so I held a chair out for her. She proved me correct by smiling warmly, saying "Thank you," and accepting it.

I sat next to her and we began the ritual exchange of life stories. She was twenty-four, had a master's degree in chemistry from Wellesley College, was a high-school teacher because she loved to teach, and had had two serious relationships, one of which had ended amicably and the other with a restraining order. She spent most of her spare time reading. Her favorite writer was John D. MacDonald, but depending on her mood, just about any author would do. An occasional guilty pleasure was reading those so-called autobiographies, which she doubted the people who supposedly wrote them even read.

"Okay, now that I've bored you to tears, what about you?"

I smiled, at least I'm fairly certain I did, and rattled off my *curricula vitae*. My name was David, as I had said. I was a student at Boston University, and I was trying to snow the faculty into giving me a bachelor's in psychology. (She actually threw her head back and laughed, if you can imagine it.) I had wasted much of my first two years in college in a series of foolish and meaningless flings, and while I wasn't looking for anything serious, I wouldn't object too strongly if it found me. I loved to watch old movies. Bogart, Olivier, Hepburn, that crowd.

She listened so attentively to my story that for a moment I was tempted to regret that hardly a word of it was true. I chastised myself for that moment. How many articles had I read on relationship websites that insisted on the importance of preserving the mystery at the beginning of a relationship for as long as possible, because the other person finds you more interesting if they have to work to get to know you? Obviously they shouldn't have to work so hard that they decide it's not worth the effort, but neither should it be so easy that the knowledge is no challenge to obtain and of no interest once gained. As in all things, a balance must be struck.

Besides, the life I had related to her, whomever it might belong to, clearly fascinated her. She asked me many questions about my college experience, about my favorite movies and actors and actresses, and what qualities I looked for in a woman. She even wanted to know about my flings. Not in organic detail, of course, but reminiscences. That surprised me. I've always heard that while a woman could technically accept that a man had had a life before he met her, she never wanted to hear anything about it.

To this day I couldn't tell you where my answers came from, but come they did. I, who normally could not sustain even the smallest of small talk, was holding this woman enthralled until some of the guests, unnoticed by her, began to leave. To employ a sports metaphor, I was in the zone.

We talked on and on, until the hall was nearly empty. The custodian stood by the door and stared at us, trolley in one hand and doorknob in the other. Reluctantly I stood up, she did the same, and we walked out. The custodian didn't say a word, but he slammed the door behind us. That said it all.

I asked Gail if she would like to continue our conversation the next day. She said she would love to, rummaged through her purse, produced a scrap of paper, wrote her phone number on it, and handed it to me. Then we said our goodbyes, went to our cars, and drove away.

But I didn't go home. Not yet. There were scenes to be drafted and a stage to be set. The second act of the performance would soon begin.

We decided to forego the traditional dinner and a movie in favor of a late picnic lunch in the middle of the wooded area behind the houses on Homer Street. This was the part of Newton where I would one day have my counseling practice. That's what I remember telling her, at any rate.

After we ate, we went for a walk. We had gone a few hundred yards when, without a word, she took my hand. I looked at her, and she gave me a shy smile. I answered it with what I hoped was a reassuring smile, and squeezed her hand with what I surmised was just enough force to make her feel "companionably intimate," or however Cosmopolitan had put it. That was one of the few pieces of advice they offered on interacting with women that didn't assume you were with the sort of woman that doesn't exist outside of porn.

I asked her to tell me about the relationship she had pleasant memories of. As I expected, I didn't have to coax her. She chattered on for maybe half an hour, and I made sure to nod in all the appropriate places to give the impression I was listening. It was only when she described how she had felt about him, how much she had loved him, that I went into receptor mode. I can only do this for brief periods, so my timing had to be just right. If my experiment was to be successful, it was crucial that I absorb what I could of her emotional state at this particular time.

Then, as I knew they would, the memories of the breakup came, and with them the emotions of sorrow and regret. Fortunately I was no longer in receptor mode, but I could see them: smoky, dark gray tendrils that writhed inside her like serpents—no, like small boa constrictors, attracted to the center of her life essence like sharks to blood in the water, trying to squeeze, slow, and ultimately stop the beating engine of her heart.

I saw them and I knew the time had come.

I pulled her close and hugged her. She was caught off guard and did not reciprocate immediately, but then wrapped her arms tightly around me and started to cry softly into my shoulder. I stroked her back, which I had learned from those movies on the Lifetime channel was the expected gesture of commiseration, and focused on the pressure on my own back. When it started to slacken, I would know she was relaxed enough.

After thirteen seconds it did. I masked my relief by pulling back just enough to take her face between my hands and tilt it up so that I was looking directly at her. I leaned in close, predicting that she would think I was going to kiss her and would close her eyes, which she did. Now.

I rotated my hands ninety degrees, so that I was cupping her chin in one hand and cradling the back of her head with the other. Before she could open her eyes, I snapped her neck.

24

I caught her before she could fall to the ground, carried her back to my car, placed her upright in the passenger seat, and sped off as fast as I could risk without getting pulled over. There was no time to lose. Soon all trace of this love that had warmed her heart would leave her cooling body, and I would lose it forever.

Luckily my home was not far away. I was eager to introduce her to her new family.

I lived in an off-campus ILG (independent living group, not a fraternity house but a lot more like one than most people who live in them care to admit) with seventeen other students. I parked in the alley that ran behind the house, opened the gate leading to the back yard, put her arm around my shoulders and mine around her waist, and led her inside in this fashion. In the unlikely event anyone was watching, they would assume I was taking her inside to sleep off a bender. That's the great thing about living in a college town. Drunkenness hides so many things.

The day before, to mark the approaching end of the school year, I suggested that we have a party. As you might imagine, nobody objected, particularly since I volunteered to supply all the food and drinks.

Boston is New York City's little brother in many respects, including the growing magnitude of its rodent problem. Almost every store stocks rat poison, and nobody thought anything of it when I stopped in LaVerde's Market and bought a box.

In addition to buying the drinks, I volunteered to serve them, and had skipped classes that day to mix them just right, without prying eyes. The fraternities were always looking for new drink recipes, and I couldn't have anyone stealing my secrets.

I proposed a toast to the imminent end of finals and got a roar of approval. They all knocked back the first round of shots, then the second, then the third. They didn't all collapse immediately, but those who stayed awake long enough to realize something was wrong were in no condition to do anything about it. When the last of them expired, I was glad. I hate noisy crowds.

I dragged everyone into the basement, found a hacksaw, and cut large holes in their chests so as to avoid damaging the hearts. I did not need a surgeon's skill, and time was short.

Throughout much of my life I've had to listen to people either rhapsodize or gripe about their relationships. This only increased when I got to college and moved in with a group of students I didn't know, all of whom seemed to thrive on late-night gab sessions, usually generously fueled by the fire-sauce. At first I didn't have a clue why they all seemed to look to me as an informal therapist, since I could never empathize with them. I've never had any great capacity for feeling. Emotions, to me, have always been interesting abstractions at best and dangerous distractions at worst.

Gradually I came to understand. They sought me out for precisely that reason, because I had an unparalleled ability to remain objective and help them examine all sides of the problem.

With much practice I developed the ability not just to *comprehend* the nature of the emotions roiling within them but to *see* them there, as the living, tortured things they were, warring ceaselessly within the existential battlefields they knew as their hearts.

And so I decided to take pity on them. The ancient Greeks believed the heart was the seat of all reason as well as of all feeling. The essence of that belief has endured to this day. Much is made of the expressions "speaking from the heart" and "speaking directly to the heart." I could do neither of these things while the heart was inside the body, because there was far too much interference from the surrounding physiology. It would be like trying to hold a conversation with someone underwater. The obvious solution was to remove the interference, and the only way to do this was to remove the body. Peel it away, reveal the heart at its most vulnerable. Then you can fully commune with it and perhaps unlock its secrets, which is the ultimate objective of any therapist.

Gail's heart was the best of all. Therefore it deserved a place of honor, away from the others, which had died harboring nothing loftier than carnal lusts and curdled self-pity. It was scarcely worth the effort to remove them, since there was nothing more to them, inside or out. But she, in the glorious gullibility of her innocence, the wonderful innocence of her love for a man I would never meet but knew so well, showed me the remnants of my own soul. In this basement, sheltered from the mindless cruelty of the world above, she in her preserve jar on the highest shelf, I in my rocking chair, both attended by the cool darkness, what marvelous conversations we could now have, she and I! And perhaps the others, in their own, smaller jars, would look upon her and learn what it was to be truly alive.

Many happy hours did I pass in this way, until I realized we could not stay there. Someone would be looking for Gail and, unlikely as it seemed, the others might soon be missed as well. So I gathered up my lonely hearts club late one night, and we set out to find a place so far removed from civilization that it would not intrude.

Close to the center of the state I came across a house standing alone on a huge plot of land. It looked uninhabited, but if it wasn't, I was prepared to remove any inconveniences.

Finding the door unlocked, I went inside and saw at once that it had been untenanted for a very long time. The gas and water were off and a thick layer of dust covered everything. Perfect. And so it was, until the day when I, still chained to the weaknesses of my own body, was arrested at a nearby convenience store, where I had gone for munchies.

I found out later why the cops were looking for me. That busybody roommate of Gail's had watched her talking to me at the reception until she had to leave. She got worried when Gail didn't come home the next day, and told the police about me. It seems there was something about me she didn't like. Probably the fact that I didn't talk to her. I had seen into her heart also, and found her unworthy.

Now here I am, waiting for my second and last date, this one with a needle. I realize that in my desire not to bore you with details that have surely been endlessly rehashed in the mass media, I have crafted an account which you might find lacking in some of the finer points. If that's so, and if you have questions to ask, by all means do so. You know where to find me.

I'm always up for a heart-to-heart talk.

MOST HUMBLE SERVANT

For some people, the three most beautiful words in the English language are "I love you." For Gordon Jerritt, on the morning of September 24th, they were "Grand Opening Today!"

He stood in the dining room of Seventh Avenue's newest restaurant, Jerritt's Joint, savoring the end result of months of groundwork. Filing the incorporation papers. Getting the loan from the bank. Buying the vacant building. Obtaining permission to renovate it. Filling out the endless forms and paying fees to all the lawyers and bureaucrats who wanted a piece. Hiring contractors who would do good work without overcharging him in every way they could think of. Ordering the furniture and making sure it was installed in the right places. Planning and designing the menu. Advertising for employees. Then, after all that, finding people who would distribute his fliers to prospective customers instead of just dumping them in the nearest trash can.

The process was enough to give him an ulcer, but it was all worth it. Here he was now, feeling fine. All the preliminary work was complete, and he was ready to begin his new life as a restaurant owner. He felt a twinge of disappointment that there hadn't been a line of people waiting for him to unlock the door, but very few businesses were successful right away. It would take time, that was all.

A dog with matted fur ambled by, saw him, and stopped for a closer look. Gordon lunged at the window and scared the mutt off.

He couldn't imagine ever moving out of Texas, but he had asked himself many times if he really wanted to have his business in Austin. It was a great town in most ways, but every other person who lived here seemed to have a dog. Man's best friend? Yeah, right. Noisy, disgusting beasts, that's what they were. Maybe he had to put up with seeing them all over the place while he lived in the city, but after he retired he was going to buy a couple of acres in one of the outlying areas. He might get a cat or two. He liked cats. But if a dog came onto his property, or just wandered too close, he'd shoot it. Let people complain. If they had the time and energy for that, they could use that time and energy to keep their mongrels under control. Anyway, there were too many stray dogs roaming around. Why shouldn't he do his part to thin them out?

He almost wished his parents were here to see this day, but decided it was just as well they weren't. They would constantly be giving him advice on how to run his business, which he wouldn't need or want, and he'd end up telling his own mom and dad to cork it. Besides, he grew up in an orphanage, had only vague memories of his parents, and hadn't even thought about them in years. No reason to start now.

What he would think about, and revel in when it happened, was how he would get the last laugh over the other children in the orphanage, the ones who had made his life there so miserable with their endless taunts about his weight. Now here he was, a business owner. The fat kid had made good. And what were they doing now? Who knew?

His size could even help his business. What better advertisement was there for an eating establishment than an owner who obviously liked to eat? Austin was supposed to be a "healthy" city, but he knew there were lots of people here who, like him, couldn't care less about good nutrition. They wanted good-tasting food and plenty of it, and he would give it to them. Let the Hollyweird types munch on tree bark or whatever the health nuts were doing now.

Suddenly he realized he was standing at the window, willing the people passing by to come inside. That smacked of desperation, and a business owner who was desperate on the first day would not be a business owner for long. He had expected the first few days to be slow, and he was prepared.

Ten minutes after he sat down with a newspaper, the door opened and someone came in.

Gordon jumped up to welcome his first customer of the day. But at the sight of him, the smile froze on his face and the words died in his throat.

His visitor looked even shorter than he was because he walked hunched over and shriveled in on himself. His clothes fit him poorly and looked as if he had pulled them out of a dumpster. His complexion was sallow, his eyes were small and close-set, his nose looked squashed, and his cheeks sagged like the jowls of a dog.

Everything about this creature, in fact, made Gordon think more of a dog than a man. As if to emphasize the point, he took no immediate notice of Gordon, the man he had presumably come to see. Instead he wandered around the room, peering at tables, examining them so closely he looked as if he were sniffing them.

"Can I help you?" Gordon asked, no longer interested in being friendly.

The man jumped, looked at Gordon, and took a few halting steps in his direction but did not get close to him, to Gordon's relief.

"I'm answering your ad," the man said timidly. "Your most humble servant, Steven Cooper."

He came closer and stuck out his hand. Gordon ignored it.

"Just what did you have in mind?" If he wanted to be a cook, he was gone. No way was Gordon letting such a sickly-looking person touch anything that would be served to the customers.

"You'll need someone to keep the place in order. Sweep and mop the floors, take out the trash, clean the bathrooms. I can do those things."

You don't even look like you can keep yourself in order, Gordon started to say, but stopped himself. He did need a janitor, and he hoped he wouldn't end up having to hire a foreigner or some college kid. This guy could at least speak English, and it was impossible to imagine him cramming for a calculus final.

"What kind of pay you looking for?"

"Whatever you can manage, Mr. Jerritt. I don't need much at all, really."

One of the things Gordon hadn't been looking forward to was holding interviews, wading through all the applications, trying to pick the best people for the positions he had to fill. Maybe he could give this poor slob a break and help himself at the same time. If he did a good job, that would be one less worry. If not, he wouldn't have to feel the least bit bad about firing him.

"You got a family?"

"No, sir. I have no one."

Wow, there was a shocker. But confirming the fact made the decision easier. No family meant he wouldn't be asking for any time off to take care of a sick kid, and it also meant he only needed to be paid...oh, let's see...

"It's six bucks an hour. No benefits, so if you're looking for health insurance—"

"No, sir. I don't need anything like that, I assure you."

That was hard to believe, but he said it, so Gordon took him at his word. "Can you start today?"

"Of course, sir. I can start right now. Perhaps by mopping your kitchen floor?"

Gordon was going to do that later anyway, but if this twerp wanted to do it for him, why not?

"All right, we'll give it a shot. All the cleaning stuff's in the kitchen. Get in there and mop the floor. And I want to be able to see my face in it," he added, just because he had always wanted to say that.

"Thank you, Mr. Jerritt, thank you!" Cooper exclaimed and stuck out his hand again, more insistently this time. Not bothering to keep the grimace off his face, Gordon shook it. The hand was unpleasantly warm and damp. Gordon jerked his hand back, but he needed two pulls to do it because Cooper held on to it so tightly.

"Yeah, whatever. Just get to work."

Cooper hurried to the kitchen to start on the floor. Gordon hurried to the bathroom to wash his hands.

What a way to introduce yourself, he thought. *Your most humble servant.* Who even said that anymore? Certainly no one in this country, and the guy's name sounded American enough.

He stopped washing and looked up, inquiring of his reflection in the mirror.

Steven Cooper, he'd said. Nothing remarkable about the name or its owner. If he passed that loathsome creature in the street, he wouldn't take the trouble to spit on him, much less get to know him.

So why did that name sound familiar?

He heard a faint jingle. The bell over the front door. Maybe another job applicant, or maybe a customer. Either way, forget the name. Probably just a character he'd seen on TV or something.

A well-dressed couple stood just inside the door, clearly waiting to be seated.

"Hello, sir, madam! Welcome to Jerritt's. Sit anywhere you like."

They chose a table near the window, away from the door. Gordon waited until they had settled themselves before offering them something to drink. Coke for him, orange juice for her. "I'll get that right out for you," he said. He rushed to the kitchen, having to keep himself from breaking into a jog.

Cooper wasn't in the kitchen. Gordon didn't see the pail or mop either.

I knew I shouldn't have hired that bum, he thought with a disgusted lack of surprise. *If he's out back sneaking a smoke or a beer, I'll—*

He had to interrupt the thought to keep himself from falling. The floor was so slick that he'd skidded on it.

It couldn't have been more than two minutes between the time he went to the bathroom and the time he came back out to see to his first customers. Cooper shouldn't even have had time to start on the floor, but it was finished. And it wasn't just mopped, it was mopped to a treacherous shine. Gripping the counter to keep his balance, he leaned over to inspect the work. Sure enough, he saw his face in it, reflected with impressive clarity.

Then he saw that someone else was reflected.

An impossibly big man, nine feet tall it seemed, was behind him, looming over him. It wasn't a static image either. The giant was wrapping a collar around his neck and forcing him down onto all fours at the same time.

Gordon whipped around and of course no one was there. But he had *felt* the hand on his neck, pushing him down with steroid-freak strength, and he'd felt the collar around his neck, choking him. He had felt it as solidly as he felt the thumping of his heart and the coldness of the sweat that had popped out on his forehead.

What in the world was the matter with him? He hadn't drunk any booze today, and even if he had, he knew his limits. He wouldn't have consumed anywhere near enough to make him trip out like this.

Get it together, Jerritt! You got customers waiting! He was about to strike himself across the face to force his mind to clear, but they might have heard that, and he didn't need anyone starting rumors that he was the kind of restaurant owner who liked to slap the help around.

That was nothing, what he'd seen. A random image from a forgotten nightmare that was still floating around somewhere in his head and for some reason chose that moment to pop into his conscious memory. It was a brain burp, simple as that. Here and gone.

To prove it, he looked at the floor again, knowing for a fact he wouldn't see that other man. He would only see himself.

He did not see the other man. He didn't see himself either. What he did see was a huge, ferocious dog.

It was running up through the floor, as if swimming up to the surface of a pool, straight at him. Its mouth was open in a silent snarl of rage, and in another second it would pounce on him and tear his throat out. He screamed and tried to jump back, get away, but he slipped and fell flat on his back.

He scrambled up to a sitting position, looking around frantically for something to defend himself with. But he didn't need anything. There was nothing there. No dog, no giant man. Just him, sitting on his kitchen floor, gasping and shaking.

"Mr. Jerritt?" he heard the male customer ask. "Are you all right?"

Cripes. Now they thought he'd had a heart attack or something. He could accept that if it would explain what had just happened, but he knew better. He also knew he had to try to salvage what he could out of this mess.

He got to his feet, straightened out his shirt, smoothed down his hair, and used a napkin to blot the sweat off his face. His hands were trembling, and he knew he still looked terrible, but it would take too long to fix those things.

That wasn't a waking relic of any dream. What it *was*, he couldn't even guess, but it clearly wasn't something he could blow off and forget about. He wasn't going to do himself or his customers any favors by trying.

Holding on to the edge of the counter for balance, and looking everywhere except at the floor, he made his way to the kitchen door and reemerged into the dining area.

"Are you all right, Mr. Jerritt?" asked the woman from her chair. The man was standing beside his.

"I'm truly sorry about this, folks, but I had...kind of a bad spell in there. I was sick for a while, and I thought I was over it, but I guess I'm not, so—"

"Oh, I understand, believe me," said the woman, getting up. "That's happened to my grandfather a few times." *Thanks, lady,* Gordon thought, *I feel a lot better now.*

"I'll be here tomorrow, though, good as new. That's a promise," Gordon said, hoping they couldn't tell he was trying to convince himself as much as them.

"Don't worry about us," said the man. "You just go home and get a good rest." And they were gone. To their credit, they didn't rush out of the restaurant. He wouldn't have blamed them if they had.

The experience in the kitchen was already fading in his memory. He didn't have the sense that anyone or anything was sneaking up behind him. He turned, just to see if that wretch Cooper was standing there laughing at him, but he didn't whip around expecting to see a monster.

An attack of nerves? Not a chance. Sure, getting this place up and running had had its share of stress, but it had been excited stress, not anxious stress. Definitely not the kind of curled-up-in-a-ball-on-the-floor-sucking-your-thumb stress that would make him see dogs coming up out of the floor.

He knew he wasn't going to figure out what had happened in there. Just trying was giving him a headache. All right, so what was his next move?

There was only one thing he could do. He hadn't been lying about having a bad spell, and he couldn't be sure it was a bizarre one-time thing. So he had to close the place for the rest of the day, and...

And what? Keep it closed? It took him months to get his business started, and he was going to end it after less than an hour? Not on his life or anyone else's. Except maybe Cooper's.

Where was that little creep? Somehow he was behind this, and when Gordon got his hands on him, he'd make him admit it. He'd beat the truth out of him if he had to. Actually, he was kind of looking forward to that.

"Cooper!" he yelled. "Where are you? Get out here now!"

No sign Cooper was willing to comply, that he had heard, or even that he was there.

"*Cooper!*" he hollered.

Nothing. His "most humble servant," who came in begging for work, had taken off after thirty seconds on the job. Gordon would have laughed his head off at a story like that from anyone else.

But if that little cockroach thought he was getting away so easily, he'd never been more wrong about anything. If Steven Cooper was his real name—and now it occurred to Gordon that he should have asked for identification, but the thought of touching anything that guy always kept on his person turned his stomach—he'd track him down and make him sorry he ever walked in the door of Jerritt's Joint. And why would he lie about his name? He'd expected to get paid, hadn't he?

As Gordon saw it, he had four options. One, he could stay here and feel sorry for himself. Two, he could go home and feel sorry for himself. Three, he could go to his favorite bar, get loaded, and very loudly feel sorry for himself. Four, he could go looking for Cooper.

Obviously he would look for Cooper. And he would find him.

When he was finished with him, *then* he'd go to the bar, to celebrate a job well done.

Just having a clear course of action to follow made him feel better. He walked out the front door, locked it behind him with a sharp pang of regret, and started off.

Assuming Cooper took off right after he did whatever he did to the kitchen floor (*don't even think about that, won't help you any, you got a job to do, focus on that*), he had maybe a ten-minute head start. Trouble was, within ten minutes of here, there were lots of places a cockroach like him could hide. It could take a long time to flush him out. But thanks to this particular cockroach, right now he had nothing but time.

There was a grimy, rundown building a couple of miles away. Most everyone in the area assumed it was a crack house, but the cops didn't seem to care as long as the addicts confined themselves to that part of town. It wouldn't surprise Gordon a bit if Cooper was a meth-head, and that seemed like the kind of place where he would hang out. On the off-chance someone there still had a few working brain cells, maybe they could give him a lead. Besides, it was a nice day, and the walk would clear his head.

At first he paid no attention to the dogs. They were always yipping their flea-ridden heads off about something or nothing. But their barking was louder than usual. Much louder. It sounded frenzied, in fact, and it was all around him, forcing him to look at them, and that was when he noticed something very odd.

Every dog within sight of him was straining at its leash, trying to get to him, a few of them pulling their owners along. Looking at their faces made it clear none of them was barking out of happiness or fear. They were all enraged. And their collective fury was directed at him.

It was crazy, unbelievable, but it was true. Every dog around him, every single one, was acting as if it wanted to rip him to bloody shreds. At least two of them were big enough to do it.

The owners, yanking at the leashes, shouting in vain at their four-footed brats, were taking their attention off them just long enough to give him perplexed looks, seeing that he was the one driving the dogs wild but not seeing how. He had no more idea of what was happening than they did, but he wasn't about to stand here and let it happen. He passed an alleyway on his left and didn't see any dogs in it. *Really* hoping there weren't any, he took off running down the alley. The frenzied barking, snarls, and growls followed him where the dogs themselves were barely prevented from going.

He was sweating now, as much from the unaccustomed exertion as from his sudden fright, and he wiped his hands on his pants. His right hand remained damp, and it had a weird, slimy feel to it. He looked at it, saw it was still wet, and rubbed it vigorously on his leg. But it remained as sweaty as before.

No. That wasn't it. He brought his hand up to his face, smelled it, and recoiled.

His hand was slick, but not with sweat. It was covered in slobber. Dog slobber.

How could that possibly be? No dog had licked his hand or been anywhere near him. He'd had no contact with any animal lately, except...

Cooper.

This was the hand Cooper had insisted on shaking. The

cockroach had put some kind of hoodoo on him, just like he'd done to his kitchen floor.

How could that funny little man have worked a trick like this? Never mind how. It didn't matter. All that mattered was that he did it, and he was soon going to be very, very sorry he did it.

Gordon came out the other side of the alley and started again in the direction of the crack den. He got no more than half a block when a Dalmatian crossed the street in front of him. When it saw him it went berserk. It arrowed at him, barking viciously, slavering with unmistakable bloodlust.

He spun and ran for all he was worth. There was a sports bar a few doors down, but the beast would be on him before he reached it. He looked around wildly for a big rock or anything else he could use as a weapon. It would've been nice if someone had left a loaded gun lying on the sidewalk, but there was nothing. He was as good as dead.

Wait! There! A door standing open! He lunged for it, made it through, and slammed it shut an instant before the dog thudded against it. He heard it scratching furiously at the door, even biting it in its frenzied hate. Was the thing actually going to try to bite clean through? Could it? Maybe, but he would be long gone by the time it got through.

He looked behind him to see where he was, but there were no other people and no advertisements of any kind. The building looked deserted, and there was no back door he could see. Well, he could hide out here, hoping that miserable dog would give up and leave. In the meantime, he would look around to find something he could use as a club for when he had to go back outside.

There was nothing on the floor but a page of the *Austin American-Statesman* and a few slivers of wood and bits of masonry, not even big enough to choke the beast if it swallowed one.

He glanced at the newspaper. An article in the middle of the page caught his attention. He picked it up, noticing that the slobber on his hand didn't come off on the paper, and read:

Leander Man Found Mauled To Death

The body of Philip Long, 44, was discovered yesterday evening, near Long's home in Leander. The body had been savaged beyond recognition, and Long was only identified by his driver's license.

There was no predation of the body, leading investigators to conclude that he had been killed by feral dogs, but Mike Howard, animal control supervisor for Travis County, admits to being baffled.

"Twenty-three years I've been in animal control, and I've never seen a dog attack like this," he said.

Long's wife, Terri, wants the owners of the dogs to come forward and accept responsibility for his death.

"No one deserves to die like that, especially not Phil," she said. "He had a hard life. He lost both his parents when he was a child. He grew up in an orphanage, and then he was bounced around foster homes. But he made it through all of that and became a kind and generous man, and a wonderful husband and father. He never hurt anyone in his life. He was walking to the store to get some soda when this happened. There was no reason for this to happen. Those dogs should be found and destroyed before they do this to anyone else, and the people whose dogs took him away from us need to be held accountable..."

The paper slipped through Gordon's nerveless fingers and drifted to the floor. Now all of this made...well, no, none of this made sense, but now it all came together.

He knew who Philip Long was. They had met as children, when they both lived in Dallas, in the Episcopal Children's Home. In a place like that, the kids tended to form themselves into small tribes to escape the crushing sense of isolation. Gordon's tribe had two other kids in it. One was Philip. Who was the other? Derek Brandt, that was it.

He remembered one other kid who was there, who had lived with them but had never been one of them. He wasn't in their tribe or in anyone else's.

Now Gordon knew why the cockroach's name had nagged at his memory. He should have made the connection sooner.

Most of the boys of Episcopal Children's Home spent their time in one of six ways: in school, doing homework, doing chores, playing football or baseball, or tormenting a shy, scrawny loner named Steven Cooper.

Gordon had taken a sadistic pleasure in seeing how cruel he could be to Steven. Not because the kid had done anything to him but because there was finally one person at the home who was lower on the totem pole than the fat kid, and he had reveled in his newfound advantage.

One fine autumn day, the children were playing flag football in a vacant lot across the street from the home. A starving stray dog wandered up to them, looking for a few scraps. It wore a frayed collar, but its owner had long since left it to fend for itself.

Derek started to chase it away, but Gordon, who even then had a strong dislike of all things canine, had a better idea.

He looked over at Steven, who was sitting under a tree at the far end of the field reading a comic book one of the teachers had lent him.

"Hey, Cooper!" he yelled.

Steven's head snapped up.

"Yeah, you! C'mere!"

Cooper looked to his left, then to his right, then pointed at himself. *Me? You want me?*

"What are you doing?" Philip hissed.

"Yeah! You! C'mere! We're gonna play a game!"

Steven hesitated, wondering why anybody would want to play a game with him. None of the boys wanted anything to do with him, and the girls were never more than coolly polite to him. But he decided it didn't matter why, as long as they did, so he flung the comic aside and bounded over.

To Philip, Gordon whispered, "Keep that dog here a minute. We're gonna have some fun with it."

Philip was confused, but knowing Gordon as he did, he had every reason to believe that whatever game they were going to play would be at Steven's expense, and he was always up for that.

Derek believed the same thing. He had nothing against Steven personally but wasn't about to stick up for him, so he eased back a little to let the other two do whatever they were going to do.

When Steven reached them, Gordon asked him, "You like dogs?"

"Well...sure," Steven said. "Who doesn't?"

"Why?"

"Huh?"

"Why do you like dogs?"

"Well...they're nice. And...and loyal, and...humble."

"Humble, huh?" Gordon smiled. "Almost like a servant, huh? 'Cause they fetch things for you and stuff?"

Steven brightened. "Yeah! Yeah, that's it! Like a pipe and slippers! I mean, I don't smoke a pipe—well, I don't smoke at all—and I don't wear slippers, but I'd like to have a dog to fetch me stuff."

"You like this dog?" Gordon asked, pointing at the hopeful-looking stray.

"Well...yeah, I guess."

"'Cause it's humble, right?"

Steven did not understand this game, but he seemed to be doing all right with it, so he continued to play along. "Yeah. I mean, it sure looks humble."

"Yeah," Gordon said. "It does, don't it? Think you can be humble like this dog?"

"Huh?"

"Simple question, Cooper. Do you think you can be humble like this dog?"

Philip thought he knew what Gordon was up to. He moved to stand on the other side of the dog. The dog's head swiveled to follow him, then went back to Gordon, who seemed to be the leader of this pack.

"Uh...yeah, I guess so. I mean, I think I'm pretty humble."

Gordon smiled again. "You think so, huh? Well, let's just find out!"

He grabbed Steven's arm and pulled him inside the loose circle that the four of them plus the dog made. Pulling that arm downward, he slammed his free hand into the middle of Steven's back, to push him down. He put all his weight into it, and he weighed twice what Steven did, so it didn't take long to force him to his knees.

Philip was ready. He grabbed the frightened dog by its neck and pulled off its collar. Once he had it, the dog ran away.

The other kids gathered to watch. Gordon, happy to have an audience focused on him but not making fun of him, took the collar from Philip. Still holding a miserable, struggling Steven down with one hand, he held the collar up for everyone else to see, then put it around Steven's neck. He held the ends of the collar and used his thumbs to push down on the top of Steven's neck.

"You're *real* humble now, aint'cha?" he yelled. "Look atcha! I call and you come running, like a stupid dog! And now you're down on all fours with a collar! You ain't no better than a dog! You *are* a dog! Say it! Say you're a dog!"

"Yeah!" Philip shouted. "Say it!"

Derek stood off to the side and watched. Whether he enjoyed the spectacle wasn't clear, but the teachers who rushed over to break it up made him wash the dishes, scrub the floors, and clean the bathrooms for a week alongside Gordon and Philip. And when other kids asked him if the punishment was worth it, he said that it was, because he'd never seen anything so funny.

Steven was excused from school and chores the next day. He spoke to no one, and no one spoke to him. The day after that, he was gone. Rumor had it he was transferred to another orphanage, but nobody was interested enough to find out for sure. He was never heard from again.

Until now.

Now Gordon understood the meaning of those images he saw in his kitchen floor. The dog was plain enough. And the nine-foot man who forced the collar on him? Had he really seemed that big to Steven, in a way that went beyond simple physical size? He was much stronger and acted far more confident. Had Steven looked up to him because of that? Was that why he'd never gotten over the prank?

"Cooper?" he called out. He would fall to pieces if he allowed himself to think about how totally insane all this was, so it was just as well that as heavy as he had always been, he'd never been good at heavy thinking. All he could do was roll with the impossibilities piling on each other as well as he could, and cling to whatever teeny hope existed that he would survive the day. And if that meant being alone in an abandoned building and reaching out to someone from his childhood, someone who was using a supernatural dog-training method to take revenge for a cruel trick played on him thirty years ago on the chance he could hear and would listen, that was pretty much par for the course, wasn't it?

Plus it seemed to do something. As soon as he said the name, the dog outside stopped barking. It also stopped scratching and biting at the door. It was quiet now. Almost as if it were listening. Maybe that didn't mean anything. Maybe it did.

"Hey, Steve, if you're listening..." he began.

No noise from outside.

"Hey, look, man, I'm sorry about what we did to you. You know, at the home, when we were kids? It was wrong, it was way outta line, I admit it, all right? But, hey, this, what you're doing now—however you're doing it—this is wrong, too!"

That was apparently not the way to get on Cooper's good side. The dog started up again, even more determined than before.

And it was no longer alone. There were more dogs at the door now. A lot more. They did not bark, but Gordon heard them shuffling and scratching.

"Cooper!" he bawled.

The dogs stopped again. This time, the silence was definitely not a good thing.

The doorknob started to turn. In the extremity of his terror, Gordon's field of vision contracted until the knob filled it. He saw it, with its faint scorings and tiny craters, turn languidly to the left, stop, and swing inward, pulling the door with it.

He saw a man standing where the closed door had been.

He heard the man say "At your service, sir."

He saw the Dalmatian spring into the room, followed by ten, twenty other dogs.

He saw them all coming straight at him.

But he couldn't hear them. He couldn't hear anything.

The last thing Gordon Jerritt ever saw was Steven Cooper backing out of the room and closing the door behind him.

The next morning a man stood on the edge of a pier next to a fishing boat, with a thermos of coffee and what remained of a box of assorted donuts. Another man walked by and called out to him: "Hey, Derek, some game last night, huh?"

"Didn't get to watch it," Derek griped. "Wife dragged me to some stupid fundraiser for her museum. Pass me that last donut, willya?"

"Get it yourself. You're supposed to be working, remember?"

"So are you, so make yourself useful and get me the—"

"Excuse me, sir?"

A strange-looking little man stood a few feet away. Neither of them had noticed him coming.

"I understand you're in need of an assistant," the fellow said.

"Huh? Oh, yeah, well, me and my partner here, we're looking for someone to help us out on our boat. But I'll tell you right off, it's pretty rough work." He looked the skinny stranger up and down as he said this, to emphasize the point.

"I assure you, sir, I can do a lot more than you might think."

"Yeah?" Derek said with a smirk. "Okay, I guess we could give you a shot. What's your name?"

The stranger said, "Steven Cooper, sir. Your most humble servant." And he stuck out his hand.

DANCE WITH A STRANGER

"But this is your hour—when darkness reigns."

Shaun Mathison had not been to church since childhood, but those words from the Gospels rang through his mind as he sat looking out the window of his shelter. For a while he had shared the shelter with others, but it was his alone now.

Soon the heavens would light up, as they had for untold millenia, and the dance would begin again. Until then, there was nothing to do but wait...and remember.

When they came, they numbered six. These scientists had chosen Ultima Thule, this tiny village at the northern tip of Greenland, as an ideal place to set up a research outpost to study the aurora borealis, also called the northern lights.

They knew what caused the lights. High-speed electrons and protons shot from the sun like minuscule cannonballs, were trapped in the Van Allen radiation belts, and channeled toward the North and South Poles by the Earth's magnetic field. Collisions with air molecules along the way gave these particles so much energy that they started glowing to get rid of it. The borealis appeared most often during magnetic storms and periods of great sunspot activity.

But their interest in the borealis was more esoteric than the reason it existed. They wanted to know if the shimmering celestial display could be used as the equivalent of an early warning system, an indication of an approaching sunstorm—a rare but spectacular event in which the sun threw off titanic waves of charged particles, sometimes enough to interfere with or disable communication and tracking devices and anything else that used electricity.

The warning system hypothesis was Shaun's, but he would have been the expedition leader regardless. He was a tall, spare man who always had a severe expression and an intense, penetrating gaze you couldn't meet for more than a few seconds before dropping your eyes. He spoke in a rapid staccato that was the verbal equivalent of machine-gun fire, and he always walked at a pace that was close to a jog. He worked with a speed and intensity that was fascinating— and a little disconcerting—to watch, always with his face set in grim concentration.

For a while, his coworkers made jokes and goofy faces around him to try to get him to smile, as tourists sometimes did with the famously humorless guards of Buckingham Palace. Nothing worked, and finally he got so irritated by these attempts that he posted a sign on his office door: "Anyone wasting valuable research time with infantile games will be disciplined." It would have been funny if he were older, but all who knew him agreed that he was far too young to be so serious.

He never talked much about anything and was not often asked to, because he had the tact of a brick and never felt the need to apologize for any remark he made, no matter how insensitive. If asked about his personal life, he made a cryptic remark or ignored the question. So the story circulated that he had endured some tragedy, but no one dared ask him. It was easier just to do what the sign said.

Despite Shaun's youth, he was remarkably old-school in some ways, one of them being that he did not like to use email. Therefore he posted a notice on the communal bulletin board that he was putting together an expedition to Greenland, for which he needed five other people.

Most who saw the sheet expected it to remain blank. Six weeks in Greenland with him? As admired as he was for his abilities as a researcher, few could stand to be in the same room with him for more than a short time.

The next morning, however, he had his first volunteer. The meticulous signature of Clyde Kirschner should have been no surprise; if anyone would volunteer for something like this, he would. And their colleagues were not sure whether he or Shaun was more deserving of their pity.

If Shaun was a misanthrope, at least he had an excuse. His work was his life, and the steady stream of papers he published was more than enough to persuade the powers-that-be to overlook his personal oddities. Clyde, on the other hand, was one of those people present in every academic hierarchy, who rose as high as they did only because they knew whose posteriors to kiss and whose papers to attach their names to. Everyone knew he stole others' ideas but could never prove it, because he always knew enough about the subject matter to say convincingly that he was pursuing his own research. All the same, everyone took care to make sure he was never left alone in their labs or offices, a task made almost impossible by his odious personality.

Some of the men had taken to saying things they knew would provoke him, hoping he would give them an excuse to hit him. They knew he wouldn't rise to the bait, though, and he never did—he had sense enough for that, at least. The women had to resort to carrying Mace. He was the main reason the company had a sexual harassment policy, which he routinely ignored because he could not be fired. Not yet.

Clyde's father had founded Kirschner Laboratories and still funded a number of critical projects, said funding contingent on a Kirschner being on the payroll. The problem was that he was a retired widower with no other relatives, and his only other offspring was a fifteen-year-old daughter. So everyone consoled themselves by having Catherine's sixteenth birthday marked on the calendar, seeing to it that there would be an entry-level position available for her, and counting down the days until they could give Clyde a big sendoff. Preferably off the nearest cliff.

Shaun intimidated Clyde as much as he did the other researchers, so he was spared what everyone else endured on a regular basis. Even so, it was not hard to guess why Clyde would isolate himself in a frozen wasteland with him for six weeks. He wanted to be able to say that he'd been an integral part of a project of this sort, directly assisting someone who commanded as much respect as Shaun did.

Later that day, Shaun found an unsigned note on his desk. It said that even if he had to take Clyde with him, no one would say anything if he lost him on the way.

The corner of his mouth twitched. That was the closest he ever came to showing amusement.

But it seemed that his expedition was doomed before it began. He needed four more people, and who would commit to such a project with Clyde?

However, by the end of the next day, the remaining blanks were filled in with the names Harold Green, David Weiss, Michael McBraen, and Vincent Pestrono. These four shared a lab three floors above Shaun. No one knew much about them; they tended to keep to themselves, but Shaun had once walked by a lab or office and heard Harold relating his genealogy to whomever was listening. Harold was, or so he claimed, a descendant of Christopher Marlowe, the great English poet who was a contemporary of Shakespeare.

It had to be understood, however, that he was an old man and forgot things easily. This was his explanation if someone asked him to bring in his family tree and he "forgot" to do so. But he was entertaining, and people liked to listen to him. He knew how to spin a good yarn, so nobody really cared if it was true.

The main function of the other two seemed to be keeping Vincent away from the more fragile equipment. Vincent was a brilliant theoretician, but he was incredibly clumsy. He had spoken of his onetime dream of being an astronaut, and the running joke was that he'd been left in the centrifuge so long he never regained his equilibrium. The unofficial division of responsibilities was that he came up with ideas for experiments, and the others kept him out of the way long enough for the experiments to be run.

There was no going-away party. Shaun hated social events, no one would have attended a gathering for Clyde unless it was his funeral, and the other four were ghosts. Everyone else knew who they were, but not much else about them. Shaun had arranged for all their equipment and supplies to be transported ahead of them, so the six of them only had to take taxis to work one morning and share a van to the airport that evening.

The rush-hour traffic was in rare form, assisted by two accidents, one with injuries. As they crawled by this one, everyone but Shaun shifted in their seats to look. A young man on a stretcher was being bundled into an ambulance. Clyde wondered out loud if the man had a widow who needed comforting. Vincent elbowed him hard enough to knock the wind out of him.

"Sorry," he said. "Was trying to scratch my leg."

"You don't look sorry," Clyde growled.

"I don't? Sorry."

Harold, Michael, David, and the driver snickered. Clyde glared at all of them, intending to dry up the snickers, but only turned them into full-blown laughs. Shaun stared straight ahead, his lips pressed into a bloodless line, ignoring all of this. From time to time his colleagues looked at him, then at the cars ahead of them. He seemed to be trying to move the traffic out of their way by sheer force of will.

They got to the airport just in time to catch the 7:30 flight to Nova Scotia. From there they caught a connecting flight to Greenland's capital, Nuuk, on Greenlandair. On this flight, they seemed to be the only non-Inuits. When the captain said "Welcome aboard Immaqa Air," the other passengers chortled.

"What's so funny?" Harold asked.

David shook his head. "Who knows?"

"Greenland has some of the harshest weather on Earth," Shaun spat out. "It's impossible to predict. In the indigenous language, 'Immaqa Air' loosely translates as 'Maybe Air.'"

Vincent, who sat next to Shaun (no one else wanted either of them as a seatmate), noticed that his hands gripped his armrests while he spoke, and relaxed a bit once he finished. This made a sort of sense to Vincent. Shaun always spoke as though he had to see how quickly he could get the words out, and looked a bit winded when he finished. Vincent had a mental image of him wringing the words out of himself as he would wring water out of a sponge.

"If the weather's so hazardous," Michael asked, "why are we flying in it?"

"Would you rather swim?" Shaun snapped.

There was no conversation for the rest of the flight. There were no children aboard, and the Inuit only speak when they must.

The captain and flight personnel stood at the front of the plane as the passengers disembarked, but said nothing to anyone. The Inuit were used to this, but the visitors were unnerved—except for Shaun, who was indifferent to friendly gestures or the lack of them.

In preparation for the voyage, Shaun had purchased some Rosetta

Stone software and taught himself some Danish in order to acquire what they needed in the airport. Danish was no longer the official language here, but he hoped it was still spoken. English was an important secondary language here as it was in most of the world, but they couldn't count on meeting anyone who spoke it. Greenlandic grammar was impenetrable, and its vocabulary seemed to be all x's and q's.

They needed three snowmobiles and a cargo sled. One of the merchants happened to have three snowmobiles left, but those were his last ones, so the price would have to be a bit higher. He could let everything go for twenty thousand kroner.

Shaun had not learned the Danish word for *ripoff* and was in no mood to haggle. He paid the man and took the sleds.

What followed was an arduous ride across dozens of miles of icy wasteland. They could see where they were going because it was too cold to snow much, but by the time they reached Ultima Thule their mouths were frozen shut. Michael and David hauled the generator off the sled and hooked it up while the rest of them set up the shelter.

"I think now I understand why these people don't talk much," David said once they had thawed somewhat. "If they did, their lungs would freeze."

"No," Harold said, "that isn't why."

"Okay, enlighten us, Mr. Expert."

Harold was always happy to educate someone. "Inuit folklore tells of a time when men could speak to animals. The words were shamanistic in character, and had an intrinsic power they called... what is that word..."

"Tengeq," Shaun answered. They all turned to look at him, but he was assembling the spectroscope and had nothing more to add.

"Right. *Tengeq,*" Harold continued. "If the words were spoken casually, they lost their power. The Inuit still believe that to some degree, so they don't indulge in idle chitchat."

"Hmp," David said. "I know some people I'd like to leave here with them for lessons on keeping their traps shut."

Shaun had instructed Clyde to bring in their food. Like the others, Clyde was chilled to the marrow, but like the others he knew better than to argue with Shaun. When he brought the last of it in, he announced, "Clyde is in the house!"

"Yeah," David said. "I was just talking about you."

"I'm sure it was a laugh riot."

"No," Michael said. "He was talking about marooning you here, which was only a nice thought. A laugh riot would be if you fell off a glacier."

"Yuk it up, retards. Maybe when we get back you can get gigs as comedians."

"Whoa!" Michael exclaimed, wide-eyed.

Clyde looked at him, amazed. "Is that really your ambition? In that case—"

"Shut up, imbecile. Everyone come and look at this!"

Michael was crouching at a window looking at the sky, and the others immediately did the same—except for Vincent, who tripped over a sleeping bag and sent himself and David sprawling. Fortunately he missed the spectroscope, which Shaun had placed out of harm's way, or he would never have heard the end of it.

What they saw through the window was a sight each of them would remember for the rest of his life. All two days of it. The sky was ablaze with ribbons of color—greens, blues, reds, and yellows dancing and cavorting in a mesmerizing display.

Vincent glanced over at Shaun, and the look on his face said it all. Even *he* was impressed.

Shaun, Vincent knew, grew up in London, where even seeing a star was a rarity because the sky was always choked with smog. When he was offered a position at Kirschner, he moved to Boston, where the viewing was not much better. Vincent himself hailed from New Mexico. Looking up at the stars every night as a boy convinced him that someday he had to visit one of them. If he was captivated by this spectacle, what must Shaun have been feeling?

That, alas, was not to be known. After looking at the borealis for maybe twenty seconds, Shaun left his spot without a word and went back to making adjustments on the spectroscope.

"Incredible," David whispered. No one argued.

"It's got a beautiful name, too," Michael said. *"Aurora borealis."*

"The name comes from Roman mythology," Harold replied, without taking his eyes off the sky. "Aurora was the goddess of dawn, and her son Boreas was the north wind." As with the primer on Inuit folklore, this seemed a surprising piece of information for him to have at his fingertips.

Vincent beamed at them and patted Harold on the shoulder. "I taught him everything he knows."

The others shook their heads but couldn't help smiling. Vincent was easy to like as long as he wasn't near anything breakable.

Abruptly, he yawned. He brought up his hand to cover his mouth, inadvertently smacking the back of David's head in the process, and the spell was broken. He looked sheepishly at David and said, "Well, I am getting tired."

Clyde made an exaggerated gesture of looking at his watch. "Yeah, it's really late. I vote we get some shut-eye."

"Didn't think it would happen so soon," Michael said.

"Me either," said David.

"Huh?" Clyde asked. "What are you talking about?"

"David and I had been wondering how much time would pass before you said something halfway intelligent."

Clyde opened his mouth to retort, but Shaun said, "I'll take the spectroscope outside and take some preliminary measurements. The rest of you should call it a night. We have a big day tomorrow." That was the last word on the subject.

Harold awoke five hours later. He knew he wouldn't be able to get back to sleep; he was lucky he had slept this long. He lay in his bag for a few more minutes, then got up and carefully made his way to the window. Shaun was still there, assiduously taking measurements and noting his findings. He thought of going outside and keeping a vigil with him, but he knew Shaun detested company, and there wouldn't be anything for him to do.

He looked around the shelter. The others would be sound asleep for hours yet. He couldn't just lie on the floor until they woke up, and he thought Shaun would understand. So he put on three layers of clothing over his thermal underwear, pulled on his parka, gloves, scarf, snowcap and snowboots, braced himself, opened the door quickly, and stepped out into the Arctic night.

Shaun heard the sound of boots crunching toward him and looked around. Harold could not see the expression on his face, but he knew it was one of irritation, which he hoped would fade once Shaun realized who it was. There was no one Shaun could really be said to like, but Harold was one of the few people he respected. Harold liked to tell stories but didn't find it necessary to talk just to be talking. That was a rare commodity. And he knew how to listen. That was rarer still.

Shaun did not acknowledge his presence, but went back to studying the borealis. Harold stood next to him and watched the sky. They stood in silence for some time before Shaun stood and stretched.

"Pity we can't take this back with us."

Harold nodded. "Yep. Makes you feel humble. Folks in Boston could use a good healthy dose of that."

Shaun snorted—his version of a laugh—but said nothing.

"Soothes the soul, too, doesn't it?" Harold said.

Shaun whipped around and looked sharply at him. Harold calmly returned his stare. Finally Shaun nodded, and his shoulders slumped a little.

"That's the main reason you wanted to come here, isn't it?" Harold spoke quietly but with conviction, as a father confessor might have.

If Shaun was surprised by the question, he didn't show it. "What makes you think that?"

"There are many places where the borealis can be studied just as efficiently, but none quite as isolated as this one. Here you don't have to work to block out the world. That's the appeal for you." Harold paused, then probed a bit deeper. "In a place like this, you still get to pretend the world makes sense."

Shaun stiffened. Harold had hit a nerve.

"But the world *doesn't* make sense," Shaun replied, almost in a snarl. "Events don't always unfold as they're supposed to. If I had learned that sooner—" He choked off the words. He hadn't meant to say that. But it was too late.

"Shaun," Harold said, "you're a brilliant scientist. No one disputes that. You do more work than any three others. You have nothing to prove to anyone, but you're always trying to prove something. To yourself, I think. That's why you always have to top yourself. To make sure everyone knows you're the hardest working, the most capable, the most knowledgeable. But everyone knows that already, don't you see? Everyone respects you. But no one *knows* you, because you've closed yourself off. If there's one thing you have to learn by the time you get to be my age, it's that what matters most isn't how much is in here." He tapped his head. "It's how much is in here." He tapped his chest.

"You don't understand," Shaun said, so softly that Harold had to lean forward to hear. "I believed that too. Once. And because I did..." His voice cracked, trailed off.

Harold put his hand on Shaun's arm, only mildly surprised that he didn't shake it off.

"What happened, Shaun? What mistake do you think you made that you have to spend the rest of your life paying for?"

Shaun took a deep breath, then another. Harold said nothing, but lowered his arm and waited. When Shaun was ready, he began his story.

"Everyone believes I left London because I was lured to Kirschner with the promise of a high salary and lots of perks. That's the story, but it isn't true. That is, it's only partly true. I was offered all that, but that's not why I took the job. Comfort and security weren't important to me then. I was an idealist. I was a fool. And I was engaged."

He paused. Harold waited.

"We were to be married on the first day of summer," Shaun went on. "Actually, she would have preferred the first day of spring, but early spring in London is always cold and rainy. Not exactly ideal marrying weather. At the time, I was assistant to a fellow named Symonds. He was head of the Department of Mathematics at University College. He was due to retire in three years, and it was an open secret that he was grooming me to be his successor. It was no secret that it was my ambition to do just that. Not for the money, you understand—professors at English private schools don't live as well as you might think—but because I had foregone a personal life for years to be the best there was at what I did. And I had to have something to show for it.

"On many occasions I went to the professor's home to help him with an assignment that had to be completed by a certain time. One day when I was there, I caught the attention of his daughter, who was on break from Cambridge."

Harold smiled. It was quick, but Shaun caught it.

"Yes. I imagine you know how these things go. She always had some excuse to come looking for me while he was attending to something elsewhere in the house. She asked all sorts of questions about my work, found it endlessly fascinating. Can't imagine why. It was mathematics after all. Then she started asking questions about me. What did I like to do for fun, did I have anyone to do it with, that sort of thing. As I said, I didn't have many opportunities for a social life. So when one presented itself to me, I seized upon it."

"Of course. Anyone would have."

Shaun smiled bitterly. "But would anyone have seen what would come of it? I didn't. The old man wasn't stupid, he had to have known, but never said a word about it. I don't think anyone else suspected. We tried always to be discreet. But I would tolerate no disrespect for her. And..."

He took a deep breath, let it out.

"And one morning, I was sitting at the top of a stairwell, making some final amendments to the day's lecture notes. Another bloke came up the stairs and asked what I was doing, and I told him.

"'Lecture notes, eh?' he said. 'Sure it's not a love letter for that little bird of yours?'

"I couldn't help it. I jerked my head up, and pressed down so hard on my pencil the point broke off.

"'I knew it!' the prat said. 'You're good, old boy, I'll give you that. But you couldn't hide it from me. I've been round the block too many times. Could smell her on you, I could. Saw it in your eyes when you looked at her. Saw how you always wanted to touch her when she walked by, but didn't dare. Couldn't have anyone sussing it.'

"By this time I was up and glaring at him. So he leaned in close, put his hands on my shoulders, and said, 'But there's something you should know, mate. You're not her first. Not by a long chalk.'

"I batted off his hands and said, 'What of it? I understand these things, you know.'

"'No,' he said. 'That's just it. You *don't* understand. You think

54

you've got a future with that one? You're nothing to her, mate. Just a way to pass the time until she's got to go back to school.'

"'Sod off,' I said, and I started to walk past him. But he grabbed my arm and held fast, and he said, 'Oh, yeah. She's got you snookered, she has. She must know you've never been to Cambridge. Why do you suppose she's never suggested the two of you take a trip there? Because she's got half a dozen blokes there waiting for her. I'll wager if she thinks about you at all, it's only to wonder how you measure up.'

"That got me so angry I took leave of my senses. I tore free of his grip, drew back and punched him. He fell down the stairs...and broke his neck at the bottom."

Harold drew in a sharp breath, but didn't dare speak. He knew that if Shaun didn't finish the story now, he never would. And he had to get this out of him once and for all.

"I should have gone for help, I know that. But I panicked. I was wracked with guilt. I ran down the stairway and out of the building, and didn't stop running until I was five blocks away. Then I forced myself to stop, and stood where I was until I could get myself under some measure of control, however long that was. It was surely enough time for classes to change, perhaps twice, so I knew the body had been found. When I got back, the police had been summoned, so I told them what happened. They questioned me most of the morning, as well as a student who'd been on the stairs above me. He was doing some last-minute revision for an exam and had heard everything. The police concluded that it was death by misadventure and decided not to arrest me. Then I went to Professor Symonds's office, told him what I had done, and tendered my resignation. He urged me to reconsider, offered me as much time off as I needed, but I couldn't work there anymore. I...I just couldn't.

"I'd been offered another job in Boston, several weeks before, as an adjunct professor at Brown University, but I'd turned it down. I went home and rang them to ask if the position had been filled. If not, I had changed my mind. They told me it was still open and that I could start as soon as I was able. I thanked them, hung up, and started to pack.

"It was while I was packing that Victoria came to see me. That was her name, Victoria. She pleaded with me to stay. Told me again and again that it wasn't my fault. It was a horrible accident, yes, but an accident, the man had been a cad and a rotter, and she would spend the rest of her life proving to me that he was wrong about her.

"I suppose some part of me listened to her. But the rest drowned her out, saying I could never again lose control like that. I had to be impervious to sentiment, always in complete control of my faculties and my circumstances. I don't even remember what I said to her. I only know that I caught the first available flight from Gatwick to Logan, threw myself into my work at Brown, distinguished myself there, eventually caught the attention of Kirschner, and the rest, as they say, is history. You know, since then I've never even allowed myself to think of her, until now."

"Well," Harold said after a long moment, "I'm not going to tell you what everyone else told you. You know it's true, even if you won't admit it to yourself. But I think I understand. Your way of protesting the randomness of the world and the caprice of life is to make sure that your own world is perfectly ordered, that your own life is rigid and unchanging. Right? And I guess that's worked well enough. You've earned the respect of the scientific community, even if that means nothing to anyone else. It's not important that you don't have a personal life if you'll never have anyone to share it with, or if you drive yourself so hard you won't live to see fifty. And if you never allow yourself to enjoy your accolades, what does that matter, as long as you have them?

"Shaun," he went on in a more serious tone, "we'll be here for six weeks, which means we'll return four days before my seventieth birthday. My grandchildren had started planning the party before I left. Do you know how that feels? No, of course not, there's no way you could. But I want you to know this: I'm twice your age, and my scientific achievements pale beside yours. For that, I admire you. But I wouldn't trade places with you for anything."

Shaun and Harold looked wordlessly at each other for five or ten seconds.

Then Shaun's lips twitched.

Then he smiled.

Then he chuckled.

Then he threw back his head and laughed.

It came pouring out of him. He was powerless to stop it, even if he'd wanted to. After a minute or so, his laughter dried up, his cheeks glistened with half-frozen tears, and his sides hurt. And he felt better than he had in a very long time.

Harold was grinning ear to ear. "That's what I'm talking about!"

"Thank you," Shaun said.

"Don't thank me, son. You gave me my present early."

Shaun glanced at the shelter. The meaning was plain.

"Don't worry," Harold said. "I won't say a word."

Shaun could take comfort in this, because he didn't know he was being watched, or that the cold, appraising eyes did not belong to anyone in the shelter.

"Have you ever thought of becoming a psychologist?" he asked.

Harold feigned shock. "What? And give up vacations in places like this?"

They walked back to the shelter and went inside. A blast of wind ripped the door out of Shaun's hand and it took both of them to close it again. Vincent, who was closest to the door, awoke with a groan.

"It's just us," Harold whispered. "Go back to sleep."

"No." Vincent got up and started to pull on his gear. "Something just occurred to me."

"What's that, then?" Shaun asked.

"The colors in the borealis correspond to the excitation of different gases in the atmosphere. While I was looking at it last night, I thought I could detect patterns in the alterations and interactions of the colors. I want to see if that's true, if it happens at intervals that can be calculated, predicted, and used as a sort of celestial chronometer."

Shaun mulled that over and decided it was a valid hypothesis. "The spectroscope's all yours. You have two hours before sunrise."

"Good. That should be enough time to make some progress." He made his way to the door. Harold and Shaun gave him a wide berth, then went to the window and watched him, holding their breath. He slipped and fell twice on his way to the spectroscope, but regained his bearings when he reached it, and settled in to make his observations. Harold and Shaun both exhaled with relief.

"I understand why you brought him," Shaun whispered.

"Oh yes," Harold agreed. "He's still a boy, but he has a bright future ahead of him. He's got a disciplined mind. One day his body might catch on."

"I just hope I'm there to see it."

The next thing Shaun knew, Michael and David were shaking him. They were trembling, but it wasn't from the cold. Their faces were pallid.

Shaun scrambled to his feet. "What? What is it?"

"It's...it's Vincent," Michael stammered. He said nothing else, only pointed a quivering finger at the door.

Shaun snatched up his parka and dashed out the door, but halted just beyond it. There, next to what was left of the spectroscope, lay what was left of Vincent.

His clothes and his body were in tatters. Harold was kneeling next to him, crying. Clyde was standing next to Harold, patting him on the shoulder because he couldn't think of anything else to do.

Shaun, with the others right behind him, joined them. Harold said the only thing he could. "I don't know. I don't know what happened. After he went outside, I lay down for a nap. I wasn't tired at all, but then suddenly I just had to sleep. When I woke up, the sun was just coming up. I came outside, and...and this is what I found. I hadn't heard a sound."

"None of us heard anything," David added.

"What should we do?" Michael asked.

They all looked at Shaun. He was the leader. He always knew what to do. They were counting on him to keep them functioning. Yes. That was his responsibility. He had to ignore his feelings. Focus on the task facing them.

"Well, we can't leave him like this. We should give him some sort of burial."

"I agree," said Michael. "But how? Even if we had any digging tools, the ground is frozen solid."

"We'll have to improvise. Bring his sleeping bag out here."

David ran back to get it. When he came back, Shaun placed the bag on the ground and started to ease Vincent into it. Harold helped him. When they were done, they zipped the bag up all the way.

"Harold," Michael croaked, "you knew him best. You should be the one to say something."

Harold looked at Shaun, who nodded. Then he stepped out a little way from the body, and the rest of them formed a loose semicircle around it. When they were ready, he closed his eyes, opened them again, and started to speak.

"I remember sitting at my lab table one day, making some notes for a paper I was preparing on the transmission of hemorrhagic fever. My door crashed open and this young boy bounded in, all smiles and knees and elbows and outstretched hand. He introduced himself by knocking my microscope off the counter and breaking it."

David and Michael chuckled. Clyde laughed, too loudly. Shaun shot him a look. Clyde choked it off.

Harold went on. "Well, this young fella was falling all over himself apologizing, offering to buy me a new microscope. Any model I wanted, top of the line. Much as I wanted to, I just couldn't get mad at him. He was too eager to please, and he hadn't meant any harm. So I told him not to worry, accidents happen, and who was he, anyway? 'Oh!' he said. 'Forgive me, sir. Vincent Pestrono, sir. At your service, sir.' I asked him what he meant by 'at my service,' and he said he'd been assigned to work with me. He was going to be my assistant. I told him there must be some mistake, I hadn't asked for any assistant, and nothing personal, but I didn't really want one. I didn't have the heart to tell him what I was thinking: that I especially didn't want an assistant who would probably end up wrecking all my equipment. Then he handed me a paper that had been signed by the man he'd been working for, saying he was transferring him to me. What the paper said was that he felt Mr. Pestrono would be a great help to me in my research.

"Well, I knew this man, and I knew what he'd been saying about somebody named Vincent when he wasn't around, saying he lived up to his name because he was a real pest, but up to that point I hadn't been able to put a face with the name. I realized what it was, of course. They wanted to have a good laugh at this poor boy's expense by fobbing him off on me. So I felt sorry for him and I said, wait a minute, come to think of it, I could use someone to help me. Well, then he grinned fit to bust, you'd have thought I told him there was going to be an extra zero at the end of his paycheck, and he was with me ever since. And it wasn't long before I started wondering how they could've let him go. He came up with some really good ideas, things I never would have thought of. But the answer was they never gave him a chance to prove himself. And I was glad I did. And when David and Michael came aboard later on, they were, too. In spite of all the times he hit one of them with a door, or a filing cabinet drawer—"

"Or stepped on my foot," David chimed in, smiling.

"Or slammed a drawer on my hand," Michael added with a laugh.

"And whenever we wrote a paper," Harold said, "we made sure to highlight all of his contributions, so when those people read the paper they'd know what they'd given up. They even tried to get him back a couple of times, and others tried to lure him to their labs, but he always said no, he was staying right where he was, because he wouldn't find a better group of people to work with." His voice cracked, and he had to pause before he could finish. "We felt the same way, Vincent. I'm sorry we never told you that before. But we're sure going to miss you."

They stood in silence with heads bowed for a little while. Then Shaun gathered up the remains of the spectroscope.

"I think we can fix this," he said. "It will give us something else to think about."

They walked as a group back to the shelter. Once inside, out of sight of the body, they could allow themselves to speculate on what had happened.

"Do you think it was wolves?" Michael asked.

"Highly improbable," said Shaun. "Contrary to popular belief, wolves rarely attack people, and when they do it's out of hunger, so they don't leave much. Besides, we would've heard them howling. We haven't heard or seen anything besides us since we got here."

"Then what—"

"It's useless to theorize without evidence. It will only waste valuable time and energy. If it doesn't come back, that's that. And if it does, we'll know then."

They knew he was right. Saying nothing else on the matter, they set to work on the spectroscope, stopping only for meals. By the time they had it repaired, the sun had set. The sky again belonged to the borealis.

Abruptly Shaun pulled on his parka and declared, "I'll take first watch."

"What?" David exclaimed. "You can't! We have to—"

"We have to make sure whatever Vincent ran into doesn't come for the rest of us."

His tone left no room for argument, but Michael was determined to find some. He opened his mouth to say something. Harold held up a hand to forestall him.

"Shaun's right," Harold said. "We do need someone to keep watch. But I'll do it." He rushed on before anyone could object. "I'll be up most of the night anyway, and the rest of you need your sleep."

"What if whatever's out there comes back?" David demanded. "You wouldn't—"

"None of us would. You saw what it did to Vincent," he said flatly. "But I can yell as loud as any of you. Probably louder, with all the exercise my vocal cords have had."

"Harold," David said, "I appreciate what you're trying to do, but it must be twenty below outside. How long do you think you could survive that? I'll go. I've never felt less like sleeping in my life."

"Ditto me," Michael said. "We can both go. If something tries to sneak up on us, we'll double our chances of seeing it."

Harold appealed to Shaun. "Will you talk some sense into them?"

Shaun shook his head. "Theirs is as good a plan as any. We didn't bring any weapons. No survey of this type ever called for them. So we'll need someone who can move fast."

Harold saw that he was outvoted and gave in. Clyde, seated on his bedroll, kept his mouth shut. He believed he knew what had happened to Vincent, but he prayed he was wrong.

If he was right, then a violent death awaited them all. And none of them would see it coming.

David and Michael wordlessly bundled up, took their flashlights, and went outside. Since there was nothing to do except watch the beams of their lights as they walked around, the other three did that for a while. Shaun found his eyelids getting heavy, and he fought to stay awake, but it was a losing battle.

He decided to lie down, just for a minute...

Harold was shaking him awake. He looked as though he had aged ten years overnight.

Shaun was afraid to ask. "David? Michael?"

Harold could manage only a trembling whisper. "You'd better see for yourself."

Shaun swallowed hard, got up and into his parka, and went outside.

They were propped against the wall on either side of the door. They might have just sat down to rest, except they were sliced open from neck to pelvis and their hearts had been torn out of their chests. But their eyes and mouths were closed, and their faces were serene. Despite the savagery of the attack, they looked as if they had died in their sleep.

Clyde, who emerged a moment after Shaun, dashed around to the side of the shelter and was noisily sick. The strength ran out of Shaun's legs and he sank to his knees. Harold knelt down beside him, put an arm around his shoulders, and gently helped him up and back inside.

"Come on," he said. "There's nothing you can do for them."

A moment later, Clyde staggered in, tore off his parka, and started packing his things. "We have to get out of here," he said, shaking.

"Clyde, panicking isn't going to help," Harold said and tried to restrain him.

"No!" he shouted, breaking Harold's grip with such force that the older man almost fell backward. "We'll all die if we stay here! This is what happened to the group that came four years ago! They—"

In an instant, Shaun had Clyde pinned against the wall. "This has happened before? You *knew* this had happened before?"

"Yeah. I...I mean, I'd heard rumors, but I didn't—"

"*What rumors?*" Shaun screamed in his face.

"There...there was a scientist," Clyde said. "Worked at a clinic in Fargo. He noticed a spike in sleep disorders during the winter. He thought it was just because of the long nights, but that didn't explain why some people were affected and others weren't. So he thought something else had to be involved. So he built this device. He called it a delta wave modulator, because delta waves are what the brain produces during REM sleep—"

"I know what delta waves are! Get to the point! What does that have to do with all this?"

"Well...so he came here to test the thing. Figured this would be the ideal place, because it stays night for six weeks in winter. Brought three others with him. Or four, or five. Depends on who's telling the story. Anyway, they never came back, so a second expedition was sent to look for them. They found them, all ripped apart. Nothing else had been touched, but the modulator was gone."

"And you didn't find any of this worth mentioning?" Shaun inquired.

"I didn't think it was true! You've got to believe me! I mean, the guy had mentioned once or twice that he wanted to make a delta wave modulator, but that was all he ever said about it. Never wrote a paper on it or anything. So his colleagues thought he gave up on it. And he didn't make any kind of announcement that he was coming here. Some time later, the word got around that he'd died, but nobody had any concrete evidence as to when or where or how."

"So it's people we're dealing with?"

"I guess so. I mean, what use would wolves have for a delta wave modulator?" Clyde said with a nervous half-chuckle.

Shaun slowly released him. "What exactly did this modulator do?" he asked.

"I don't know. Like I said, no one had ever seen it work."

"What was it *supposed* to do?"

"Um...well, when it was activated, the brain of anyone standing within a certain distance in front of it would be forced to generate delta waves. The theory was, this would make the person go to sleep and dream. I guess he thought that was important because in some sleep disorders, the person can go to sleep but they can't have dreams, and they keep waking up."

Shaun's eyes narrowed. "And just how do you know so much about an experiment that was hatched in North Dakota and never written up?"

"One of his former colleagues used to work at Kirschner. We shared an office for a while. One day I saw some notes about it on his desk, talking about what materials he would need to complete the experiment. That's how I found out it was never finished, at least not to his knowledge."

"And you memorized the details so that later on you could pass off the idea as your own."

"Yeah." Clyde could not deny it, but at the moment they had bigger worries than intellectual property theft.

"There's something I don't understand," Harold said. "If someone in North Dakota built this thing and didn't tell anyone, how would someone in Greenland know what it was and what it did?"

"There's no telling why they took it," Clyde said. "Maybe it was just an interesting trinket, something they'd never seen before."

"Interesting enough to kill five people?" Shaun yelled. "And three of us?"

"That's why we have to get out of here! They're going to come back and finish the job! We have to take a snowmobile and get help!"

In a blind panic, Clyde ran outside without his parka. Harold, still wearing his, took off after him. "Come back here, you fool! You'll freeze to death in minutes!"

Harold soon caught up to Clyde, who was shaking like a rag doll in a high wind. He wrapped his arms tightly around him and led him back to the shelter with as much speed as he could manage.

Clyde collapsed. Hypothermia was already setting in. Harold tried desperately to get him on his feet. Shaun ran outside to help—and that was when he saw them.

"Behind you!" he shouted.

Too late.

The figures were cloaked in dark hooded robes. That was how they had approached unseen. The nearest one raised a spear above his head and drove it through Harold and into Clyde, pinning them both to the ice. They spasmed, then went limp and still.

Another of the figures approached Shaun. His brain screamed at him to get away, but his legs had gone deaf. He was rooted where he stood.

"Do not be afraid." The figure had reached him. Its voice was soft and feminine. Under the circumstances, it was not exactly a relief to him that she spoke English.

She pulled back her hood, and Shaun found himself looking at a woman who might have had her pick of fashion magazine covers anywhere else. She had alabaster skin, dark green eyes, and jet-black hair that cascaded to her shoulders in soft, graceful waves. Once he'd seen her face, she pulled her hood up. It was a cold night.

There were four others with her, including the executioner. They stood at a distance between him and the snowmobiles, but he could see that they were huge. His chances against even one of them were zero. The fight would be over before it started.

So be it. But he would at least know whose prisoner he was.

"Very well," he said, "who are you?"

"We are the servants of the Great Capering One," she answered. She gestured at the borealis, which did seem to be capering above them. "The secret of the lights has been entrusted to us. It is our sacred duty to protect it from outsiders."

"You mean you killed five people just to keep them from looking at your precious borealis?" Shaun demanded.

"You do not understand. The Spirit of the North Wind has blessed us with the lights. To allow anyone else to witness our ceremony would be a blasphemy to him."

"Ceremony?"

She pointed. "There."

The other four were now leaping and cavorting. At first their movements seemed to be random, but as Shaun watched, a pattern emerged. As the borealis flashed and writhed in the sky, they imitated its motions as closely as they could. The activity of their dance rose and fell with the activity of the borealis and changed with the predominating colors. Yet they were not just stumbling around. Shaun had never liked to dance, but to him their choreography looked flawless.

Vincent was right, Shaun thought. *Not in the way he believed, but he was right.*

"We cannot allow outsiders to witness our ritual," the woman said, "but neither do we wish anyone to suffer. Each time, before we came, we summoned the mists of sleep to fall upon you." She removed a black rectangular object from the folds of her cloak. "With this."

"What is that?" Shaun asked, though he already knew.

"We do not know. It has a great power we do not understand. Four winters ago, others like you came, and they brought it with them. We consecrated them to the North Wind, and we found this box. One of us picked it up and saw that it was smooth and dark, except for this small piece of silver, the talisman of the box. He touched it, it moved, and the rest of us fell asleep. He was unable to rouse us, and he believed we must have been possessed by the magicks of the box. But when he moved the talisman the other way, he was able to awaken us easily. The box has the power of sleep and waking, and for that we revere it."

Shaun saw no reason to improve her understanding of how the modulator worked. She had the basic idea, and he knew technicians whose explanations would have been even more primitive. However, there was something he had to know.

"Why am I still alive?"

"Because I have chosen you."

"Chosen...?"

"To dance with me."

"But..." He tried to get his mind around this. "I'm an outsider. I'm not even supposed to live, much less be your...dance partner." He felt laughter bubbling up in him at how silly that sounded, but forced it down. He didn't know how that would be interpreted, and he was completely at their mercy.

"Normally that is so. But we are permitted to make exceptions, should we wish it."

Shaun took stock of his situation. If he refused her offer, they would kill him. Maybe they would put him to sleep first, and maybe they wouldn't. If he accepted, that meant he agreed to live among them, and he would never be allowed to return home. Was that such a bad thing? There was nothing in Boston for him. There never really had been. Also, if this woman was to be his mate, or however they thought of it, he reasoned that he could do worse.

"What is your name?" he asked.

"You will not be able to pronounce it until you learn our language. But for now, you may call me Emma. One of those who came before left writings in which he spoke often of a woman with that name. She held great meaning for him. I do not know her, but I honor her."

"Oh. Well...it's nice to meet you, Emma. I'm Shaun."

She seemed to like this greeting. "It's nice to meet you, Shaun."

She did not seem interested in a handshake. Maybe that was just as well.

CROSSED LINES

It was Donna Bloom's day off, and she was looking forward to sleeping in and not doing much of anything. The doorbell put the kibosh on that dream, and on a somewhat naughtier one.

With surprise and not a little annoyance, she put on her robe and slippers and went to see who it was. Surprise because she almost never had visitors, and annoyance because this one had the nerve to call at 7:24 a.m. One of the few things she hated about living in the Midwest was that many of the people here really did get up before the chickens.

She opened the door. No one was on the porch. She looked up and down the street. No one was in sight.

Her head was already filling with nice evil thoughts of what she'd like to do to the person responsible for this hilarious practical joke when she glanced down and saw a small package, wrapped in plain brown paper. She picked it up to examine it. Her name and address were neatly printed on it. There was no return address.

She didn't dare bring it inside. There were all kinds of possibilities about what could have been in the package, and few were good. Still, she had to know what it was. She knelt down and unwrapped it.

The tape was weak and the paper came off easily, to reveal what appeared to be an ordinary answering machine.

It was a useful present, but she couldn't imagine who could have given it to her, especially this way. If visitors were rare for her, phone calls were rarer. Unless you counted telemarketers, but who did? She was an anachronism because she did not have (or need) a cell phone, only a land line.

She closed the door, shivering and stamping her feet. She loved South Dakota's beauty and tranquility. Its winters? Not so much.

As she connected the machine to her phone, she thought she had the answer. Her mother was the ultimate morning person, often up and about by five. Also, she loved to go for runs, and her route sometimes took her by Donna's house. This was on purpose, because she had tried for months to get her daughter interested in running with her, but finally gave up. That must have been it: she dropped off the package during her run and stopped just long enough to ring the doorbell so as not to lose her momentum. That would also explain why she hadn't bothered with a return address.

Donna called to thank her.

"Hello?" the voice answered brightly.

"Hi, Mom, it's me."

"Oh, hello, Donna."

After acknowledging her identity, her mother fell silent and waited for her to say what she wanted.

"I just wanted to thank you for the machine."

"Machine? What machine?"

"You didn't leave an answering machine on my doorstep?"

"Certainly not."

For a moment she thought her mother was putting her on, but knew that was utterly foreign to her character. Donna was lighthearted by nature and loved to laugh, but this was not because these were supposedly character traits typical of overweight people. It was because she did not want to be like her mother, who exemplified the stereotype of the mirthless, no-nonsense Midwesterner. If she said she hadn't left the machine, she hadn't. But then who did?

These thoughts went through Donna's mind in half a second. "Oh," was all she said out loud.

"Someone gave you an answering machine?"

"Yes. It was wrapped in brown paper, and there was no return address on it, so I thought it might have been you."

"Well, it wasn't. Are you coming for lunch today?"

Donna sighed, but made sure it was inaudible. Her mother had never had much use for chit-chat. "Yes. What time?"

"11:30."

"I'll be there."

"See you then. Enjoy your machine. Of course it's not likely you'll get much use out of it—"

"Goodbye, Mother," she said and hung up. It was fortunate that Mrs. Bloom took no great offense to being hung up on. Donna found herself doing it whenever her mother made a jab at her weight or lack of a social life, which she now did regularly.

It was not Donna's ambition to be a spinster, but as she had repeatedly tried and failed to explain to her mother, she was content with being single even at what her mother considered her advanced age. She was twenty-six. More importantly, she was content with her appearance. If a man couldn't live with that, she couldn't live with him.

She looked at the clock on the wall behind her. Twenty minutes to eight. She wanted to trade in her car today, and figured she might as well start getting ready since she was up. So she showered and dressed (and dressed, and dressed—the sun was just now making its grudging appearance, so it was a balmy minus ten), and went out.

The car dealership opened at nine, so she had time for breakfast first. She went to a local coffee shop that she frequented, which the waitresses found somewhat odd because she did not drink coffee. But they boasted the best sausage biscuits in the tri-county area, and she was not inclined to argue. Instead she treated herself to two of them, along with two bananas—the children she took care of loved bananas and had gotten her hooked on them—and a glass of milk.

She took her time with her meal, but was still the car dealership's first customer of the day. The salesman was extremely accommodating, probably because she wanted another Honda and was trading up for a newer and more expensive model. By the time she got back home, she was in such a good mood that she sang along with the radio.

She walked by the kitchen, and what she saw made her look again.

There was a message on her machine.

This day was off to a roaring start. She even allowed herself to fantasize for a moment that it was the devastatingly attractive graduate student who worked at the local library, calling to ask her out. But whoever it was, it was impolite to keep them waiting. She played back the message.

It was a man's voice. But it was not the grad student. And it was definitely not a social call.

"Look out! *Look out for that truck! D.B.!*"

A terrified scream.

Then the squeal of slammed-on brakes.

Then silence.

She stared at the machine, too stunned to move or even to think. Slowly she lifted her hand and pushed Erase.

The machine beeped once and the message was gone, leaving her to grapple with its meaning. Had it been addressed to her? They had used her initials. Some of the locals had a habit of referring to certain people and places by their initials or in some other verbal shorthand, but no one she knew did that. The caller ID identified the number as Unknown.

The phone rang. She cried out and jumped back.

She recognized the number, but could not make her hand move to the receiver. The phone rang once, twice, three times, and at the end of the fourth ring she picked it up.

"Hello?"

"Hey, Donna! Glad I caught you. I was just making sure you were coming over to Mom and Dad's for lunch."

She nearly collapsed with relief. It wasn't another trick. It really was her brother, Keith.

"Donna? Hello?"

"Oh, sorry. Uh, yeah. Yeah, I'll be there."

"Are you okay? You sound a little spaced."

"Oh, yeah, I'm fine, I just...I didn't sleep well last night, so I'm kind of out of it."

"No problem. Just get Dad to tell you one of his war stories. That'll put you right out."

"I heard that!" yelled a voice in the background.

"So anyway, it's at 11:30," Keith said. "Mom told you that, right?"

"Yeah. I talked to her earlier. Should I bring anything?"

"No, just bring yourself. *Please.*"

"I'll be there," she said and hung up, wondering yet again how he could stand it.

Donna talked to her parents as infrequently as possible, but Keith was still living with them while he worked his way through college. His entreaty was not out of any great desire to see her but out of his conviction that it was always better to spread the misery.

Their parents had wasted their lives, and they knew it, and they made sure everyone else knew it. Not surprisingly, few were willing to be the sounding boards for their lifetime of accumulated bitterness, so the two of them got it all.

Donna looked at the clock. 11:07. That left her just enough time.

At 11:28 she pulled into their driveway. Keith was outside waiting for her, and not because he enjoyed the bracing cold.

"What's the forecast?" she asked.

"They're in rare form. I'd say a ninety percent chance of yelling."

"I was afraid of that. Okay, let's get this over with."

Their mother had made baked chicken with mushroom sauce, green bean casserole, sweet potatoes, and fruit salad. Whatever else she was, they had to admit she was an incredible cook. Her father was living proof of this fact. Until two years ago, he hadn't known how much he weighed because their scale only went up to three hundred pounds. He hated exercise, always had, but when he finally couldn't take another day of his wife's relentless nagging, he agreed to go walking with her, then running. Eventually he came to like it ("I told you so" was her favorite sentence, and she got plenty of use out of it over this), and began to shed his excess poundage. Now he proudly pointed out that he was literally half the man he used to be.

This turned out to be a mixed blessing, however. Once her mother no longer had a reason to criticize him for his weight, she came down on Donna with full force. Her father, who had been her ally on this issue if on no other, joined with relish in the attacks. He told her constantly that if he could lose his weight, there was no reason she couldn't lose hers.

As soon as they were all inside, they sat down to eat. Donna took four bites before she looked up and noticed her mother watching her like a hawk.

"What are you doing?"

"I'm just making sure you don't eat too much."

72

She dropped her fork in frustration. "Mom, I'm not going to eat too much."

"It's a mother's job to make up for what a child lacks. Everyone has an internal mechanism that tells them when they've eaten enough. Yours is obviously broken, so I have to fill in."

Donna had promised herself that no matter what happened, she would not cry in front of her parents. She dropped her head to hide her moistening eyes, but her chest heaved with helpless anxiety.

"Phyllis, leave the girl alone."

Donna looked up, incredulous. Did her father just speak up for her?

"Frank, you know good and well that if I leave her alone, then so will every man on Earth."

"That's beside the point. The girl has no willpower, and we have to accept that. If she wants to be a fat cow, that's her business."

She looked forlornly to Keith for support, but knew she would get none. As long as they were picking on her, they would leave him alone. Sure enough, he was staring down at his plate, shoveling in his food. This brought him no criticism because he was pencil-thin, but he hoped he would be finished and far away from the table before they got around to grilling him for the gazillionth time on what he intended to do with his life.

She had to handle this herself. "I have to go," she said, and stood up.

"What do you mean, you have to go?" asked her mother. "You just got here!"

And it feels like I've been here for a month. "I just remembered, there's something I have to take care of."

"Sit down and eat," her father said. "Whatever it is, it can wait."

"No, really, it can't. I have to go." She ran out before they could say another word. They looked at each other, shrugged, figured maybe it was her time of the month, and went back to their own meals.

Once Donna was in her car, she permitted herself a few seconds of wracking sobs before she got herself under some measure of control. Then she started the engine and lurched out of the driveway, grateful no one was coming down the street. She drove home as fast as she dared.

She walked in the door, slammed and locked it behind her, and made a beeline for the bedroom. She was going to sleep for a week, no matter what her employers said.

Passing the kitchen, she saw something out of the corner of her eye.

A light was blinking on the answering machine. She had a message.

Before she could stop herself, she had walked over to it, her body acting of its own accord and blithely ignoring her brain screaming at it to stop. Some unseen puppeteer lifted her arm, extended her index finger, and brought it down on the Play button.

"Look out for that truck! D.B.! D.B.!"

She stabbed the Erase button, cutting off the sound of squealing tires. She let loose an anguished scream at the same time and fell to the floor. All the strength had gone out of her. She lay there for a few seconds, then crawled, then stumbled to her bedroom and collapsed on the bed.

It was half past three when she woke up. The sun was already low in the sky, and shining directly through her window. She shielded her eyes and sat up, feeling a bit better but still black and blue with psychic bruises.

She emerged from the bedroom. The answering machine was directly in her line of sight.

There were no messages.

She mouthed a prayer of gratitude, but decided this had gone far enough. She went to the phone and pressed *69, the callback function. We're sorry, your call cannot be completed as dialed. *Of course not. Why should this be easy?*

So she called the police. Rather, she tried to call the police.

The receiver informed her that this call could not be completed by erupting in a near-ultrasonic screech that almost ruptured her eardrum.

She held the receiver as far from her as she could and tried again. The same thing happened. The phone service out here was not always a hundred percent reliable, one of the few disadvantages of living in the boonies.

All right, if she couldn't call them, she had to go down to the station and talk to them in person.

Some day off this was turning out to be.

One of the good things about living in a small town was that maybe there wasn't much to do, but there was never any traffic to speak of. Barely ten minutes later she arrived at the police station and went inside.

"Can I help you?" asked the desk sergeant.

"Yes. I'd like to report some phone calls I've been getting."

"Are they harassing calls?"

"Well...not exactly. I don't know. They're just...weird."

"Why don't you tell me about them?"

She did. When she finished, the sergeant rubbed his chin and said, "You're right, miss. That is strange."

"Isn't there something you can do?" Donna pleaded. "Maybe trace the calls, find out who's making them?"

"Doesn't work that way, I'm afraid. You say the messages only last a couple of seconds?"

"That's right."

"Not nearly enough time for a trace, even if we had reason to do one," the sergeant said.

"You don't think this is worth doing anything about?"

"I understand your worry, miss, but we've gotten complaints like this before. Always turns out to be somebody's little joke. Whoever it is, they're bound to get tired of it soon, if they haven't already."

"Officer, whoever's making these calls isn't joking. There's real terror in his voice."

"Miss, you're still young, but you'll learn this soon enough. There are some real sickos out there, and they got some mighty strange ideas about what's funny. But at this point, there's really nothing we can do. My advice to you is to just go home and try to relax."

Donna thanked the sergeant and left. She seethed with frustration, but knew he was right. She hoped he was also right about her gentleman caller's short attention span.

But she was not going to test that theory just yet. She got home, hurried inside, and jogged across the living room, determined not to look to her left. But she ignored too much of her peripheral vision, barked her shin on the corner of her coffee table, and went sprawling. As she got up, she happened, just for an instant, to glance toward the kitchen.

Her message light was blinking.

You're not going to answer it. You are not.

What am I, stupid? Of course I'm not going to answer it. I'm going to go into the bedroom, get undressed, get into bed, pull the covers over my head, and wait for this day to be over.

Okay, good. So we're in agreement. Right?

Right.

Her mind and body had consensus, but her mutinous legs carried her into the kitchen anyway. She looked down at the machine and sighed heavily. The blinking red light teased her. She had to know.

She pressed Play.

"Look out! The truck! D.B.!"

That was it. She punched the Erase button and decided two things. First, she was going to call her employer and tell her she was taking tomorrow off. Maybe there were some jobs where it didn't matter if you were a nervous wreck, but that of a nanny was not one of them. Second, she was going to unplug this machine, take it to the city dump, and ask the custodian to drop it in the incinerator and allow her to watch.

She dialed her employer's number. The phone rang three times. Four. Five. Seven. Ten. Eleven. She called the cell number, with the same result.

She hung up, bewildered. Leslie Blanchard was a real estate agent and could never afford to miss a call from a potential client, yet her machine was off and she wasn't answering her phones. Either of those by itself might not be a big deal. Both of them together warranted checking out. She might be in some kind of trouble.

Leslie's Explorer was parked in the driveway. Now Donna was really worried.

She knocked on the door. It was not closed all the way, and her knocks inched it open. Cautiously, she looked inside. Leslie sat on the far end of the sofa, weeping quietly.

"Leslie?"

Leslie jumped at the sound of her name. She looked at her guest as if trying to remember who she was.

"Leslie? Are you all right?"

Donna didn't know why she asked that. Leslie's eyes were red from prolonged crying. Whatever had happened, she was miles from all right.

"Oh...Donna," she said at last. Her eyes were glazed; she seemed to be trying to focus them. "This really isn't a good time."

"Leslie, what's wrong?"

Leslie could say only "Dennis" before she broke down again. Dennis was her husband. Had he been in an accident? Was he in the hospital? No, Leslie would be there, not here. Had he left her, maybe? They had always seemed to have a blissfully happy marriage, but you never knew anymore.

Donna sat next to her and put her arm around her. "Leslie, tell me what happened. Maybe I can help."

"It was two hours ago," Leslie finally managed to say. "The police just left. They told me everything. He had a green light. They said he had a green light. We had run out of bananas and he had gone out for some more. He was on his way home. He was almost home. But the truck hit him." Then she collapsed into uncontrollable sobbing. Donna could only wait until it petered out on its own. When it did, she said, "It was on the answering machine."

The words ripped through Donna. "What? What did you say?"

"When I got home." Leslie was barely intelligible now. "We had a new machine hooked up to our phone. I thought he had bought it. There was a message on it. Somebody yelling 'Look out for the truck, D.B.' And then the police came..."

Donna would get no more out of her, but she didn't have to. She knew everything now.

There was one thing she knew above all else. She had to get rid of that machine.

Leslie didn't see her leave. There was no point in saying goodbye.

In South Dakota in winter, night fell quickly. By the time Donna was on the road again, it was full dark. She saw nobody out and about, which was a good thing. In her present state of mind, anyone who crossed the street in front of her did so at his own peril.

What *was* that machine? Was it some kind of...relay to the other side? Did it pick up messages from...?

Then she had a horrifying realization.

The message was always the same, as were the initials. D.B.

Donna Bloom.

Dennis Blanchard.

And now Dennis was dead.

The light ahead of her turned yellow. She had to beat it. She gunned the engine.

She never had a chance.

The semi hadn't been there a moment earlier. She would have sworn it hadn't. But now here it was, barreling down on her, its headlights filling the world. Had she caught a glimpse of what was written above its cab, she might have laughed. She didn't even have time to scream before the Dole Bananas truck slammed into her.

The man opened his front door early the next morning and looked around, but no one was there. He was about to close the door when he noticed something on the porch. It was a small package wrapped in plain brown paper. He had just picked it up to examine it when his wife appeared beside him.

"Oh, no," she said. "Darryl Burke, what have you bought now?"

Field Trip

March 1, 8:24 a.m.

I can't believe it—I'm actually in Egypt! Maybe it's lucky the flight didn't last any longer than it did, the captain might have thrown me out of the plane. But I don't care what Islam says about excitable women, this is a once-in-a-lifetime opportunity. And to think, my professor offered it to me! I always thought she was annoyed with me because I kept offering her suggestions about what to teach in class. Professors like to do things their own way, but from the first day I met her I knew she was open to new ideas. Why else would she be teaching a course in Alternative Religions? And why else would she have taken such an interest in me?

I have to go over how it all happened again, so I can be sure this isn't all a dream. That's also why I've brought you along, my faithful diary, to serve as a record of everything I did and saw while I was here.

Okay, let's see...it was the end of the last class before the weekend, so naturally the other students were only thinking about how to scramble their minds and bodies. I, however, was focused on how I could make Professor Carlson's class even better. So I walked up to her desk (she got kind of an exasperated look, but I know she only does that because the other students always see me talking to her and she doesn't want them to think she's playing favorites) and suggested that we do a project on ancient Egyptian mythology. She looked at me for a second and raised her left eyebrow the way she does when somebody says something really interesting (as you might imagine, that doesn't happen a whole lot) and asked me to sit down and tell her what I had in mind. Surely the fates were with me—this was the first time in months I've had an idea to share with her and she didn't have a faculty meeting or something right after class. So I suggested to her that perhaps we could organize a field trip to Egypt, maybe study the hieroglyphs on a few sarcophagi, or whatever those things are called, and talk to some of the natives and get the real story on their beliefs. I never cease to be amazed by how biased and ignorant our textbooks can be. And she said that was a great idea, and since I was the one who thought of it, I should have the honor of going to Egypt myself and interviewing some of the holy men!

I don't mind telling you that absolutely made my day. Imagine, me ever thinking she didn't like me! It just goes to show you how wrong our opinions can be, doesn't it? And then she told me not to worry, she'd take care of everything, I should just come by her office on Monday morning and there would be a plane ticket waiting for me. I got so excited I jumped up and hugged her. I apologized, of course, you're really not allowed to do that, but she said not to worry about that either.

The head of the Liberal Arts department is retiring at the end of the year. I'm going to nominate Professor Carlson as his successor.

March 1, 11:37 a.m.

You'll never guess where I am now. I'm inside a tomb! No, I'm not dead, in fact I've never felt so alive! When I got off the plane, there was a man waiting for me. I love the way these people talk, it sounded musical when he said, "Miss Dimwitty?" That's not really my name, of course, it's just the professor's little joke. Besides, she can hardly be expected to remember all her students' names, and Dimwitty is close enough to Dunwiddy. So I said, "That's me!" and he laughed—the people here are so friendly!—and took me out to a waiting taxi. We rode for a while, and I was chattering the whole way, I was afraid that maybe I was getting on his nerves, but he just smiled and nodded and asked me questions, which surprised me, nobody ever asks me questions. And then...you won't believe this. The taxi took us out to a waiting camel, because I would be going to a place in the actual desert where I could examine some of the ancient writings for myself. He explained they would still be readable because Egypt's hot, dry climate is ideal for preserving written text. Talk about the authentic experience!

So the camel brought us here, to a pyramid that served as a tomb for some of the lesser figures in the ruling hierarchy, but before that (in the time of the 26th Dynasty according to my guide), it was the center of worship for one of ancient Egypt's most important deities. He told me to wait here—I can't believe how cool it is inside, maybe because not that much sunlight ever gets in—until he comes back, because he has to bring someone back for me to talk to and the person lives in an area unsuitable for a lady. And he gave me a huge backpack full of food and water to sustain me while I wait, and a bedroll to sleep in if I got tired—he had warned me that he might be a long time coming back, life in the desert can be very unpredictable.

Just try to find a man that thoughtful in the States!

March 1, 4:19 p.m.

Did I say a thoughtful man in the States? About now I'd settle for anyone.

It's been five hours since he left me here—I never told you his name, did I? He told me everyone calls him Anka (no, not as in Paul Anka, though he gets that a lot). It's a shortened version of his real name, which is a real tongue-twister. Are you ready for this? His honest-to-goodness name is Ankh-af-na-Khonsu. (I asked him to write it down for me.) I didn't want to sound stupid, for all I know, that may be a common name here, but I couldn't resist asking him where it came from, and am I glad I did, because you won't believe what he said.

The ancient Egyptians believed in four principal gods, each of which rules an Aeon of two thousand years. At the end of that time the reigning god yields to the next god in an event called the Equinox of the Gods. Bet it beats the Winter Ball by a mile, huh? Anyway, around 500 BC, a Priest of the Princes ended the Aeon of Isis and heralded the Aeon of Osiris. His name was Ankh-af-na-Khonsu, and my guide says the original priest was the beginning of an unbroken line of priests, of which he was the last until eleven years ago, when his first son was born. (One guess what his name is!) I know that people in this part of the world are famous for telling stories, but man, I hope this one is true.

I also hope he comes back soon. Time may not mean much in the desert, but it sure does to me.

March 1, 7:52 p.m.

Still no sign of him, but at least I have company now.

About an hour ago, two jackals came in and sat down just inside the entrance, and they haven't moved since then. I was a little worried at first, because jackals are scavengers like vultures are, and seeing vultures in the desert is never a good sign. But you know, I actually think these animals were sent to help me. A little while after they came, a vulture did show up at the entrance and the jackals chased it off. It might've been hoping it could peck my eyes out while I was asleep. I've heard vultures like to do that. But with my new protectors standing guard, that's no longer a worry.

And that's not all they do, it seems. They also helped me make my greatest discovery yet. They kept looking at a corner of the tomb at the opposite end from me. I kept trying to see what they were looking at, but all I could see was sand and more sand. Then a gust of wind blew some of it off what looked like an old book. Well, you can just imagine how excited I was—this book may have been here since the time of the pharaohs! Immediately I went over and lifted it out. The cover is ornate, lettered in gold leaf. I didn't believe it at first either, but I'm looking at it with my own eyes! Obviously it was made as some kind of chronicle for the reigning monarch, whoever that was. The problem is the title is in the language they spoke at that time, I think it's called Cuneiform. Or maybe Sanskrit, or Akkadian. One of those. Duh, why would it be anything else? But it might take a while to find someone who can translate it. I'm scared to open it, it's been sitting here so long the pages might crumble to dust if they're disturbed. But when I get home, this book is going straight to a museum and I'm going to be famous!

I just hope nothing happens to you, dear diary, because I'll be telling my grandchildren about this trip and I want them to be able to read you for themselves.

March 2, 6:04 a.m.

I was kind of freaked when I woke up. My guide still hasn't come back, and I was starting to wonder if something had happened to him. He had warned me about the place where he was going. But I forgot all about that when I saw the book.

The wind must have blown it open during the night, and I found that the pages, while of course brittle, can still be handled carefully. At first the pages were blank, which got me to thinking maybe the person who made this book didn't live long after that. I don't think ancient Egyptian monarchs were generally known for their sense of humor. But then the most amazing thing happened. As I was looking at the page, writing appeared on it. In English, yet! And this is what it said:

The tale of the Sun is a jocular one,
For he is a prankster, you see.
He looks from on high, where he reigns in the sky,
And wonders what fools we must be.

The tale of the Wind cannot help but portend
The truth of what must be your fate.
It comes and it goes, and wherever it blows,
It curses the small and the great.

The mightiest hand penned the tale of the Sand;
It could have been no other way.
Kings rise but to fall, and the gods, one and all,
Bear witness to this very day.

The biggest mystery is how a book as old as this one obviously is could have its text in modern English. I think I know the answer, it's just too incredible to believe. But maybe if I write it down I'll see that it makes sense after all, so, here goes.

Egyptian myth mentions something called the Akashic Record, the place where all things past, present, and future are written down. Do you suppose this is something like that? Some kind of a...I don't know, some kind of magic book? That it shows whoever's reading it whatever they need to know in language they can understand? If that's true, then I've got to figure out what I'm supposed to learn from it. One thing is clear: this is a book like no other. I can understand why it's been hidden so well, a lot of people would do anything to get their hands on it. When I get out of here, I'll have to keep it under lock and key until it's in good hands. And that means, first of all, sneaking it through Customs. There's no way I can risk letting them examine it, they might destroy some of the pages.

For whatever reason, this book's wisdom has been entrusted to me, and it's my duty to share it with the world. I must not fail. I will not.

March 2, 9:16 a.m.

If I was wondering about the nature of this book before, what just happened was more than enough to remove all doubt.

I had finished my last water bottle and I was really getting worried because I know how quickly you can dehydrate in the desert. The book was open right in front of me, and I noticed there were four stanzas, where before I know for a fact there had only been three. I started to snatch it up but caught myself—I have to keep reminding myself how fragile this book is. So instead I left it where it was and leaned over it to read:

All things with a name must return whence they came.
Despair not, but rather take heed.
What flows like a breath through this chamber of death
Of life is the source and the seed.

As soon as I read that, I noticed the light glinting off something deeper inside the pyramid. I went to see what it was, and what did I find? A tiny pond, right in the middle of the tomb! How could I not have seen it before? Maybe it rained sometime during the night, some of the rain seeped in under the walls, and it just popped up. However it got here, I knew I had to fill my water bottles from it before it dried up, so after drinking as much as I could, that was what I did. And this time I'll ration my supply.

I'm starting to wonder what these jackals really are, though. They haven't eaten or drunk anything since they got here. They just sit at the entrance, watching me. And something really unsettling happened earlier this morning. No one had come back for me, so I thought I should go outside to see what I could see. But as soon as I got near the entrance, the jackals started growling and snapping at me and I had to back away. I tried a couple more times and the same thing happened.

It looks like these jackals were meant to serve a dual purpose. They're not just here to keep other animals from coming in. They're here to keep me from getting out.

March 2, 8:48 p.m.

A full day has passed, the sun is setting now, and still no sign of Anka or anyone else. I'm starting to wonder if he's ever coming back.

One good thing: at least I won't have to worry about starving for a while yet. I still have lots of food left, and I haven't been hungry since I started drinking the water from the pond. Maybe it's got special minerals in it or something. I don't suppose it really matters.

The only thing I can do is get a good night's sleep and hope things look a little better in the morning. I had thought about sneaking out while the jackals were asleep, but no such luck. Not only do they never eat or drink, they don't seem to need sleep either. They just sit there looking at me, perfectly calm as long as I don't get too close to the entrance.

I just had a horrible thought: what if Anka never planned on coming back for me? What if he didn't go to meet any holy man? What if he just left me here to die?

No. That doesn't make any sense. This trip was set up by Professor Carlson, so he's obviously a friend of hers, and she would never let anything happen to me.

I guess I should just sleep now. If I'm just being paranoid, it's because I'm so tired, and if I'm right...well, there's nothing I can do about it.

See you in the morning.

March 3, 7:35 a.m.

Well, it's morning, but I don't feel better. I feel ten times worse.

Most of that is probably due to the fact that I just passed the longest night of my life. I must have woken up every hour, so thirsty it felt like my throat was coated with sand. I swore I would ration my water supply but I couldn't help myself. Every time I woke up I would open a bottle and guzzle half of it. The pond is still there, and so far I've been able to replenish whatever I drink. But how long can that last? The water will be sucked into the ground before long—I'm amazed that hasn't happened already—and there's no telling when it will rain again.

Something else that hasn't done my mood much good. As soon as it was light enough I happened to glance at the book and I saw there were two more verses in it.

Where knowledge abounds, all of Heaven resounds,
The better the wise to esteem.
Those who have it not should more humbly have sought,
For nothing is as it may seem.

If you, when hard-pressed, have pursued what is best,
Then shall Yaru pursue you in turn.
But if by your pride to yourself you have lied,
By the hand of Lord Set you will burn.

Okay. From what I remember of what I've read about their mythology, I know Yaru is their heaven. Osiris, one of their main gods, became the god of the dead after he was murdered by his brother Set and resurrected by his wife with the help of another god, Anubis. Anubis then became the god of embalming, I guess because he had such a knack for it.

Wait a minute, that reminds me of something...

Wait, I have to drink some more water.

That's better. You can't imagine this thirst, it feels like my insides are turning to dust.

On the way here Anka and I were discussing a few things about his religion, specifically the animal iconography. He told me Anubis is the god that's depicted with the head of a jackal, it's not Osiris, as I had thought. I pointed out that the most important aspect of tolerance of other beliefs is not to make a big deal about little mistakes like that, and after all one god is pretty much like any other, right? Maybe I shouldn't have said that, I could tell I had offended him...

Hang on, I need another swig of water...

Anyway, I could tell I had offended him, but he didn't say anything and I figured, no harm, no foul.

Did he bring me here to punish me? Did they do something like this in the time of the first Ankh-whatever-his-name-was?

No, that's silly, there's no way he could...

Needed some more water. I can't *believe* this thirst!

There's no way he could have set this up. Jackals can't be trained like dogs can, and what about the book? How could he possibly have...

I needed a minute there, it's getting hard to see. Still plenty bright outside, that's weird, but I don't feel so good. Getting hard to write too. Body's getting stiff. Is it possible this water is poisoned? Is that why...

Sorry. Had to drink some more, poisoned or not.

Crazy random thought: since the jackals are servants of Anubis and he was the god of embalming, maybe it's actually embalming fluid, huh? Watered down, of course.

Feel sleepy now. Have to take a nap. Maybe when I wake up Anka will

A telephone rang late the following evening. It was answered on the second ring.

"Hello?"

"It is done."

"Good. I knew I could count on you."

"As I listened to her speak so freely of sacred matters of which she is so ignorant, my duty became clear. Those such as her disturb the harmonies of the cosmos."

"She's on her way back, then?"

"You will see her tomorrow."

"Excellent. You perform your duties perfectly, as always. And please don't be offended when I say this, but I hope it will be a long time before we speak again."

"Do not concern yourself with such trifles. I have lived a long life in service to the gods. However long it will be before I am needed again is already known to them, may their will be done in all things. Peace be with you, Linda Carlson."

"And with you, Ankh-af-na-Khonsu."

True to his word, a package arrived for her with the next morning's mail. She shut her door, sat at her desk, and opened it. Inside was a blue backpack bearing the name "Heather Dunwiddy" in permanent marker. She smiled. So few things were permanent.

She stood the backpack upright and opened it. It was half-filled with sand, almost enough to obscure the only other things inside: a diary and a larger book. Carefully she reached inside, lifted out the book, set it on her desk and opened it, reading the seven poetic stanzas written in it. Of particular interest to her was the last.

Whatever you try, you live only to die,
As is dirt washed away by the rain.
Presume not to stand with the Sun, Wind, and Sand—
In the end, they are all that remain.

Photo Album

There were times Geneviève Petillon found it hard to believe the day Charles Duchamp asked her to marry him had been the happiest of her life. As is often the way of these things, he hadn't had much to say to her since then, and today everything she had been waiting to say until the right time—which she now realized was never going to come—erupted in a torrent of mutual recrimination. She barely gave him time to pick up the phone before she fired the first salvo.

"Why do you even want me to marry you? So you'll have someone besides your mother to cook for you, is that it?"

"You know perfectly well why I have been so busy! I have been building a home for us to live in—"

"Charles, how many times do I have to tell you? I'm a city girl! I always have been, I always will be! Maybe living in a cabin in the middle of the woods is your idea of heaven, but for me it's a reasonable facsimile of the other place! Can't you at least think about living in Montreal? It's so beautiful here—"

"I respectfully disagree. It's crowded. It's expensive. Sometimes it's tolerably clean. But beautiful, no. For that, there is no comparison to my village."

"Lourdes-du-Blanc-Sablon is a thousand kilometers away! When would I ever see my family?"

"Now you're being silly. Whenever you like, of course."

"Whenever I like in the summer, maybe. Half the roads between here and there are impassable in winter and the phone service becomes a crap shoot. We'd be cut off from the rest of the world for half the year! Is that really what you want? What am I saying? Of course it is."

"We have been a family of the outdoors since the time of my

great-grandfather. You knew that when we met, and as I recall you thought it was wonderful. Or perhaps that was one of your little jokes, yes?"

One thing Geneviève did not think was so wonderful about Charles was his temper. She heard it rising in his voice and instinctively extended an olive branch.

"Charles, please, let's be reasonable. Lourdes-du-Blanc-Sablon has incredible natural beauty, I readily admit that. But you know it doesn't have much of anything else. It's no kind of place to raise a family—"

"My family believed otherwise."

"I'm sorry. I didn't mean it like that. Look, we can find a way to resolve this. Let me come up for the weekend and we can talk it out, face to face, okay?"

"That is a fine idea. My parents will be pleased to see you again."

He said this in a stiff, formal way. Once he had been offended he was not difficult to appease, but it took a little while for the chill to leave his voice. She decided she would take what she could get. "Great! Let's say, Friday at six?"

"Very well. You remember where we live, yes?"

It's not exactly hard to find, there are no other houses within four kilometers of yours. She choked off this thought and said simply, "Yes. I'll see you then."

"Au revoir." And he hung up.

Not for the first time, Geneviève wondered what she was getting herself into. Charles could be adorable when he wanted to be. The problem was that he could also be a few other things, a fact of which her mother reminded her every chance she got.

"You're convinced he's not a violent man," she would say, "and you're probably right. We all like him very much, you know that. But you also know how stubborn he can be. And don't forget, he has a quick temper and a lumberjack's strength. That combination worries me. It should worry you also."

She therefore decided her mother did not need to know about this last conversation.

The next morning she took her eight-year-old nephew to soccer practice, but her thoughts were still too full of what had happened the night before. After running two red lights and narrowly avoiding several accidents, she asked her brother to take him back home—much to the dismay of her nephew, who had briefly allowed himself to hope that someone in his boring family had finally learned how to drive.

Montreal had the traffic problems of any big city, but traffic was nonexistent once she left it. She had planned to get to Lourdes-du-Blanc-Sablon by six, and arrived with forty minutes to spare. Charles' parents were waiting outside for her, and they smiled and waved when they saw her pull into the driveway.

She couldn't help but smile back. From the day Charles had introduced her to them, they had treated her as their own daughter. Whatever happened with Charles, this would not be a wasted trip.

No sooner was she out of the car than Mrs. Duchamp enveloped her in a choking embrace that almost brought her to tears. By the time they separated, she noticed that Mr. Duchamp had already unloaded her car. She had no time to remark on this because Mrs. Duchamp was already ushering her inside. She sat Geneviève on the couch with a plate full of freshly baked cookies and a pitcher of orange juice on the table in front of her before she could ask where Charles was.

"He'll be back soon. He's been working all day, so he wanted to go for a walk in the woods before you got here. It's his favorite way to relieve stress, you know."

Yes, she did know. What remained to be seen was how much stress he had to relieve.

The pale, slender woman sitting in the house was so different in demeanor and temperament from the hulking, ruddy man walking through the woods behind it that an observer might have found it hard to believe they were acquaintances, let alone engaged.

Charles Duchamp would have had no trouble being taken for a lumberjack even without his flannel shirt and knitted cap. He was six feet five, two hundred ninety pounds of brawn and sinew, with a broad face, a thick, squat neck, and massive, calloused hands, each attached to an arm that could lift Geneviève over his head without effort.

Understandably, her parents' first reaction to him was markedly different from that of his parents to her. Her mother was reluctant even to let them go out after dinner until her father made two compelling points: he was a perfect gentleman despite his rough appearance; and what man, no matter how drunk, would make a move on her while she was with him?

Now he was strolling through the woods that were his second home. Had he known Geneviève was at the house waiting for him, he would have gone back and insisted that she come for a walk with him. He knew she could only voice her objections while surrounded by the urban sprawl and barely controlled chaos that was Montreal. But out here, in the serene majesty of God's cathedral, she could not help but see things his way. And his family would help to persuade her—why, they took better care of her than her own family did! What possible reason could she have for not wanting to live near them?

Also, he would have much to teach her here. Nature had so many secrets that so-called modern medicine was only beginning to catch on to, things he had known most of his life. For almost any common illness or injury he could point to the plant that could treat it and show her how to make the remedy. And their sons would grow big and strong here, with the crisp, clean air and water, so much room to wander around in, and plentiful and natural food. He never wondered that she was so small, subsisting on the slop that city people ate. Just being out here never failed to give him a feeling of sublime tranquility.

He sat down under a tree to enjoy it and to listen to the music of the woods. The singing of the birds, the chittering and scurrying of the small rodents, the rustling of the leaves, the pealing of the bell...

That last sound snapped him out of his reverie. There were no bells here. The nearest bell tower was nearly a two-hour drive, and even here sound couldn't carry nearly that far.

It was faint, but there was no doubt it was the tolling of a church bell. Charles got up and set off in search of the sound.

After a few minutes he came to a clearing with a shallow valley that he knew intimately, except now there was one minor difference. At the bottom of the valley stood a small, white clapboard church with stained-glass windows. The bell in its steeple would be calling the faithful to worship, if there were any.

"*Nom de Dieu,*" he whispered, crossing himself.

Although Charles was a devout Roman Catholic, there would normally have been no reason for him to do either of these things. But these were decidedly not normal circumstances, for two reasons. One, he'd been here three days ago, and this church was not here then. Two, he knew this church. It was called Our Father of Saint Christopher's, or if you wanted to be picky, Notre Père de Saint-Christophe. He was baptized in it as an infant. Six years later there was a wedding in it. He'd had the flu and could not attend, but he remembered that wedding. It was the day the church burned to the ground.

All his family ever told him was that the fire was caused by an electrical short. The official accounts provided no other details, and no one would answer his questions. Shortly thereafter, the church and the wedding became forbidden subjects in their household. This seemed to be the prevailing sentiment in the village, because those who died in the fire were buried in unmarked graves, and the church was never rebuilt.

While he ruminated on these things, his legs drew him ever closer to the church until he realized with a start that he was about to walk into it. He stopped and looked at the gleaming white walls that might have been painted yesterday. He started to walk around them, admiring the tableaux depicted in the stained glass artwork, when he noticed the bell had stopped ringing.

I must be the only worshipper today, he thought, and continued on. The mosaics were beautiful, but not what he would have expected. There were no renditions of the Last Supper, or of Jesus on the cross, or of any of the apostles. Instead there was only...

C'est impossible.

But there it was. Rather, there he was. He stared at a red and blue window featuring a stern-looking portrait of Charles Duchamp.

He could not even allow himself to believe it was just a Biblical figure that looked like him. He had never seen a rendering that reminded him of himself, and he knew for a fact that the Israelite wardrobe of two thousand years ago did not include knitted caps and checkered shirts. But that's what this person was wearing because, all common sense to the contrary, this person was *him.*

Mouth agape, he looked at the next window. This was also a picture of him, but in this one he was walking through the woods.

In the next window, he stood in front of a log cabin.

In the next, he was inside.

Then he was holding hands with a much smaller woman—a woman who, upon closer scrutiny, turned out to be a credible likeness of Geneviève.

He rounded the walls, stupefied, his legs propelling him slowly forward as if independent of his higher brain functions, which were a little busy at the moment.

Then they were sitting down to dinner at a table covered with plates and bowls of food.

Then there were children with them, three boys and a girl. He could not help but grin at this one.

When he saw the next one, he smiled rapturously and clasped his hands in front of his chest in a gesture of silent gratitude.

It was not a single large portrait but four smaller ones. In two of them, the older boys were sound asleep. In the third, Charles was tucking in their youngest son and kissing him on the forehead. In the fourth, Geneviève was reading their daughter a bedtime story.

That brought him back to the front of the church and the first window.

Overcome by this spectacle, he knelt where he was and began to pray, asking God to reveal to him if what he saw was real. The scenes in these windows, the expressions on everyone's faces...he had scarcely dared to hope that he and Geneviève would know such happiness.

"Charles! Charles Duchamp!"

"Mère Sacrèe?" he responded at once. Then he realized with a twinge of embarrassment that it was not the voice of the Holy Mother calling him, but the voice of his own mother.

He started to call out but stopped himself. At once he understood how he could make everything right with Geneviève. The solution was so simple, yet so perfect.

The source of their conflict was her perception that she was not a big enough part of his life, that her feelings were not as important to him as they should be. He could remedy that, starting right now. With this church.

Whatever had happened here so long ago, it was a foregone conclusion that his parents would not want their only son's wedding to be held in a place they refused even to speak of. They would not be able to prevent it, but that was a battle he wanted to put off as long as possible. In the meantime, he would tell only Geneviève of this place. They would take a walk in the woods and he would bring her here, and he would tell her that it was a surprise for the rest of the family. Until the great day, only the two of them would know of this place.

There were few things a woman liked better than her betrothed sharing a secret with her and no one else. He could think of no greater proof of his sincerity.

It came together in his mind with such clarity. How could he not have seen it before? That wasn't important. He knew what he must do now.

His mother was a long way off, coming from the north. He headed off as quickly and quietly as he could towards the east, moving in a semicircle so that he would approach her from that direction.

"Charles!"

"Oui, maman!" She turned to see him cresting a small hill, cheeks flushed from his hike.

"Where have you been? Geneviève has arrived! She is waiting for you!"

"I am sorry, *maman.* I must have lost track of time."

"Well, come along. She will be delighted to see you!"

As indeed she was. The moment he walked in the house, she ran up to him, threw her arms around him, and buried her head in his chest. He hugged her with care—when he was overcome with emotion he sometimes forgot how delicate she was. Finally they separated and looked each other over.

"You look wonderful, Geneviève. I am delighted to see you again."

"So do you, and so am I."

"Dinner is nearly ready, my dears," said Mrs. Duchamp. "Charles, go and wash up. Geneviève, if you would like to rest before we eat, Pierre has put your things in your room."

"Thank you, *maman,*" she said, smiling. Whenever she came to visit, the guest room was always referred to as "her" room. They never came out and said so, since they didn't want to influence her decision, but she knew they would be overjoyed if she moved in. Now that she was here, she had to admit the idea at least merited consideration.

After Charles was born, Mrs. Duchamp learned she could not have any more children. She barely survived giving birth to this one. They had doted on Charles all his life, but they had always wanted a daughter. When Charles and Geneviève told them of their engagement, Mrs. Duchamp insisted she start calling her "mother," which she was happy to do. Mr. Duchamp did not care either way, but from the beginning he too had gone out of his way to make her feel welcome.

Mrs. Duchamp was used to preparing large quantities of food, since Charles' appetite matched his size, but tonight she made enough to feed a platoon. She always did this when they had company, even if it was only Geneviève, who could not eat very much. Charles understood this better than his parents and ran interference for her when his mother tried to force thirds on her. She looked at him gratefully. The food was wonderful but she was already full to bursting.

Dinner conversation was animated. It alternated randomly between English and French, and often got so loud a listener might have thought they were drunk or fighting. But Charles was in particularly high spirits, and Geneviève preferred to feed off his energy rather than question it. They talked about everything under the sun except the impending wedding. His parents knew the subject of living arrangements was still a sensitive one.

After everyone had consumed as much as they could—which still meant they would have leftovers for the better part of a week—and Charles had helped his mother with the dishes (Geneviève had wanted to help but was told the only thing she was allowed to do in their kitchen was help herself to whatever she liked), his parents retired to their room, leaving the two of them alone for the first time since she got there.

"I have something to show you," he said at once.

This caught her off guard. She came here intending to talk about where they were going to live, but he was in such a good mood that she was loath to do anything to spoil it. "What is it?"

"It is in the woods. Not far." He got to his feet, and she scrambled off the couch. He towered over her when she was standing. When she was sitting, looking up at him was enough to give her vertigo.

"Come." He extended his hand and she took it, having to suppress the impulse to wince when he squeezed. She once saw him crush a tennis ball on a dare, so the gentleness with which he held her hand was all the more pleasantly surprising.

Twenty minutes later she was staring at the church, as awestruck as he had been. She knew this clearing also. It had been months since she last saw it, but it had been exactly the same when Charles saw it three days ago. While it might have been possible to build this church in so short a time if a construction crew worked around the clock, the Duchamps would have heard the racket and gotten legal injunctions to stop the work. They would have seen it as blasphemy to build anything here, even if they didn't know what it was. Mr. and Mrs. Duchamp would have gone straight to the courthouse, and Charles would have gone straight to the workmen. He could be very persuasive when he wished to be.

She looked at him. He nodded. "I know. That it is here is amazing enough. But you must see the windows!"

Except for a few occasions with his family, she had not attended Mass since she was a child, and could not help smiling at his childlike enthusiasm about the stained glass windows. They looked like the windows that adorned any Catholic church.

Ten seconds later her smile had been replaced with gawping amazement. They walked around the church twice, each time examining the tableaux as closely as they dared. When she finally found her voice, she could only stammer. "How... how is this possible?"

"I cannot even guess. But this can be nothing but a miracle from the Lord."

Geneviève did not believe in God. Charles and his parents knew that, but never made an issue of it. At the moment she was unable to argue with him, even had she been so inclined.

"I've seen this place before," he added.

The admission startled her. "What?"

"It was here when I was a small boy. It was called Notre Père de Saint-Christophe. I was baptized in this church, and when I was six, there was a wedding here. I could not attend because I was ill, but I will always remember the day." He stopped talking and stood in thought.

She had seen pictures of him as a child. Incredibly, he was frail and sickly then. But she could not imagine any virus daring to attack him now.

"Go on," she encouraged, and gave his hand a small squeeze.

"Something happened the day of the wedding. The church caught fire and burned."

"How horrible!"

"Yes," he said sadly. "But what was strange was what came after. Fires are a part of life here, although sometimes a tragic one. But the papers said nothing about it except that it was caused by a fault in the electrical system. Nothing was said about the wedding or who was in attendance. Papa had gone while Mama stayed home to tend to me, and I heard them whispering about it that night in their room. One of them would shush the other when they got too loud. Clearly they did not want me to overhear."

"But why should that be? It was a tragedy, but as you said, it was an accident."

"Yes, that is what I said. But I don't believe it's true."

"I don't understand," Geneviève said.

"Nor do I. My parents refused to answer any of my questions about what happened, and finally I was told not to ask any more. Years later, whenever I tried to raise the subject in casual conversation with the people of the village, everyone would stop talking, then I would be told that no one spoke of that day or of that church. Then they would change the subject, and it would be as though I had said nothing."

"The church was never rebuilt?"

"No. And I don't know where the people who died in it are buried, which can only mean they were buried in unmarked graves. Normally that is reserved only for people accused of the most heinous crimes."

"Wow. Well, something happened in this church on that day, and it wasn't just a wedding. That much is obvious."

"I was thinking..." Charles started to say.

"Yes? What were you thinking?"

"That a church like this would be perfect for our wedding."

She looked at it again. "You know what? I wasn't thinking about that until you said it, but now that you have, I agree completely. In fact, why bother looking for a church like this? Why not this church?"

He looked at her with a broad grin. "I had hoped you would agree. But that means we must solve the mystery of what did happen here so we may put everyone's fears to rest. It would not be much of a wedding if we were the only ones in attendance."

Now it was her turn to grin. "Charles, one of the first things we learned we have in common is that Agatha Christie is our favorite author. But we must be pragmatic. I am not Jane Marple, and you are not Hercule Poirot. How could we ever hope to solve a mystery like this?"

"By doing what they would do. Looking for clues."

"And where do we start looking?" Geneviève asked.

"The logical place is the library," Charles said. "We can access the online archive of the local newspaper back to when the village was incorporated. It shouldn't take long to find the articles that tell of what happened. As I said, the accounts were sketchy, but it would be a solid beginning."

"And if we research the history of the church, that might provide useful information also."

"A good idea. We can start on that in the morning. But as long as we're here, shall we go inside and have a look around?"

"After you, *Monsieur* Poirot."

"Thank you, Miss Marple."

They found what they expected to find. Two columns of pews, each seven rows deep, all as highly polished as the hardwood floor, and a humble pulpit with a lifesized rendition of the crucified Christ on the back wall. It could seat perhaps a hundred and forty people, which would be plenty. It did not have a reception hall, but that was of no importance. The reception would be in his parents' house. They would hear no arguments even if he wanted to make any.

"I don't see anything strange about this place," Charles finally said. "Apart from its windows, and the fact that it's here at all, I mean."

"This is going to sound strange," said Geneviève, "but...I can't help feeling that the fact of this church being here now, in the way that it is...that it's part of some greater purpose, some...some grand design, maybe. I think that's why I'm not as disturbed by this as I guess I should be."

"*Exactement!*" Charles exclaimed. "Almost as though it were put here specifically for us to find!"

"Charles, do you think...do you think that whoever's up there—"

"He usually likes to be called God."

She suppressed the urge to laugh; he was serious. "All right...that God intended for us to get married in this church?"

"That is the only explanation that makes sense. Nothing else could possibly account for how this church could simply appear here, why no one else has seen it, and most importantly, the images in the windows."

"But why would it matter to God where we get married? More to the point, why would He go to all this trouble?"

"Nothing is too much trouble for Him. But your questions are good ones. I believe that will be an important focus for our researches in the morning. But we should go back now. It will be dark soon."

They hurried out of the church and back up to the house. They were so intent on watching for any obstacles ahead of them that they did not see the church doors close soundlessly behind them.

His parents were already asleep, so they eased the door open and crept inside. He walked her to her room and stopped at the door.

"Sleep well," he whispered. "We have a big day tomorrow."

"I can hardly wait."

She kissed him goodnight and disappeared inside her room. He went to the kitchen to make himself a sandwich. He was not really hungry, but eating helped him concentrate, and the sound of her door closing behind her was a reminder of something that had been troubling him: the fact that they were not sleeping in the same room.

It was not a question of propriety. His parents would not have cared. Geneviève understood the problem but did not know what to do about it. Neither did he.

Charles tossed and turned throughout the night, but otherwise slept like the dead. In this regard, his size presented a special problem. If he should chance to roll on top of her, she would not be able to budge him, and he might suffocate her without waking. His parents, dreading the prospect of their daughter-in-law being afraid to share a bed with her husband, had promised to find a solution before the wedding, but so far they had made no progress. He was too tired to think about it tonight, so he made a note of it in his prayers, undressed, and climbed into bed. He was asleep almost instantly.

Half an hour later, he flipped over. His arm fell on the nightstand and sent it crashing to the floor. He grunted once and was still.

Geneviève awoke at about seven-thirty and shambled into the living room to find Charles sitting on the couch leafing through a magazine. He looked up and smiled when he saw her.

"Good morning, sleepyhead."

"Good morning," she said, choosing to believe he was kidding. "Where are your parents?"

"They had to go into town to run some errands."

"Oh. Then we'll have breakfast when they get back?"

"Actually, we've already eaten. We decided to let you sleep in."

She was certain he was joking until she glanced into the kitchen and saw the dirty dishes in the sink. That decided her. By any means possible, she had to persuade Charles to move to Montreal with her. She loved his parents dearly, but getting up at the crack of dawn every day was simply not an option.

"Are you hungry?" he asked. "We saved you a little something."

"Oh, no, thank you. I'm still full from last night. Also, I'm anxious to get started."

"I thought you might be. I've been thinking about the best way to proceed."

"And?"

"I believe answers can be found in Saint-Augustin."

"Why should we go to another town?" she asked.

"Whatever happened obviously terrified everyone in the village. Even now, all these years later, no one will speak of it. Not only would an investigation be fruitless, but someone would certainly tell my parents what we were doing."

"I understand," she said. "And Saint-Augustin?"

"It's close enough that they might have received news of what happened, but not so close that they would see the harm in relating the story to an outsider. Particularly if you purchase something while you are there."

"Just me? Aren't you coming?"

"Among other things, detective work requires the ability to ferret out information," Charles said. "You can make a stranger feel comfortable enough to speak freely. I cannot."

"So you see," Geneviève said, "being small has its advantages."

"True enough."

"All right, while I'm ferreting, what will you be doing?"

"Research at the library," he said. "Later we'll compare notes, and hopefully get a much better idea of what happened."

"Sounds like a plan," she said. "And I remember passing Saint-Augustin on the way here."

"People from the city are something of a curiosity there. Your accent will give you away at once. And if you say you are coming back from Lourdes-du-Blanc-Sablon, there's every reason to believe they'll tell you all you could wish to know."

"Suitably embroidered, most likely."

"That is a risk, yes. But we should be able to separate fact from fiction."

"I've never tried to do anything like this before. I can't believe how excited I am about it!"

"Are you sure you won't eat something?" Charles asked. "It could be a very long day."

"Yes, I'm sure. Besides, you'll have to stop your mother from shoving food down my gullet again tonight."

That brought forth a deep, hearty laugh. "*Touché.* I will see you tonight, then."

"Count on it." She kissed him quickly and left.

On the way up to see Charles, she had been so focused on the necessity of seeing him and resolving their dispute over where they would live (*which we still haven't done,* she thought—*is that why I'm so excited about this little diversion?*) that she hadn't paid much attention to the scenery around her. Now, with not much to look at ahead of her, she found her gaze constantly being drawn away by the awesome spectacle on her left.

This road followed Canada's eastern coastline. To her right was rolling prairie, with mountains hazy in the distance. To her left and below her, surging and frothing as though it might reach up and swallow her at any moment, was the Atlantic Ocean in its endless glory.

She shivered with the proximity of it. Montreal was not landlocked by any means, but its rivers were of a manageable size and you could coexist with them without feeling insignificant. But this was too much, especially given what the realities of her situation would be. If she were to live in Lourdes-du-Blanc-Sablon, she would have to go to larger towns for...well, just about everything, and she would have to look at this every time. Would she get used to it? Eventually. But did she want to? The answer to that was a resounding no.

It would take nearly two hours to get to Saint-Augustin. She compensated by lowering her sun visor and folding it back so that it partially covered her window. The difference it made was negligible, but any port in a storm...no, that was definitely not the metaphor for right now. As it was, her knuckles turned white every time her car was buffetted by a passing semi.

By the time she reached the turnoff, her fingers were stiff from gripping the wheel so hard for so long, and she stopped at the first tavern she saw. She needed coffee. Lots of it.

About a dozen people were inside, and they all looked up as she entered. Most promptly went back to whatever they were eating, but a few of the men followed her progress as she walked to a corner booth and collapsed in the seat.

A waitress was there within seconds. "Can I help you?"

"Large coffee. Black. Please."

The waitress, whose nametag identified her as Sandrine, said, "You got it. Be right back."

Sandrine came right back bearing a menu and a huge mug filled almost to the brim with dark steaming liquid. The mug was too hot for Geneviève to touch, so she just breathed in its vapors.

"Where are you from?" Sandrine asked.

"Montreal. Actually, I'm on my way back there. End of my vacation, back to work."

"Where did you go?"

"I spent a couple of days in Lourdes-du-Blanc-Sablon."

Sandrine stopped in the middle of gathering up her tip from the next table and turned back to face her. "Lourdes-du-Blanc-Sablon? Do you know about the church?"

Bingo. "I'm sorry...the church?"

Rural storytellers were a curious breed. They would happily talk your ear off if it was a subject on which they could educate you, or at least entertain you. But if it became apparent you were milking them for details, they would clam up. So Geneviève asked this question with what she hoped was a blank look.

Apparently it was good enough. The waitress's eyes lit up and she said, "Oh, yeah. Quite a story, too. Don't imagine you'd want to hear it, though."

"Why do you say that?"

"It's kind of a long story, and you're obviously in a hurry. I mean, seeing as you're just stopping for coffee."

Geneviève smiled. She knew how this game was played. "Well, you know, I'm not in that big a rush, and I'm always in the mood for a good story...that wouldn't be bacon I smell, would it?"

"Fresh from the smokehouse, sweetie," Sandrine said proudly.

"Why don't you bring me some scrambled eggs, bacon, and a couple of slices of toast. And keep the coffee coming, please."

"Coming right up." Sandrine took the menu and was gone, soon to reappear with a plate of victuals. Geneviève hadn't been hungry until now, but one look at her beloved cholesterol and she was famished. She was nearly half finished when Sandrine returned to freshen her coffee and ask if the food was all right.

"Yes, it's fabulous," she said around a mouthful of eggs. She swallowed, then asked, "What were you saying before? About the church? I've seen lots of churches in this area. A lot of them are beautiful, but none of them struck me as odd."

"Oh, you wouldn't have seen this one." Sandrine said this in a whisper, but the other patrons heard. Some of them glanced her way, exchanged knowing smiles, and went back to their food.

Geneviève caught this and wondered. Many of these hamlets had their own ways of amusing themselves at strangers' expense. Was she about to see one of them? Her accent marked her as a *Quebecoise*, which meant her status among the locals was lower than that of Canadians of other provinces. But it wouldn't do much good to tell them that the raging secession arguments had never made any sense to her. She could only hope that Sandrine wasn't making up what she told her as she went along.

"Okay, I'll bite. Why wouldn't I have seen it?"

"Because it isn't there!" Sandrine paused for dramatic effect, then went on. "See, what happened was..." She glanced at the empty seat. "Do you mind?"

"No, not at all."

Sandrine slid into the seat, leaned in close as if she were about to confide a secret, and said, "Like I was saying, there was a wedding there, about...oh, must have been about twenty years ago. One of my cousins went, and he came back and told me all about it. And he says, sure, it was a lovely service and all, but the darnedest thing happened right at the end. The bride and groom were off in a corner, fighting about something. They were trying to keep their voices down, but voices have a way of carrying in church, and the people close by could hear what they were so brassed off about. It was the twenty-second of June the day they got married, and it was seven or so, but it was still plenty light out. So they figured they'd just light the church with candles, all romantic, you know? So they brought in about a million red and white candles, put 'em all over the place, and they had white lace curtains over the windows to filter the sunlight. Made a really nice effect, too. It was dark enough so it looked cozy and intimate, but not so dark you were tripping over things. The whole evening was perfect. Except it wasn't. See, rumor had it somebody in the bride's family was some kind of devil worshipper. Black Masses, all of that." She crossed herself, went on without missing a beat. "So somebody figures he'll be a wise guy, sneaks in a black candle and lights it in a corner by one of the windows."

Sandrine paused in her narrative. "That's just the story, mind. You won't find anyone who can prove anyone did any such thing."

Geneviève nodded quickly, encouraging her to continue, which she did. "So the groom happens to look over that way, he sees this candle and goes ballistic. The bride's trying to be reasonable, she says it's not doing any harm, it's just burning there, minding its own business, right? Besides, the more candles, the better, because the Blessed Mother would see them, take pity on the supplicating bride, and bless her with a fertile womb. Apparently she'd been married before, but the guy left her because she couldn't have children. What a prince, huh? Anyway, then the groom heads over there to take the candle and throw it outside. She's trying to stop him, and he starts waving his arms around, he's in such a high dudgeon, and he knocks the candle over. It hits one of the curtains, and the curtain goes up like it's made of flash paper. Well, somebody had just opened the door because he was leaving, and at that instant there's a gust of wind like you wouldn't believe. Blows the doors wide open. Fans the flames, sparks are blowing everywhere, a lot of the other candles get blown over. Well, that summer was really dry, and the wood that church was made of was really old, and they had a bunch of tablecloths, so you can guess what happened. Quick as anything, the whole thing's ablaze. My cousin was standing right by the door, that was the only reason he got out with his life. The supporting timbers went up—some of them were rotting anyway—and the roof came crashing down, crushed everyone still inside."

"*Nom de Dieu*," Geneviève said in a horrified whisper—the first time she had ever spoken God's name aloud since her first (and last) communion.

Sandrine nodded. "*Oui.*"

"But..." Geneviève decided it was time for at least a sanitized version of the truth. "I have...well, I used to have friends in that area, and now that you speak of it I remember a conversation with them several years ago about that event. They said the papers barely mentioned it."

"Of course not. What would they have said? They could hardly report the opinion everyone had about what happened."

"What did everyone think it was?"

Sandrine leaned in even closer and spoke just loud enough for Geneviève to hear. "That it was God's judgment. They had let the Evil One into their church, and God opted for some old-school payback, give them a taste of what He did to Sodom and Gomorrah. They never rebuilt the church, those who died in it were buried in unmarked graves, and to this day the subject is out of bounds."

Charles had told Geneviève that last part. Given the context, it was no surprise that the topic would be a forbidden one.

She ate while she listened, and had just swallowed the last forkful of eggs. She thanked Sandrine for the food and the story, paid the check, left a generous tip, and exited the restaurant. She walked rapidly to her car and sat in it for a minute to digest this fantastic tale, then drove back to Lourdes-du-Blanc-Sablon.

Charles was waiting for her on the path, a few hundred meters from the house. She stopped and he got in.

"Drive around for a while," he said. "I must show you the town."

"What?"

"I left a note for my parents that I would show you the town today. That way, they would not ask questions. Therefore I must show you the town."

"Why? You're in my car now, and if we go in together—"

"I will not lie to my parents."

She puzzled over this for an instant, but told herself that thinking too much about any aspect of this affair was not a good idea. Instead she reversed down the path and eased out onto the main road.

They made only a perfunctory circuit. Even Charles had to admit not much of the town itself was worth seeing. But while they were out, he said, "There was only one article on record about what happened. It said nothing I didn't already know. It was believed that the fire was started by a fault in the electrical system, and there would be an official investigation, but there never was. That was the last anyone ever said of it. Did you have any luck?"

"You have no idea! I stopped in a restaurant for breakfast—"

"I thought you said you weren't hungry." He sounded a little hurt.

"I wasn't, really. I had just stopped in for coffee. The waitress and I got to talking, and I told her where I was coming from, and she asked if I knew about the church."

Charles' eyes widened.

"Exactly," she went on. "I didn't want to make her suspicious, so I told her I had seen a lot of churches around here but didn't see anything remarkable about any of them."

"Very good. And then?"

"Then she said there was quite a story attached to this particular one, but I probably wouldn't have time to hear it because I was in a rush to get wherever I was going. She knew I was in a rush because I only ordered coffee."

"In other words," Charles said with an appreciative laugh, "the price of hearing this story was that you order breakfast."

"That's right. And you won't believe what she said."

She recounted it in as much detail as she could remember. When she finished, Charles was rubbing his chin, deep in thought. "Yes," he said. "That explains a lot. We take our faith very seriously here, we always have. If someone had defiled it in that way, the actions taken were certainly appropriate."

Geneviève sensed a doxology coming and tried to head it off. "If the church was lit by candles, then the electrical system wasn't being used at all. That means the paper told an outright lie. Journalistic fabrication is a criminal offense!"

"One that was committed for the greater good," Charles declared. "Besides, do you think anyone would be interested in prosecuting a sin of omission that was committed twenty years ago?"

"Charles, we really should think about this. The more we find out about that church, the worse an idea it seems to get married in it."

"That's what this is all about, isn't it?" Charles asked.

"What are you talking about?"

"The reason you came here in the first place. You want to call off the wedding."

"What? No! I—"

"Yes. But you couldn't say so honestly, so you resorted to subterfuge. You knew if you insisted on the one thing I could never agree to—that we live in Montreal—I would refuse to go through with it. Then my parents would blame me for the demise of our relationship, and you could return to your beloved *city* with a clear conscience."

"Charles..." She was on the verge of tears, so she swerved to the shoulder, came to a stop, and faced him. "Charles, how can you say that to me? How can you even think that?"

"Because...never mind. Let's just forget it."

"No, I won't just forget it! Charles, I want you to look me in the eye and tell me that you truly believe any of what you just said. That I've given you any reason, any reason at all, to have so little faith in me."

He went on staring down at his lap. "I must have time to think. Take me home."

"Charles, we have to talk about this! Please! We—"

"Please...take...me...home."

He still would not look at her, but his voice, faint as it was, held a hint of menace. Subtle, barely there, but enough to scare her witless.

Burning with shame, shocked into mute compliance, she did as he asked. When they pulled up in the driveway, he got out and went in the house without so much as a backward glance. He slammed the door with such force that the windows rattled.

His parents were not home, or they would have come out to meet her when they saw she did not come in with him. Just as well. She was in no condition to face anyone, least of all Charles. Not knowing what else to do, but needing to do something, she got out of her car and started to walk through the woods. She wept silently, but a thousand thoughts clanged through her head.

Was he right? Did she secretly want to call off the wedding? Was that why she was so inflexible on this one subject? She had always known how much he hated city life, and truth be told, he'd never had much reason to like it. It was obvious how much this life agreed with him. He was incredibly strong, glowing with health, and overflowing with vitality. What right did she have to demand he give up a life he knew and loved for one he detested?

And the other side of the equation? Why couldn't she live here, with his parents? His question had been a fair one, but she had refused even to consider it. Why? Because she would have to do without a few conveniences here? So what? Here was a tightly knit community, an environment ideal for growing children, in-laws who adored her and never left any room to doubt it, and a husband who would be devoted to her. What were boutique clothing stores and twenty-four-hour supermarkets compared to that? She had asked him when she would ever see her family if she moved here, but she hardly ever saw them now, even though they lived less than half an hour from her. The visits she did make were out of duty and as brief as she could get away with. And she had wanted Charles to think she couldn't move here because she would be too far away from them?

With a surge of guilt, anguish, and self-loathing, she realized he had known the secret desires of her heart better than she had.

She knew what she must do. She would return to the cabin, tell him he had been right, and beg his forgiveness. He would probably scream at her, vent his anger and frustration, but she would expect that—in her present state of mind, she would welcome it. She would stand meekly, not even meeting his eyes, and take whatever he saw fit to dish out...

That last phrase dampened her resolve.

Whatever he saw fit to dish out.

What would that entail? She had enraged him, that much was plain. What would he do if he saw her now? He had never been inclined to violence before, but he had never been so angry before either. And he could snap her neck as easily as she could snap a pencil. She had to remember that.

There was only one thing to do. She had to get in her car and return home. The only belongings she brought with her were some clothes and a few toiletries. Forget them. She would leave a note for his parents, explaining everything, apologizing profusely, thanking them for their hospitality, and asking them to have Charles call her when he had calmed down. She would attach it to the door and—

"Ouch!"

She looked up at what she had collided with. She hadn't been looking where she was going, and she saw without much surprise that she was back at the church.

"This is your fault," she said. "You're the cause of all this trouble. The townspeople were right. If there really is a devil, then you're his sanctuary. Well, maybe I can't get rid of the devil, but I can get rid of you."

She scanned the ground for rocks, heavy pieces of wood, anything that could be used as implements of destruction.

After a few seconds she spotted a piece of granite the size of her palm. That would do for a start.

She picked it up and drew her arm back, ready to hurl the rock as hard as she could through the window facing her. She did not. Her arm slowly dropped back to her side, clutching the rock in nerveless fingers.

The window had changed.

She crept forward for a closer look, hoping against hope that this was some sort of optical illusion. But this was no trick of the light.

The portrait in this window was no longer of Charles. It was of her, walking down a long pathway, away from a house. The house was small, indicating that it was far away. The people standing in front of the house were reduced in size to maintain the scale, but there was no mistaking who they were. The man in the middle was much larger than the man and woman flanking him.

It was Charles and his parents. She was leaving them.

Dreading what was now on the other windows but needing to know, she walked slowly around the church.

In the next window she was driving back to Montreal. The ocean was at storm tide, its waves rearing up as if about to submerge her, car and all.

According to the rest of the windows, she made it back safely, but it might have been better if she hadn't.

She was sitting in her apartment, which was now dark and empty, as were the eyes that stared out of her gaunt face. She looked as though she had lost thirty pounds.

Then she was in another church, about to marry a man she did not know. His expression was cold and severe. Hers spoke only of privation and misery.

Then it was late at night, and she was lying alone in bed. The look on her face was one she had seen many times before, in chocolate-fueled conversations-slash-rants with her girlfriends. It said that her husband would not be home tonight, that this was a common occurrence, that she knew where he was, and that she wondered if that was where he spent the affection he could never spare for her.

In the next window she was kneeling, hands clasped tightly in prayer, face upturned to a gloomy sky. She was praying—pleading—for deliverance, but God had left her to the fate she had brought on herself.

Then she was kneeling in front of a grave. She caught a glimpse of the name engraved on the stone and turned away in agony, but was forced to turn back as though her face were being held between invisible but irresistible hands.

Ever since she was old enough to think about having children, she had wanted a daughter. The only name that would do was Stephanie. The simple headstone bore only two words. Stephanie Petillon.

She shut her eyes and screamed, a wordless prayer that this would not be. But she opened her eyes again and it still was.

There was one more window. She couldn't look at it, but she no longer had a choice.

She inched around to the front of the church, eyes squeezed into slits, taking deep, ragged breaths.

This last one showed Charles and his parents in yet another church, with a few others in attendance. The ceremony was a funeral.

In the open coffin, at eternal but artificial peace, skin creamy white except for the mark on her throat where it had been sewn shut…

She backed away in horror, and only then did she realize she was still holding the rock. With a strangled cry, she flung it away and buried her face in her hands, violently shaking her head, trying to shake those terrible images out of them.

At some point she must have collapsed. When she could finally bring herself to look again, she was sprawled out on the ground. But that wasn't the only thing different.

The church was still in her field of vision. What she saw there could just have been a projection of a last, desperate hope, or more likely the beginning of her brain's total meltdown. As before, she had to be sure.

She inched forward, not daring to turn away or even blink, lest the window change back again. It didn't. It almost seemed to be inviting her to examine it as closely as she liked.

All the windows had reverted. They were again a pictorial record of the life of idyllic happiness they had shown her and Charles.

This was the life that could be...but so was the other one. That, she understood now, was the message of the windows. This church's personal sermon, simple but effective.

Mess with me, and I'll mess with you.

Almost before she was aware she was moving, she was running as fast as she could back to the cabin. She had to explain this to Charles, somehow make him understand, and she realized she was praying for wisdom and guidance. Why not? If she could believe the things that had happened since she came here, as it seemed she must, then it wasn't that hard to believe in God. Particularly since He, whoever He was, appeared to be her only hope of escaping whatever had moved into these woods.

She rounded a hill at top speed and ran, literally, into Charles coming the other way. The collision with his immovable bulk knocked her flat.

"Geneviève! Are you all right?" He extended a hand to help her up. She took it gratefully, and as soon as she was on her feet, launched into a teary, garbled apology. He held up his other hand, and her voice trailed off.

"I shouldn't have gotten so angry," he said. "I realize now what you were trying to tell me. Not that you don't want to get married at all, but that you don't want to get married here. It will be no trouble to find another church nearby—"

She tried to make sounds while he talked, but none were immediately forthcoming. Finally she stammered, "The church! Charles, I have to show you something! It showed me something a few minutes ago! Let me show you—"

"Easy, easy. It's right over there. Show me what you mean."

They walked back, Geneviève having to trot to keep up with Charles' long strides. What they saw a moment later brought them both to a halt.

The church's doors stood open.

A single black candle burned inside.

She wanted to look at Charles, to ask him if they should go inside, but she could not take her eyes off the candle. Nor could he. Its flame was steady but illuminated nothing around it. It was a point of light surrounded by absolute darkness.

Then there was nothing else in the world except the flame, drawing her to itself.

It was hypnotizing her. Both of them. By the time she realized this, they were inside the church. She turned just in time to see the doors slam shut behind them, plunging them into night. The sun was shining outside, but in here there was nothing. It was as if they were no longer in the world. Maybe they weren't.

Charles let go of her hand and took off running at the doors, intending to smash them open. He might have done it. But just before he reached them, they were blown open by the wind, a gust of hurricane force that knocked them to the floor.

It also knocked the candle to the floor and onto a trailing lace curtain neither of them had been able to see in the darkness.

The curtain was engulfed in an instant. The fire raced across the ceiling, a living thing, frenzied and ravenous, driven by the wind.

Geneviève was held immobile by the force of that demoniac gale, but Charles was struggling to get up, to break the invisible shackles.

"Come on, Charles!" The wind snatched her words away before they left her mouth, but she shouted them anyway. "You can do it!"

The wind was strong. Charles was stronger. Slowly, strenuously, he managed to stand. But he never got the chance to enjoy his victory. An instant later, the supporting timbers went up in flames (some of them were rotting anyway) and the roof collapsed on top of them.

The next day, two policemen scoured the charred grass where the church had been. They were not told there had been a church here, only that two people had died in a forest fire of unknown but suspicious origin. And the only reason anyone was here was that one of the bodies was identified as Geneviève Petillon, a resident of Montreal. So two of Montreal's finest were dispatched to investigate.

Of the other victim, they knew only his name, Charles Duchamp. The local constabulary told them that. Apparently his family had taken his body and fled. The first cop shook his head at this. People did some bizarre things. But the scene they were examining was no less macabre.

"What do you make of it?" he asked his partner.

"I haven't the faintest idea. This grass is completely burned, but nothing else has been touched. What was here, anyway?"

"This was the site of a church. Notre Père de Saint-Christophe. But I had to learn that from a contact in Saint-Augustin. None of the locals would tell me anything."

"Why would they keep quiet? Makes them look like they have something to hide."

"That's what I wanted to know. So I did some digging before we got here. The church was founded about seventy years ago by a descendant of one of the original settlers of Lourdes-du-Blanc-Sablon. And he thought it would be fitting if the inaugural service was the baptism of his first child."

"That's natural enough."

"Yeah. But what followed wasn't natural at all. There were complications in the pregnancy. The uterine wall had thickened, and the baby was crushed trying to get through the birth canal. It was born dead."

"Didn't the doctors know that would happen?"

"They couldn't find anything wrong with her in any of the tests they did. But these were country doctors and this was seventy years ago. They wouldn't have known about endometriosis."

"Endo-what?"

"Exactly. But because this man was an important member of the community, he couldn't afford to lose face, not for any reason. His wife was already half-mad with grief, and he had to do what he could to settle her down. That meant the ceremony had to continue as planned, and he arranged to have the particulars kept quiet. They paid off the priest to do it right away, since obviously they couldn't wait eight days. The man never told anyone, but the story got out later through his wife, who by then was in a mental hospital and telling anyone who would listen and quite a few people who wouldn't."

The second officer looked down at the ground where the church had been, and backed onto the untouched area. "You mean…the first ceremony to take place in this church…"

The first officer finished the sentence. "…was the baptism of a dead child."

The whereabouts of Charles' body and family were a mystery never to be solved, but the mortal remains of his fiancée ended up on a dissecting table in Montreal's St. Pierre Hospital. The resident pathologist, Dr. David Berrault, and a third-year medical student, Michelle Fourchet, did the autopsy.

"The cause of death is obvious," Dr. Berrault said. "The poor girl was crushed and burned. But do you notice anything about her?"

Michelle peered down into her abdominal area, where he had subtly gestured. Then she looked up. "Incipient endometriosis."

"Very good. It's not as easy to spot in women who have never given birth. For that at least, she can be thankful. In the unlikely event she had been able to conceive and carry the child to term, it would probably have been born dead."

Three years later, a young couple walked through the woods where the Duchamps had lived. They had married eight months earlier. He had taken a one-year sabbatical, and they chose to spend part of it driving up the Atlantic coast from Massachusetts, where they lived, up to Nova Scotia, and back again, stopping wherever they wanted.

"I can't believe how beautiful and peaceful it is here," said the woman. "Maybe we should think about settling here."

"You say that about every place we stop."

"I know, I know, but this area really has possibilities. The people are friendly, the cost of living is low, there's no crime to speak of, and no pollution or noise."

"It is really quiet here," he agreed. "I can even...wait. Do you hear that?"

"What...yeah! Yeah, I do. It sounds like...a bell?" she guessed.

"Yes," he said. "A church bell. What would a church be doing way out here?"

"Let's go and see it. Maybe there will be a priest there who's got a blessing for me. Nobody else has been much help."

"Margaret, I told you, not every woman gets pregnant right away. It doesn't mean there's anything wrong with you."

She sighed. "I guess you're right."

"I know I'm right. But let's follow that sound. I've never heard such a beautiful bell in my life. We have to see what kind of church could have it."

CARAMEL

On a cold, clammy autumn night, Edward Hench was going home. This was not his preference.

He would stay only long enough to change out of his work clothes, take a shower, cool down with a little TV, and head out again. That was the idea. His wife had a different one.

He had tossed his keys on his dresser. When he emerged from the bathroom, they were gone.

Rebecca had hidden them and refused to tell him where. To be fair, that would defeat the purpose of hiding them. The ensuing argument ended with her saying, "You're going to get some exercise and start getting healthy if it kills you!"

She stomped off to the bedroom and slammed the door before he could decide how to respond to that. Not that it mattered. He was not in the mood to say anything to her. That was no surprise; over the last few years it had become increasingly rare that he was ever in the mood to say anything to her.

Although they had frequent disagreements, some of which were very loud disagreements, she was not at her core a disagreeable woman. However much he might hate to admit that, he knew it was the truth. He also knew she was genuinely concerned about his health, and he knew the massive amount of sugary, fat-laden snacks he consumed on a daily basis was not doing his health any favors.

He just wanted to go for a little drive, he said. She knew where that little drive would take him: right to Caramel, the small pastry shop that had opened a few months ago, less than a mile from their house. So she informed him that he would get his keys back in the morning. She knew he would not let them out of his sight again after that, but she didn't know what else to do other than try to stop him from indulging his gargantuan sweet tooth this one time.

"Why don't we go for a walk?" she suggested. "The cool night air will do you good."

He responded that he would go for a walk alone, because the silence would do him more good.

"Why are you being so stubborn about this?" she yelled. "Do you have a death wish? Is that it? You know diabetes runs in your family!"

"So what? I'm not diabetic."

"Well, it's only a matter of time, if you keep stuffing your face with donuts and cinnamon rolls and anything else you can get your bloated hands on!"

"That doesn't guarantee you'll get diabetes any more than smoking guarantees you'll get lung cancer!"

The shouting match went on for another few minutes, but there was no clear winner. Rebecca finally told him to go on and take his walk, she knew where he was going and would be amazed if he could make it there and back, then gave him her wonderfully ironic parting shot and left the room. Edward wasted no time in leaving the house.

Before he made it to the pastry shop, he started to puff and wheeze. There were no park benches along his route, so he had to sit on the curb to catch his breath, and he was dismayed—and faintly alarmed— by how long it took him to do this.

Was Rebecca right? Was he being pigheaded? Pastry-headed, even? Would he put himself in an early, extra-large grave if he kept this up?

Maybe, but so what? Nobody lived forever. To take a somewhat morbid view, there were advantages to dying in early middle age. He would not have to watch himself become stiff and weak, lose more of his physical and mental faculties year by year. And to put it plainly, "until death do us part" had not seemed like a burdensome pledge sixteen years ago when he had made it, but now? Now he had come to the conclusion that if he had to spend the rest of his life with Rebecca, he would much prefer it if that did not mean another forty or fifty years.

If that was a selfish and fatalistic line of reasoning, fine. It suited him well enough. He would live the remainder of his life as he pleased, and the rest would take care of itself.

His breathing was almost back to normal, so he hauled himself up and set off again. Finally he saw Caramel in the distance, but what he saw made him stop.

It was closed.

How could that be? It was open until nine, and he'd left the house before eight. Surely it hadn't taken him that long to get here.

He looked at his watch. 9:22. It hadn't taken that long, it had taken longer. He'd made this torturous walk for nothing. Worse, Rebecca would rub his nose in it when he staggered back home empty-handed because he was so out of shape it took him an hour and a half to cover a distance of maybe four-fifths of a mile.

Maybe he wouldn't have to admit defeat just yet. Maybe, just maybe, the owner was still inside and he could induce her to take pity on him just this once and open her shop long enough to sell him a cinnamon roll. He had a ten-dollar bill in his wallet. He would give it to her for one roll that cost $1.19 with tax and tell her to keep the change. Surely she couldn't say no to such a tidy profit.

He chose to ignore the fact that he was thinking like a drug addict who was craving a fix and told himself he had to take the chance. He'd come all this way, and it was just a little farther. He resumed walking toward the shop, but after a few more steps he stopped again.

The lights in the shop blazed on. The sign above the door flashed "Open."

He looked at his watch again. No, he hadn't read it wrong before. It was 9:24 now. From this distance he couldn't see anyone inside, but he continued to see the Open sign above the door.

Was it a mistake? Some kind of electrical short? A hunger-induced mirage?

Who cared why the sign said Open and the lights were on? It did and they were. He had to run up there and knock on the door if it was locked. If the owner was in there, he would bring her out to see who was banging on her door, and he would tell her the sign said her store was open. If she said it was a mistake, he would say that all he wanted was one cinnamon roll. He would show her the ten as proof of his sincerity. Proof of his need.

He would try the door first. Just in case.

He pulled on the handle. The door swung open.

Unable to believe his luck, he rushed inside and stood in front of the counter. In their display case were the decadent cinnamon rolls and everything else the talented baker made herself, in all their glaze-laden glory.

He started to call out, but before he could open his mouth, a woman emerged from a side door.

She was not the owner. The owner was a compact, gray-haired woman in her mid-sixties. This woman had dark hair, stood five-nine, and looked about thirty. The owner's daughter, maybe? Edward knew nothing about the owner's personal life. She was extremely good at baking. That was all he needed to know.

The young woman crossed to the other side of the counter, smiled, and said, "Good evening, Edward."

How did she know his name? He'd never told the owner, and she'd never asked. Still, however she knew him, she had opened the store after hours, as if on his account alone, so it would hardly do to ask questions.

"Good evening," he said. "I'd like a cinnamon roll, please."

"Certainly...but perhaps you would like to try something else."

"Something else?"

"A new confection I've invented. I've only just perfected the recipe, at least I think I have. Would you like to be the very first to try it and give me your honest opinion? Whatever your opinion is, I'll give you two cinnamon rolls for your help, on the house."

Edward could hardly believe his luck. Surely Heaven was smiling down on him out of the overcast night sky. "Yes!" he said, before she changed her mind and retracted her offer. "I would love to try it."

She opened a small drawer below the display case, brought out a small piece of chocolate, and handed it to him. He popped it in his mouth and chewed, rolling it over and over on his tongue, his eyes closing in bliss. Small moans of pleasure escaped him.

Finally, when he could not chew it any more, he swallowed it and felt it slide languorously down his throat. When he opened his eyes again, he saw the young woman smiling at him. She had a pretty good idea what he was going to say, but he said it anyway.

"This is the best chocolate I've ever tasted. You're going to make a fortune with it, I'll tell you that right now. Are you the owner's daughter?"

"No, she's a family friend," the woman answered. "I just like to help out from time to time. She's not here now, and I am, so I took it upon myself to open the shop and maybe make a bit of extra money. Every little bit helps, right?"

"You can say that again. Although, since you did say it, I don't think she'd be happy to know you were giving away her merchandise. I'll gladly pay you for the cinnamon rolls and for however many of those chocolates you have."

"Thank you, Edward. That's very nice of you. It's really good to know you like my chocolates so much."

"*Your* chocolates? *You* made them?"

"Yes, I did. But please don't tell anyone."

"Why not?" Edward said. "I told you, when you start selling those chocolates, you're going to clean up."

"That's why I want everyone to think they're hers," the woman said. "She's retiring soon—I would ask you to keep that to yourself also—and she needs to make all the money she can in the time she has left. I don't need anything, and as I told you, I'm glad to help her in any way I can."

"Well, you're certainly going to help her with those. Everything she makes is terrific, but your chocolates are going to be her biggest sellers. How much for everything?"

"Good question. I haven't decided how much to charge for the chocolates. How much money did you bring with you?"

"Ten dollars," he said. "I'll pay you that for the two cinnamon rolls and a dozen of those chocolates, and it will be a bargain."

"Sold!" She bent down again and resurfaced with a small paper bag. She then scooped out two rolls, put them in another paper bag, and handed the bags to him. He fished the ten out of his wallet and gave it to her, and she rang up the sale.

"Thank you for stopping by," she said.

"Are you kidding? Thank you for being here. One more thing before I go, though."

"Yes?"

"How do you know my name?"

"Louise has told me about you."

"Who?"

"The owner."

"How does she know my name? I never talk to her. You can see I didn't know her name either."

"I don't know, but she does. At least she knows what she's told me, which is that you're her best customer."

"Well, she's going to be seeing a lot more of me when she has these in her case," he said, holding up the bag. "And you can tell her I said so."

"I'll do that. Good night, Edward."

"Good night...um, what's your name?"

"You can call me...Caramel," she said.

"It suits you," he said, although it didn't really. Her skin was not caramel-colored but very pale, as if she came from a northern climate that did not see much sunlight. Canada, maybe, since she had no discernible accent. Probably it wasn't her real name. She did say that she wanted to maintain her anonymity. But he would not press her. She wanted him to call her Caramel, so Caramel it was.

"Good night, Caramel."

"Good night, Edward."

He walked out of the shop with a spring in his step, or as much of a spring as his girth would allow. No sooner was he out the door than he dug another chocolate out of the bag and put it in his mouth. Again his eyes closed, as if his brain wished to close off that sensory avenue in order to focus only on the sense of taste, which was now as happy as it had ever been.

He opened his eyes only to look out for obstacles in his path and so didn't see that, less than a minute after he left the shop, its lights went off and its sign went dark.

By the time he got home, the lights were off there too. Rebecca must have decided it wasn't worth waiting up for him and gone to bed. Thank goodness for that. He had already finished off the chocolates and the rolls, so he tossed the empty bags in his garbage can and went inside. The door was unlocked. Good of her to remember he didn't have his keys.

When he woke up the next morning, the other side of the bed was empty. Rebecca always got up before he did, and he heard her bustling around in the kitchen. He pushed himself out of bed and went into the living room, certain he was in for a lengthy serenade from the sharp end of her tongue.

But all he was in for was a surprise. She was sitting at the table as always. When he appeared, she glanced up at him, said "Morning" and went back to her crossword puzzle. It was hard to tell if she was upset, but they had long ago entered the phase of their marriage in which he saw no point in trying to guess her emotional state if she didn't see fit to tell him.

His place at the table was marked, as it was every morning, with a banana, a glass of orange juice, and a bowl of oatmeal. After those delectable chocolates, the sugar-free gruel would taste even worse than usual, and it usually tasted like liquid cardboard.

He didn't want to start the day with a fight, though, and he could eat the banana and drink the juice. That might appease her for now. He sat down and ingested them as fast as he could without choking, so he could be up and out before she started in again about what he was doing to himself.

But she didn't start in, didn't say a word, didn't even look up at him. She remained hunched over her crossword, alternately scribbling and thinking. She did not even ask him for help with any of the clues, though it was unlikely he would be of any assistance to her if she did.

He got up, threw the banana peel away, put the glass in the sink, and headed for the bathroom. He left the oatmeal untouched. This drew no comment.

Could he dare to hope she was tired of fighting with him and had decided to let him do what he wanted? Judging from her stoic demeanor, that seemed to be the case, but he hurried out of the living room before he found out it was not.

While he was in the shower, it occurred to him that he had to get his keys back. Since he hadn't been able to find them himself, he had to ask her for them. It also occurred to him that she might be saving her ammunition for when he did, but he had no choice. He didn't think she would volunteer to drive him to work every morning and pick him up every evening just to make it harder for him to go out at night.

He finished his shower, toweled off, and went into the bedroom to get dressed. His keys were on the nightstand.

Were they there when he woke up, and he simply hadn't noticed them? It hardly mattered. The important thing was that he had them back now, and he was going to keep them in his slacks from now on.

He dressed quickly, grabbed his briefcase, and went out the door. He did not kiss Rebecca goodbye; they had stopped doing that years ago. She did not wish him a good day, but even that ritual had become sporadic. He had far more bad days than good at work, regardless of what she said.

He was a middle manager for a construction company. They, like everyone else connected with real estate, took a devastating hit when the bottom fell out of the market. They were forced to fire many of their contractors because there was just no work for them. Who went and who stayed was never Edward's call. That was up to the people who occupied the corner offices he had never seen and probably never would. He, however, was the designated bearer of the pink slips, so the anguish and the anger of those he fired fell solely upon him. It was no good explaining that he did not make those decisions, since those who did make them were invisible and untouchable.

Sometimes there was a car in his reserved parking space when he got to the site. It was impossible to miss the placard denoting the space as his, just as it was impossible for him to miss the disdainful glares he got from the workers. He knew what those glares meant, and he couldn't disagree. Who was he to think he could lord it over them when he wouldn't last an hour doing the work they did?

It was useless for him to say he was only trying to do his job and get through the day, same as them. So he said nothing, ignored the stares, and pretended not to hear the muttered comments.

Today there was no car in or next to his space. Thank goodness for small blessings. Also, today was a paper day, when he had to stay in his office and catch up on the backlog of bills and correspondence.

That meant he would not see anyone else all day unless they came to his office, which no one ever did except out of dire necessity. Therefore, while he did not exactly enjoy paper days, he was far more sanguine about them than were most middle managers.

And today, unlike most days, he had something to look forward to. Right after work he would go to Caramel and buy as many of those chocolates as were on display, assuming there were any left. He could always count on a pick-me-up in the form of a cinnamon roll or apple fritter, but this went well beyond that.

He treated himself to lunch at an Italian restaurant down the street from the site. There were lunch wagons that came in every day, but he had only gotten his food there a few times before he was set straight on the stupid notion that he could ever be one of the guys. After that, he typically went to McDonald's or Subway. But today he had earned the right to splurge a little, so he ordered chicken parmesan, spaghetti with meatballs, garlic bread, and a bowl of caramel-apple crisp for dessert. He even had a glass of white wine. Since he almost never drank, that was enough to give him a pleasant buzz for much of the afternoon.

The workday ended at five, but he liked to stay until six. The parking lot was empty when he emerged, and most of the rush hour traffic had cleared. He drove straight to Caramel and waited impatiently behind four other people. He noticed with surprise that none of them ordered the chocolates, until he looked into the display case and saw why. The chocolates were not there. Nor were they mentioned in the price list.

When he was up, he asked Louise if she still had any chocolates.

"Chocolate what?" she asked. "Chocolate donut holes? They're right here."

"No, no. The special chocolates. The ones that were just made."

"I don't know what you're talking about."

"Okay." He looked around to make sure no one else was coming in, and leaned over the counter to whisper. "I'm talking about the chocolates Caramel made. At least she told me her name was Caramel, but maybe it isn't. She didn't want anyone to know she was helping you, and don't worry, I'll never tell anyone. But she made these special chocolates, and last night she gave me some—"

"Whoa, whoa. What do you mean, 'helping me'? Nobody helps me. This is my shop. And you only got your usual cinnamon roll yesterday."

"Right, that was when I got off work. But I came back last night after you closed. She was here, and she let me in—"

"Somebody was in here after hours?" she demanded.

"Um, yeah," he said, getting confused. "She likes to help you out, because you're a friend of her family. She's in her late twenties, maybe early thirties, she's a couple of inches taller than me, and—"

"I don't know any girl like that. And you say she was *in here*?"

"Yeah, behind the counter, right where you're standing now. She let me in and asked me to try—"

"What were you doing here after hours?"

"I had to walk here, and I got here too late. I saw the shop was closed, so I started to leave, and then the lights came on. The door was unlocked, so—"

"You're talking horseradish. I always lock my door."

"Look, I'm telling you—"

"Yeah, I know what you're telling me. And I'm telling you there's no way any of that could have happened like you say it happened. I run this shop alone, always have, always will. I don't have any assistants, name of Caramel or anything else. You must've been dreaming. Simple as that."

Edward opened his mouth to argue, but closed it again. What could he say? It was impossible that those chocolates, the young woman, and the strenuous walk here and back had been a dream. He seldom remembered any detail of his dreams, and when he did, they never made much sense to his waking mind.

Neither could he make himself believe she was playing a prank on him. She never displayed a sense of humor. She did not crack jokes with the customers, never laughed or smiled at a funny remark. And it would take a consummate actor to convincingly fake the indignation she showed at the idea that someone else had entered her domain without her knowledge, claiming to be her assistant.

Nothing would be gained by staying on this course, so he said,

"You're right. Must've been a dream. Sure was a vivid one, though. I'd like a cinnamon roll."

She seemed more than willing to let the matter drop—perhaps relieved that her most reliable customer wasn't going to come unglued in front of her—and completed the transaction without another word. He paid for the roll, took it, and walked out with no idea what to make of what he was told. He *knew* it wasn't a dream, knew that like he knew he was awake now.

But if it wasn't a dream, what was it?

He was in such a muddle over that when he got home, it did not fully register that Rebecca was not there. There was a plate on the table for him, turkey slices with mashed potatoes and peas. Somehow the sight of such a normal meal was comforting, so he sat down and ate it.

Rebecca walked in the door as he swallowed one of the last mouthfuls of turkey. She stopped, not believing what she was seeing, and stared at him. He stared back at her, just because he didn't know what else to do.

"Just...leave those in the sink when you're done," she finally said. "I'll wash them later."

"Okay," he said.

Before she left the room, she looked over her shoulder to confirm that he was indeed eating the meal without a murmur of protest. This was what she'd been trying to get him to do for years, so the last thing she wanted to do now was make a thing of it. She left him in silence.

That evening, while she lay in bed and read one of the Harlequin novels she liked, he sat in the living room and watched a movie on cable. Well, sort of. The television was on and he was looking at it, but none of his attention was on the story, and five seconds after it was over he couldn't have said which movie it was. He only picked it because it offered a respite from thinking for a sufficient amount of time.

When the closing credits began, he looked at his watch. 8:35. Late enough to see if he could get some answers. He shut off the TV and went out for a walk.

If he drove to Caramel, it would still be open when he got there. He could drive around aimlessly until after it closed, but he sensed a door had opened last night and he had stepped through it. A door that connected his dull, normal world with...someplace else. He also sensed he could not drive to the door. That was against the rules. The rules of what, he couldn't even guess, but rules had to be followed. He had walked to the door last night, and he had to walk to it tonight.

He set off at a brisk pace but could not maintain it for long. Last night's indulgence had taken its toll, and by the time he got close enough to the shop to read the sign, sweat was pouring down his face in spite of the pleasantly cool temperature. He had to wipe the perspiration out of his eyes to see the storefront clearly. It was dark.

What time was it? After ten. Considerably later than when he came last night. Did that matter? He didn't think so. It only needed to be after business hours.

He continued to walk to the shop. Now no more than a hundred feet from the door. Seventy-five. Fifty.

The lights came on. The sign flashed Open.

He knew the door was unlocked. Maybe it had been locked a minute ago, but it was unlocked now. He walked in, stood in front of the counter, and waited. A few seconds later, Caramel emerged.

"Good evening, Edward," she said, but did not smile. "I understand you and Louise had an interesting conversation today."

"That's not the half of it. What is going on here? She doesn't know anything about you, or at least she says she doesn't, and the chocolates..."

She did not cut him off, but held up a hand to silence him. His words came out with so much momentum that it took a little while for them to taper off. When they did, she said, "It's all right, Edward. It's my fault. I should have explained it to you."

"Explained what?"

"The reason Louise is retiring. It's...well, to put it delicately, retirement was not her idea."

"I don't understand," Edward said.

"She's becoming eccentric in her old age," Caramel told him. "Not senile by any means, at least not yet, but, well, stubborn. It's an insult to her for anyone to suggest she needs help running the business. Maybe with light housework, which I also do for her, but never with her pride and joy."

"So when she said she had no idea who I was talking about..."

"It's hard to say. Maybe she really didn't."

"You're not saying—the early stages of Alzheimer's?" It couldn't be. That was too horrible. Sure, the old broad had her quirks, but...

"We don't like to think about that, obviously, but we can't rule it out as a possibility. We're all keeping an eye on her, but we make it a point not to interfere as long as she can continue functioning as well as she always has. That's why I've decided not to introduce the chocolates, not yet. She's so set in her routines that the change would upset her. Can you understand?"

Could he understand an inflexible personality? He'd been living with one for more than half his adult life.

"Yes, I get it," he said. "Is there anything I can do to help?"

"Just go on giving her your business. But please don't mention me again, or the chocolates. For now, let those be our little secret. I'll be here with them every night after hours. When you want your cinnamon rolls or anything else, you go to Louise. When you want the special chocolates, you come to me. Deal?"

"Deal!" he exclaimed. "I'd like another dozen, please."

"Coming right up. But I guess we should set a price. Shall we say, five dollars a dozen?"

"Sold."

He walked out of the shop with eleven chocolates in a bag and one in his mouth. When he turned a bit later and saw that the lights were off, he did not find it strange. On the contrary, he concluded that since he happened to be the one to discover Caramel and her wondrous chocolates, she decided to share them only with him until she could safely sell them in the open. Such are the thought processes of the truly lost.

The following evening he went to the shop after work and bought his usual cinnamon roll, and Louise acted as though the conversation of the previous day never happened. Edward did not want to consider the possibility that for her, it hadn't. Creeping dementia or not, she remained a great confectioner. Not as good as Caramel, or whatever his enigmatic new friend's real name was, but good enough that she deserved to keep working until the day she just couldn't handle it anymore.

When he got home, there was a plate for him on the table. Baked chicken with a side of squash. Rather than touch off another spat with his wife, he decided he could humor her by eating the chicken—similar to the way in which an unhappily long-married man who is flattered by the attentions of another woman sometimes decides the woman he's stuck with really isn't so bad after all. Sometimes.

Because Rebecca was a competent cook in her own right, he had no trouble eating the chicken. But he drew the line at squash. He scraped the disgusting vegetables into the trash.

Every night for the next two weeks, he walked to the shop and Caramel was there. (He did experiment with driving there once, idled out front for ten minutes, then got out and walked to the door, even pulled on the handle, but nothing. So it seemed he had correctly guessed that rule of this odd but delightful little game.)

He always stayed and talked with her for a while. Unlike her crusty friend, Caramel was friendly and outgoing and asked him all kinds of questions about himself, his job, and his home life. She was reticent and evasive about her own life, but the hormones and sugar coursing through his body—both at dangerously high levels—kept him from caring. He only cared that she was interested in him in a way no one had been for decades. He even allowed himself to flirt with her, and she flirted back. By degrees their banter became, shall one say, less and less appropriate for a man in his situation.

Rebecca never asked where he went on his long walks. She probably assumed he had finally decided to take her advice and start getting in shape, in baby steps, which were all his body could handle. Although he wasn't doing anything wrong, even if the secret meetings with Caramel made him feel a bit like he was slipping out to meet his mistress, it was a delicious secret in more ways than one.

But if he'd never had much reason to learn the old saying "All good things must come to an end," he got a crash course in it on the Tuesday of the third week.

When he walked in that night, Caramel came out to see him and told him without preamble that there were no chocolates.

His face fell. "What?"

"There's something you have to do for me, Edward."

"Uh...sure. Are you out of a certain ingredient? Do you need me to get it for you? That's no problem, I can—"

"No. Ingredients are not the problem. I need you to do something for *me*."

His hands rested on the counter. She accentuated the personal nature of her request by laying her hand on top of his with the word *me*.

He broke out in a sweat that had nothing to do with the rigors of the walk. "Wha, what, what do you need me to do?"

She looked at him a moment to be sure she had his full attention. No worries there. Then she leaned over the counter, and he did the same in reflex. Their faces scant inches apart, her eyes drilling into his, she said:

"I need you to kill your wife."

He stared at her, utterly uncomprehending. His ears heard the sounds and his brain attached the intended meanings to those sounds, but the sentence hung in the air between them like a stream of oil that could not be absorbed into the medium into which it had been dropped.

Finally it sank in. He drew back from her, but only to stand up straighter. His hand stayed where it was, covered by hers.

"You...you want me to..." He could not finish the sentence. She did not finish it for him. She just went on looking at him, not smiling, not blinking, needing to know he had processed the requirement.

He shook his head in short, animated jerks. "No. I...I can't. I can't. Are you crazy? Kill my wife? I can't."

His denial, however, was that of a man who had been deprived of something he wanted very badly and was trying to decide how far he was prepared to go to get it.

"Kill your wife," she said again. "Do that for me, and you can have all the chocolates you want. You may have me also, if you wish. But until you do this for me, you may have nothing more from me."

She took her hand off his. Her hand was cold. Its absence was colder.

"Please," he whimpered. "You can't ask me—"

"You have to go now, Edward."

"Wh..." He looked at the door and the abyss of night beyond, into which he was being exiled.

He turned back to her, silent but begging, a pathetic expression of naked need on his face. Caramel tightened the screws.

"You have to go now, Edward. Go home and kill your wife. When that is done, what I have will be yours for the asking. Until it is done, our business is finished. You have to go now, Edward."

The lights behind the counter went out. She had not moved. She stayed where she was, staring at him from the darkness, reaching out to the darkness in him.

He backed toward the door, unable to take his eyes off her. Her head swiveled to watch him go. Their eyes were locked, and he saw no possibility of reprieve in hers.

Something pressed into the small of his back. He gasped and whipped around, but it was only the metal bar of the door. He put his hands on it, but turned back to look at Caramel once more, with a desperate hope that she would let him off the hook at the last minute, as the angel stopped Abraham on the brink of sacrificing his son Isaac.

She was there, unspeaking, motionless as if unbreathing. He saw in the shadowed depths of her eyes that there was no hope for him.

He walked out and heard the lock turn behind him. There was no way she could have gotten to the door that fast. But how she did it was irrelevant. The other row of lights cast faint tendrils into the night around him, but those too were snatched back.

The road stretched ahead of him into the darkest night of his life. He started for home.

When he got to his front door, he turned the knob without thinking. He was too shaken to notice that the lights were off or to remember that his keys were in his pocket. The door was unlocked. It wasn't very important. They lived in a quiet neighborhood and did not have much worth stealing.

He slipped into bed without undressing. Rebecca was already asleep. She was facing away from him, and he lay there, looking at the back of her head. For a moment he thought about waking her, telling her of the terrible bargain he'd been pressured to make, and swearing to her that he would never do anything to hurt her. Not anymore. From now on he would be a good husband. He would stop fighting with her about his diet. He would let her help him get healthy.

But only for a moment. The impulse faded and he slipped into a fitful sleep.

The next morning, he was so irritable from the forced withdrawal that when he saw the bowl of oatmeal on the table, it was more than he could take.

Rebecca sat in the chair across from his, doing her crossword. He looked at the oatmeal, then at her, and said, "What is that?"

"What is what?" she asked without looking up.

He marched to the table, picked up the bowl, and slammed it down. "This!"

"It's your oatmeal. Eat it before it gets cold."

"I'm not eating this glop. You eat it!"

"I don't need it."

"You think I do?"

"You're the one whose blood is turning to syrup, not me."

"Oh, you think that's funny? Like syrup? What, 'cause I'm so sweet and slow or something? Ha ha, big joke!"

She did not respond.

"Well?" he shouted. "You gonna answer me?"

"When you say something worth answering, I will."

He snatched up the bowl and threw it at the wall, shattering it. The oatmeal flowed in a sticky mess down the wall and pooled on the floor.

"Feel better now?" she asked the paper.

His hands itched to grab that paper and stuff it in her mouth until she choked on it. He grabbed his forearms hard and stalked out of the room.

If she ever looked up at him, it was after he'd turned his back on her.

By the time he got to his office he had the beginnings of a headache. He cadged some Tylenol from one of the other supervisors, but it did no good. As the day wore on, the headache spread from his temples and got steadily worse until his head was encased in a semicircular vise.

When he left for the day, the pain had leveled off to somewhere just short of intolerable. He went to the pastry shop to get a cinnamon roll, but also to see if the chocolates were available, if there was just one, in a corner of the display case, unnoticed by Louise or the customers.

The only chocolates he saw were the chocolate donuts and donut holes that were there every day. He bought two of the donuts and half a dozen of the holes in addition to his roll, to see if they would take the edge off his craving. They did not. Whatever Caramel did to make her special chocolates, they were the only ones that would do. He knew that as well as he knew the terrible thing he had to do to get any more of them.

Did he really have to do it? Maybe if he walked there tonight, he would see that she had relented.

He set out at 8:30 that evening. The walk did not seem to take as much out of him this time. Maybe that was because he was consumed with his destination, unable to spare much thought for anything else. Maybe it was because his body was growing accustomed to the exercise.

Or maybe it was because he was not as concerned about the ache in his legs as he was about the tremor that had developed in his hands.

The lights were off when he got there, as they always were at first. His breathing quickened as he approached. Finally he reached the door and pressed his face against it, as a hungry child would. Nothing. No sign, no lights, no Caramel, no chocolates.

For an instant he considered breaking in and taking them. They should be easy to find, in one of the drawers under the display case. He could take off his jacket, wrap it around his fist, and punch through the glass. Louise had probably never installed an alarm system, since she took the cash and the unsold pastries home with her each night. If he did it quickly, he could be in and out before anyone noticed anything amiss, and later he would anonymously slip her the money to replace the glass.

Dream on, he told himself. Caramel would have thought of that and would not have left the chocolates in there. Not when they were meant to entice him to commit a homicide.

Already he had reached the point where he was willing to commit lesser crimes to get them. Breaking and entering, petty theft, destruction of private property.

If he was prepared to do those things to take the chocolates—and there was no use fooling himself, if there was the slightest chance they were in there, he would be doing them now—was he prepared to do the one thing that would earn them?

Impossible. Unimaginable. He and Rebecca had their problems, but every couple did. He was no murderer.

Was he really so sure of that?

Until a few seconds ago, he was no thief either. Technically he still wasn't, but absence of the opportunity for vice was not really the same as virtue.

He slumped against the door. The cold glass soothed his head a little as waves of nausea washed through him, only partly from the withdrawal.

He straightened up, jammed his hands in his pockets to try to stifle the worsening tremors, and walked away without looking back.

Tonight's battle was his. But they would get harder to fight with each passing day, until...what? Would he do this unthinkable thing? Was he seriously so far gone that he would murder his wife for a few pieces of candy?

With every pulse of his pounding head, every cramp that seized his stomach, the automatic answer to that question became more difficult to remember.

Time for a big fat reality check. He had become a junkie, no two ways about it. There was some highly addictive substance in those chocolates, and he was hooked on it as surely as if it were booze or heroin. The only thing to do was check himself into rehab. They would do a complete workup on him, take a blood sample, isolate the chemicals that were doing this to him, and devise an effective treatment. The detoxification process would be a waking nightmare, the worst experience he had ever endured, but it was the only way he could free himself from the grip of his compulsion.

Almost at once he began to work a dodge on himself, to talk himself out of this radical course of action. It wasn't necessary to go into rehab like some strung-out loser or a celebrity doing the currently fashionable thing. He wasn't *addicted* to anything, that was ridiculous, he was stronger than that, he was just coming down with something. Maybe that swine flu everybody was so hysterical about. All he needed was to rest, take a few days off work. None of the men who had to report to him was likely to miss him. Take some vitamins, drink lots of liquids. He'd be his old self again in no time.

Before these thoughts had time to sink roots into the softening meat of his brain, he passed out.

He regained consciousness in a hospital room. He tried to sit up, but could not. Movement glimpsed from the corner of his eye made him tilt his head to look. It was Rebecca, seated in a chair next to his bed.

"What happened?" he asked in a hoarse whisper.

"Somebody was out jogging last night and found you unconscious by the side of the road," she told him. "They called an ambulance, and you were brought here. Apparently you cracked your head a good one on the pavement, but the doctor says you don't have a concussion. Guess that thick skull of yours does have its uses."

"What else did..." He was so short of breath that he had to take a deep one just to finish the question. "What else did the doctor say?"

"Sugar coma. There's some fancy medical term for it, but the point is your blood sugar was so high it's a wonder your veins haven't turned into Pixy Stix."

The image surprised a laugh out of him, but it came out as a weak, dry chuckle. As a child, like most of his generation, he had loved Pixy Stix, the giant straws filled with a powdered candy that was practically pure sugar. But his laughter shriveled and died as the other thing she said hit home.

"I was...in a coma?"

"Yep. Well, coma's a strong word for it. You were only out for nineteen, twenty hours. But while you were out, you were *out*. You babbled some in your sleep, but you never woke up."

"I did?" He'd never talked in his sleep in his life. Not that he would really know if he had or not, but no one had ever remarked on it before now.

"Yeah. Something about how you had to kill me to get the chocolates."

The syrup froze in Edward's Pixy veins.

"I...said that?"

"It wasn't hard to convince the doctor it must've been a snatch of dialogue from a scary movie you saw once. He's heard people say a lot stranger things when they were delirious."

She shifted in her chair and leaned over so she was looking almost straight down on him.

"Now the question is, Ed...what are we going to do about this?"

"I...I don't..."

"I think you do. You spilled everything, just about. How you've been going to that sweet shop after hours to get the special chocolates from some young dish who calls herself Caramel. How she finally told you you couldn't have any more until you got rid of me. Like I said, everybody thinks it was some late-night horror flick you got stuck in your head, but I know you, Ed. You might moan or grunt sometimes when you're having a bad dream, but not once in sixteen years have you ever talked in your sleep. That's why I figured that whatever you were talking about, it wasn't anything Hollywood put in your head. So I went down and had a chat with Helen—"

"Who?"

"Helen. The woman who runs the sweet shop."

"No. No, her name is Louise."

"Who told you that?"

"Car—" he started to say, but snapped his jaws shut. Rebecca was already more than half convinced he hadn't raved in his delirium but had confessed to a heinous crime he'd come frighteningly close to committing. If he answered her question, he would remove all doubt.

That one syllable was enough to do it. "'Caramel,' were you about to say?" she asked with what sounded like serene interest.

He did not answer. She took his silence for assent.

"Thought so. You've been sneaking out for strange chocolate with this Caramel person, and she told you the woman who runs the shop is named Louise?" She waited for an answer, got none, went on. "Well, that's not her name. It's Helen. Middle name Jean, last name Carter. She doesn't know about any Caramel or about any weird chocolates."

"That's what Car...what she told me," Edward said. "That Louise, or Helen, or whatever her name is, maybe she just didn't remember. She's run the shop by herself for so long that she can't accept the idea of needing any kind of help with it, and with her early Alzheimer's—"

"Her what?" Rebecca asked sharply. "This Caramel person told you Helen has Alzheimer's?"

"She wasn't diagnosed with it yet, but she was beginning to slip, and was going to have to retire soon. So Caramel was lending her a hand, in secret."

"That what this girl told you? Well, I guess it figures that it's totally wrong. Helen got herself checked out a few weeks ago and she's fit as a fiddle, body and mind. She could keep working until she's ninety if she has a mind to."

"That doesn't make sense. She told me—"

"Yeah, I gather she told you a lot of things. But what I'm telling you is what Helen told you. There is no Caramel. Never was. Helen closes her shop at nine o'clock at night, and it stays closed until she opens it again at seven o'clock in the morning. She even asked all her close friends and everyone in her family about the girl you described to her. Not a one of them knows anybody like that."

"But I was coming back from there when I passed out!" Edward said. "And that was way after it closed. How do you explain that?"

"You weren't far from the shop when they found you, that's true enough, but that doesn't prove anything. On top of that, police make rounds of the town all through the night, check on all the businesses. They've never once seen that place open when you say it was."

"It was only for a few minutes each time. It's closed right up until I get to it, and it closes again right after I leave."

Rebecca did not reply to that. She chose to let him think on that statement so he could hear how it sounded.

He was still too weak to sit up, so he hoisted himself onto his elbows to bring his vantage point closer to hers. "What are you saying? That I've gone nutso? That I imagined all that?"

"That's for you and a shrink to decide," Rebecca said. "I don't care if you went out for walks and dreamed up some young tart who made amazing chocolates for you and nobody else. But I do care that you were planning to kill me. Yeah, I think I care a little about that."

Edward flopped back onto the mattress. "Becky, I never...okay, all right, yeah, I guess I did freak out a little there for a while. I admit that. But I swear to you, I never would've gone through with it. I would've killed myself first."

"Is that so? Like when you threw the bowl against the wall this morning because you wouldn't eat the oatmeal? And then you stood there staring at me like you wished I'd catch fire and burn up right there? I didn't have to be looking right at you to see that."

Edward's chest hitched and his vision blurred. Everything she said was the truth. He had no more excuses for himself, and he broke down and wept. Rebecca handed him a tissue from the dresser by the bed, but made no other gesture.

"I'm so sorry, Becky," he sobbed. "You were right about me. "Everything you've been saying all these years, about how dumb and selfish I was, you were right. I had to keep eating all those sweets, even when I could see what they were doing to me, what they...what they almost made me do there at the end. Look, if you...if you want a divorce, you can have it. You can do better than me, and I'm the first to admit it. But if you give me another chance—I know I don't deserve it, but if you give me another chance—I can change. I'll start doing right by you. I swear it."

Rebecca looked at the floor, thinking that over. "I can do that, I guess. I've already poured sixteen years into you, and I guess they haven't been all bad. Besides, I don't have time to start all over and break in another man. The doctor says they're about ready to spring you, so I'll go down and check you out. What do you want for dinner tonight?"

"Anything," Edward said eagerly. "Anything you make, I'll eat it and like it. Even if it's more of that oatmeal."

"Oatmeal for dinner? Don't be disgusting. How about lasagna and a salad?"

"I'll eat every bite."

"Good to know."

He was discharged soon afterward. They went home, she cooked the meal, and he was as good as his word. He even asked for seconds and got them. Then he insisted that she let him do the dishes. She had no objection.

"I need to run to the store anyway," she said. "I'll be back soon."

"I'll be here," he swore. "I'm not going anywhere. Not ever again."

"Well, you don't need to take it that far. I wouldn't mind too much if you kept on going to work."

It was a few minutes after nine when she left, so Caramel was closed, but Rebecca pulled up in front of the shop, got out, walked in the unlocked door, and made her way behind the counter to the office in back. She rapped on the door twice and went in.

The office lights were on. Helen was seated at a small table.

"Did it work?" Helen asked.

"It's early days yet, but so far it's worked wonders on him. What on earth did she put in those chocolates? They drove him clean out of his head."

"Experimental formula, never intended for public consumption. She won't tell me more than that. But I don't have a chemistry degree like she does, so I probably wouldn't understand it anyway. Well, that's what I get for helping to put her through college. But I told her about the situation with your husband and she was willing to help out. If you don't mind my saying so, your methods seemed a bit extreme. Oh, I guess they solved the problem, and I don't say I disapprove of them, but are you sure there wasn't a better way?"

"With Ed, you don't have a lot of options," Rebecca said. "He can be as stubborn as a mule, and frankly he's not much smarter than one. Normally I can deal with that. But we're just getting by as it is, and a chronic illness like diabetes, with all the medications and everything else that comes with it, that would have buried us. He's in such bad shape already, nobody will give him health insurance unless we pay an arm and a leg for the premiums. And I would've had to take care of him when he got too sick to work or do anything around the house, so more than likely I would've worked myself to death even before the diabetes finished him off. I wasn't about to go through all that just because he didn't feel like giving up sweets. Trying to reason with him didn't do any good, and lecturing him didn't, and nagging him didn't, so I decided to see if I could scare some sense into him. I would've walked out and left him to his fate if this hadn't worked, but I had to try one more time to save him, and me, from himself."

"Guess that little chat you had with him in the hospital did the trick," Helen said. "How'd you know he'd pass out on the way home?"

"I didn't. But between the sugar, his weight, the walks, and the stress, it was only a matter of time before his body gave out. When he woke up in the hospital, he was too scared to question anything I told him. And you had him convinced you didn't know about any girl named Caramel or about any after-hours goings-on in your shop."

"It's a shame to lose such a good customer, but I'd feel a lot worse if I lost him to death and my pastries had anything to do with it. But tell me something, Mrs. Hench. If his body had held up long enough, you don't really think he would've tried to kill you, do you?"

"I'd like to say I know him better than that. But if there's one thing I've learned, it's that you can share another person's life with them and never really know them. We all have our secrets. I do, you do, your niece does." Rebecca looked toward the storage cupboard and called out, "Isn't that right, Hannah?"

A young woman emerged from the cupboard.

"You can call me...Caramel," she said.

Mirror, Mirror

I.

"Get a move on, you guys! We're going to be late!"

Normally Jackie just said "hey" when she poked her head into the breakfast room. But today was not a normal day, as she had been reminding the others for a week.

"Will you cool it?" Claire yelled back. "The carnival's not even open yet!"

Jackie had gotten most of the way to the bathroom. She came back, sat at the table, and said, "That's why we have to go now. Before all the yahoos get there."

"Yahoos?" asked Richard. "There are no yahoos here. I think there's some kind of municipal ordinance."

She mumbled into her bowl of cereal, "Yeah, well, there should be some kind of ordinance to keep out the—"

"Don't." Claire jabbed a manicured finger at her. "Don't even start with that."

"I'm just saying—"

"I know what you're just saying. And I'm just saying I'm not in the mood for any of your racist diatribes."

"Hey, girls, cool it." Richard had put on his peacemaker hat. "I don't want any fighting today, okay?"

"Leave her here and there won't be," Claire said. "Simple."

"Excuse me?" Jackie said. "Who died and made you queen of the freaking universe?"

"I don't have to be queen of the universe to be queen of my

world. And my world has no room for your medieval narrow-minded hogwash. Especially not today."

Tom saw that Jackie was gathering steam and made a preemptive strike. "All right, that's it. Listen up. This is my day off, it's 76 degrees, not a cloud in the sky, and you two are not going to ruin it. You call a truce right now or I'm leaving both of you here."

Jackie and Claire both had retorts ready, but Tom held up a finger, cutting them off. "One or the other. Which is it?"

The women glared at each other. Then Claire said, "He's right. We don't get many days like this. And I intend to enjoy this one. With or without you. Detente."

Jackie rolled her eyes to mask her unfamiliarity with that word. "Fine. Truce."

"Okay then!" Tom said, pushing back from the table. "Is the van all packed?"

Richard arched his eyebrows. "You're asking me? You're the OCD one here, remember?"

"I'm taking the day off from being the deep thinker. You could use the practice."

"Ha ha. It is to guffaw. Hey, you know, maybe that could be the start of a song. What do you think about that?"

"You don't want to know. Just tell me if the van's packed."

Richard ran through a mental checklist. "It should be."

"Then let's hit the road." Tom stood up and knocked a pile of papers to the floor.

"Hey, be careful!" Richard said. "I spent five days on that!"

Jackie bent down and started to gather up the papers, but she sighed when she recognized what was on them. The first eighteen measures of an original song.

"Rich," Jackie said, standing up, "you have a lot of talents. But it's time you faced facts. Music isn't one of them."

"Um, Jackie, you're my girlfriend, remember? That means you're supposed to say girlfriend stuff like it's so great that you keep persevering, don't give up, it's gonna work out, you'll be famous."

"Exactly. I'm supposed to say that stuff. And I can't. What does that tell you?"

Richard looked at the others for affirmation, but got none.

"I hate to admit it," said Claire, "but she's right on this one. We're not saying you don't have a lot of creative energy. You do. You just need to find another outlet for it."

"Like finding a creative way to come up with the three months' rent you owe me," Tom suggested.

"Look, you guys, I've heard all this before. And I'll have you know I get great ideas for songs. It's just that somebody else always thinks of them first. Like, if 'River of Dreams' had just come together in my head a bit sooner, it would've been my song instead of Billy Joel's."

Tom smirked at Claire. "Sure. That's all it is. And if he'd been born thirty years earlier, he would've been the one to write 'Bohemian Rhapsody.' It's not like Queen really needed that one."

"No," Jackie countered. "It has to be forty years, so he could have written 'Eleanor Rigby.' The Beatles had enough other hits, right?"

"Why stop there?" asked Claire. "Instead of forty years, why not two hundred and forty? And instead of one song, why not Beethoven's entire repertoire? Or Mozart's? And while we're at it, let's throw in Tchaikovsky! Maybe not everything of his, because some of it is just depressing, but at least *The Nutcracker!*"

Tom shook his head. "I don't know. Living before there was electricity? He lived on cold soup for three days that time the power went out."

Richard sat through this exchange with his arms folded. Finally he said, "Are you through?"

"If we've gotten through to you," Claire said. "Rich, at some point you're gonna have to go out and get an actual job. You can't just sit here scribbling notes on paper hoping you'll eventually be discovered and land a songwriting gig on *The Voice.* It doesn't work that way."

"What do you want to do?" asked Jackie. "Go on welfare and be a part of the underclass with the—"

Jackie choked off the rest of the question, but it was too late. Claire seized on it.

"No, what about that?" she asked, ignoring a warning look from Tom. "Let's explore this whole idea of the underclass. Now, for someone in the underclass to get out of it, they have to get a good job, right?"

Jackie said nothing. She already knew where this was going.

"And that means," Claire went on, "that if someone is interviewing them—someone like you, say—and their résumé says they can do the job they're applying for, doesn't it work a lot better if they're not fired before they're hired?"

"Look," Jackie said through gritted teeth, "I already told you. They didn't look like they could do the job."

"Ah, I see! So you're a telepath. They were really just looking to score some easy money, and they cleverly disguised the fact by applying for jobs they were obviously unqualified for instead of going on the dole or just knocking over some gas stations. But you were too smart for them. You plucked that knowledge right out of their heads and foiled their insidious plot. But it only worked with those three. Somehow you managed to miss the guy who applied as an accountant and then 'misplaced' three hundred thousand dollars. Or the system programmer who was always asking other people what he was supposed to do when this or that happened. Could it be that your amazing ability is only activated by a certain amount of melanin in the person's skin? So the white people just slip under your radar?"

"Enough!" Tom yelled.

"I'm done," Claire said.

"Me too," declared Jackie, who got up and left the room.

When she was gone, Claire looked at Richard.

"Don't," Richard said. "You've asked me before."

"And you have yet to give me a sensible answer," Claire said. "So I'll ask you again. You're a kind, nice-looking, intelligent guy. You could have had your pick of kind, nice-looking, intelligent girls. You did not have to settle for *that*. Why did you?"

"I...I just...you just don't understand. When I first moved here, I was lonely. I didn't know anybody, and I thought I had to have a girlfriend. And she was the first one who showed any interest. And it seemed like it would be cool to be going out with an older woman. Anyway, I didn't have the nerve to try for someone better."

"And now you'll probably never get the chance, even if you break up with her. Have you heard what the other girls are saying? Any guy who—"

145

"Any guy who would be with her isn't worth their time. I don't know, maybe they're right."

"Now you're being ridiculous. I would have gone out with you myself if I weren't already dating Tom."

"Oh, yes," Richard said to Tom. "Have I thanked you for that lately?"

"I keep tellin' ya, buddy, you snooze, you lose! And in your case, I mean that literally."

"Huh?" asked Claire.

"The freshman mixer where I met you? He wanted to go too, but he crashed out instead."

"Hey, it's exhausting doing nothing all day!" Richard said. "Most people don't realize that. Anyway, we can't all be track-and-field gods like you."

Claire and Tom shook their heads at each other. Then Tom looked at his watch and said, "I'll go get her. We really should be hitting the road." He left the room. Claire went to get her purse. She paused in the doorway, spared Richard a final pitying glance, and was gone.

Richard smacked his head with his keys and threw them against the wall. He sighed heavily, went to pick them up, and left the house. The forty-minute ride to the carnival was completed in silence.

"This is it?" Claire asked when they arrived.

There was a ferris wheel, a merry-go-round, a coin toss booth, a funhouse, and a cotton candy booth. That did seem to be it.

Jackie curled her lip in disgust. "I don't get it. It looked so much better in the brochure."

"Let me see it," Richard said. She handed it to him, and they clustered around him to study it.

They were at the location specified, and in the picture they could see everything they were looking at now and a great deal more. Including throngs of people, not one of whom was here. Except for the four of them, the fairway was deserted. Even the cotton candy booth was empty.

"Maybe it's not open yet," Tom said.

Jackie checked her watch. "It was supposed to open at nine, and it's after ten."

Claire shivered despite the pleasant warmth. "Can we go somewhere else? This place is giving me the creeps."

"Me too," Jackie said. "There's a great water park not far from here."

"Yeah!" Claire exclaimed. "I know the one. Let's go there."

"Well, now, hang on," Richard said. "Let's not be hasty. I see a golden opportunity here."

"What are you talking about?" Tom asked.

"Look around. What do you see? Or, more to the point, what don't you see?"

"Any decent rides," Tom replied.

"Any food stands," Claire added.

"Any other people," Jackie chimed in.

"Bingo!" Richard said, pointing at Jackie. "No other people. And what does that mean?"

"That everyone else is smarter than we are," Tom said.

"No! Focus, people. It means no crowds. No ticket-takers. No concessioners. Which also means no waiting, no limits on the rides, and most important of all, no money!"

"Yeah, but come on," Claire said. "Nothing here is worth the effort even if it's free!"

"What about the funhouse?" asked Richard.

They looked down the fairway and to the right. The sign "Hall of Mirrors" was fastened to the roof of the most dilapidated structure of them all.

"Are you crazy?" Jackie cried. "That building looks like it should have a Condemned sign on it!"

"No kidding," said Tom. "Look, let's just forget this and—"

"Come on, guys!" Richard cajoled. "Where's your sense of adventure?"

Claire snapped her fingers. "I knew I forgot something!"

"It's somewhere else," answered Tom. "Anywhere else."

"Yeah," said Claire. "Mine is at the bottom of that huge corkscrew slide at the waterpark."

Richard knew when he was outgunned. "Okay, okay. But this trip doesn't have to be a total wash. Let's just go in the funhouse. Those are always worth a look, right? We'll walk around it for a couple of minutes and then we'll leave."

The others grunted their assent and they walked to the funhouse, where yet another disappointment awaited them.

They expected the usual assortment: a mirror that made you look short and squat, another that made you look ten feet tall, and so on. Here there was only one mirror and it did not distort their reflections at all. It was wide enough that the four of them could stand in front of it without touching, but otherwise it looked completely ordinary. It was not on the wall, but on a stand about half a meter in front of it.

Tom was dumbfounded. "You have got to be kidding me. Richard, we have mirrors like this at home. Not as big, but whatever. We could've just stayed there."

"Hey, wait a second," said Jackie. "What's that on top of the glass?"

Claire stood on tiptoe to look. "It's an inscription. Really small."

Tom peered up at it. "I know what it should say: 'Mirror, mirror on the wall, who's the dumbest one of all? If you're reading this, you are!'"

Richard ignored the remark and moved closer to Claire. "Can you read it?"

"I think so." She brushed away a coating of dust and recited what was there.

"Make a wish, but do not talk,
Then once around the mirror walk.
Reflect upon the looking-glass,
And may your wish not come to pass."

"May your wish *not* come to pass?" asked Richard.

Claire shrugged. "That's what it says. I like the play on words, though."

"What play on words?" Jackie asked.

"Reflect. It refers to your reflection in the mirror, but you're also supposed to reflect on the reflection. As in, think about how you see yourself."

Jackie looked doubtfully at Tom, who said, "She's right."

"Well, anyway," Jackie said, not wishing to discuss anything that made her feel stupid, "whoever put that there doesn't seem to understand the concept of wishing mirrors."

"Or maybe they do," said Tom, "better than most."

"And on that note," Richard said, "may I just take this opportunity to say, *huh?*"

"You know that old saying. 'Be careful what you wish for. You may get it.'"

"You sound like you actually believe in this stuff."

"What I believe in is covering my bases," Tom said. "You oughta try it sometime."

"Let's be real," Richard scoffed. "If I walk around this mirror, the only thing that'll happen is I'll come out with spiderwebs in my hair."

"Go ahead. Might be an improvement."

"Sounds like a dare to me," Jackie said.

"That it does," Richard agreed. "And far be it from me to walk away from a dare."

"Okay, then," Tom said, "the mirror awaits. Start walking."

Richard approached the corner of the mirror, then turned back to address his audience.

"I make this journey on behalf of the little people, in the hope that one day they, too, might have mirrors of their own to walk around like idiots."

Tom made a show of looking at his watch. "Time's a-wastin'. Git a-goin'. Or are ya yella?"

"I'm going, I'm going. But I would like to say one more thing."

"And that is?"

"That is the worst Old West impression I've ever heard."

"Opinion noted. Now off with you."

"Right."

Richard squeezed between the stand and the back wall, and they heard him take two steps. Then they heard only silence.

He emerged from behind the mirror, and the others were gone.

"Okay, you guys, very funny. Where are you?"

Silence.

"All right, come on! Joke's over!"

He left the funhouse and looked around the carnival grounds.

There were now other people walking around, but only a few. It should have been easy for him to spot his friends. But they were nowhere to be seen. There were eight vehicles in the parking lot. Their van was not one of them.

They would never ditch me here. Even if they would, they didn't have enough time to get out the door, let alone make it to the parking lot. And even if they could have, I would've heard that van start a mile off.

Therefore it was triply impossible that they could be gone. But they didn't seem to know that, because they were gone all the same.

II.

"Hey!" Tom yelled. "You get lost back there?"

No answer.

They exchanged nervous glances. He went up to the mirror, looked behind it, and announced, "He's not there."

"What do you mean he's not there?" Jackie said.

"Just what I said. Look for yourself."

She did, and cast a frightened look at Claire.

"He...he's gone."

"That's impossible," Claire said. "He can't be gone."

"Yes it is, and no he can't," Tom said. "But he is."

"Could there be a trap door?"

For lack of any other explanation, Jackie jumped on that one. "Yeah! Maybe that's it. He stepped on it and fell into a cellar or something." She chose—they all chose—to ignore the fact that they would certainly have heard some distinctive sounds had that happened. "We should go for help."

"There's nobody else here," Tom pointed out.

"And if you're right, he could be hurt," said Claire. "So we have to find him now."

"So...where do we look?" Jackie asked.

"Behind the mirror, where else?" Claire shouted. "That's where he was when he...when he..."

"So who goes?" asked Tom.

"What do you mean, who goes? We all go!" Jackie said.

"We can't all go. Someone has to stay here."

"But—"

"No, he's right," Claire said. "If there's a trap door, we have to know exactly where it is, or we might all fall in. And if Richard is hurt or unconscious, we might end up that way too."

"All right then, who goes?"

"He's your boyfriend," Claire noted.

"Now wait a minute—"

"She's got a point," said Tom. "Look, we'll be standing right here. If anything happens, we'll see it right away and then we'll know what to do. There's nothing to worry about."

"Oh, yeah," Jackie grumbled. "Like it's not a staple of horror movies that there's always someone stupid enough to say that."

"Look," Claire snapped, "the longer we stand here arguing, the harder it's going to be to help Richard."

"All right, all right! I'm going." Jackie faced the back of the mirror, took a deep breath, and started in. They saw her walk two steps into the darkness before she vanished.

There was no secret passageway built into the wall, no trap door built into the floor. She did not fall anywhere. She was just gone.

Tom and Claire looked anxiously at each other, and when Jackie came around the other side of the mirror...

III.

"Excuse me?" said Richard.

The man in the Harley-Davidson t-shirt stretched tightly over a prodigious beer belly had just paid a dollar to the barker at the duck shoot. Funny, Richard didn't remember seeing a duck-shooting booth when they got here.

"Yeah?" Harley-Davidson said.

"Um, I think I lost my friends. I was wondering if you might have seen them. Guy with long brown hair, about your height, kinda buff? Two women, a brunette wearing a Mickey Mouse t-shirt and a redhead wearing a purple halter top and white shorts?"

The guy shook his head. "Nope. Ain't seen no one like that." The barker also shook his head.

Richard thanked the men and started to walk away.

"But you might try Information."

"Information?"

The barker hooked a thumb over his right shoulder. "Yeah. Other side of the fairway, just past the Ferris wheel. You can ask there, they might know."

"Thank you, sir." Richard sprinted off in the indicated direction, and Harley turned back to the barker with graphic warnings of what would happen to him if the game was rigged.

Richard ran past the Ferris wheel and saw a small white booth marked "Information." Shouldn't they have noticed that before? No matter. He ran up to the booth and noticed that its dark-haired occupant looked very much like...

"Claire?"

IV.

"What kind of a mirror is this?"

"I don't think it's a mirror at all," Tom said. "I mean, yeah, it's a mirror because we can see ourselves in it, but obviously it's something else."

"What *is* it?" Claire asked plaintively.

"How should I know? But it's got our friends, so we should go in after them...right?"

"I don't want to go in there. But I don't want to stay here either."

"Staying here's not an option. We have to do this. But we'll hold hands so we don't get separated."

"Definitely."

He stepped up to the edge of the mirror. "Ready?"

"Are you kidding?"

"Me either...ow!"

"Sorry." She loosened her grip on his hand.

They were both behind the mirror when Claire's hand grazed a nail sticking out from the wall. She jerked her hand back. Only for an instant. It was enough.

Tom looked back, and they saw the same thing.

Each saw the other wink out of existence.

Claire rushed out from behind the mirror, already knowing what she would find.

Tom was gone. She was alone.

V.

The woman looked up. "I'm sorry?"

Richard's burgeoning hopes were dashed. No, this wasn't Claire. But maybe she had seen her.

"Excuse me, miss. Have you seen a muscular guy with long brown hair? He's with two women. One is a redhead wearing a purple halter and white shorts. The other's a brunette, looks like you. She's wearing a Mickey Mouse t-shirt."

"No, I'm sorry, I haven't seen them. Are they your entourage?"

"My what?"

"You're some kind of artist, aren't you? An actor, maybe? No—a musician, right?"

For a moment he was too stunned to speak. No one ever said that to him unless they were playing a joke on him.

"Well...yeah, I am. How did you know?"

The woman smiled. "In this job you get a sense of people. And usually, there's not much to sense. The same boring people asking the same boring questions so they can get around this boring little carnival—I'm not supposed to say that, but it's true—before they go back to their boring little lives. But you...there's something different about you. Something kind of off-center. I don't mean that in a bad way. It's like you don't live well in this world because you don't really belong to it."

"Whoa! That's it exactly! You're, like, the first person to get that!"

"I'm the information girl, remember?"

"Yeah. Right. But anyway, I've gotta find my friends, so is there someplace—"

"Who are your influences?"

"Huh?"

"Your musical influences. Is there a certain style you try to emulate in your own music?"

"Um...no, not really. But Claire—that's my friend who looks like you—she was saying I should've been born like thirty years ago, so I could've written this one song Queen wrote."

"Who?"

"Her name is Claire. We all went in the—"

"No, no. You said this one song that a queen wrote?"

"No, not *a* queen. Queen. The rock band."

She looked at him blankly.

"You gotta be kidding. Queen! You know, 'We Are the Champions'? 'Bohemian Rhapsody'? 'Princes of the Universe'? You saw the movie *Highlander*, right?"

"Sure. But there was no music like that on the soundtrack. It was mostly Irish and Celtic. Period music."

"You're putting me on. Are you telling me you've honestly never heard of Queen?"

"I'm sorry, I honestly never have."

A connection began to form in Richard's mind. He didn't know quite what it was, but it prompted him to ask his next question.

"What about Billy Joel?"

"Who?"

"Billy Joel! He toured with Elton John all last year!"

"I don't think so," the woman said. "Elton John had six concerts in New England and I went to all of them. But it was just him. Nobody named...what was it?"

"Billy Joel. 'River of Dreams'? 'My Life'? 'It's Still Rock and Roll to Me'?"

She shook her head.

"Okay, what were the songs Elton John played?"

"Goodness. Let's see...'Crocodile Rock', 'I'm Still Standing', 'That's

Why They Call It the Blues', 'Candle in the Wind', 'Don't Go Breaking My Heart', 'Tiny Dancer', 'Daniel', 'Circle of Life'..."

Same one, all right. "There was nobody on stage with him, playing another piano?" Richard asked.

"No."

"Nobody with a New York accent?"

"That would describe this one jerk who hit on me at the Hartford concert, but nobody who was performing."

"Okay, all right, I get it. This is all a gag. They put you up to this, right? Ha ha, you guys, very funny. Come on, where are you hiding?"

"Okay, I really have no idea what you mean," she said.

"Sure you don't. We were having a discussion this morning about how I should have written the songs of Billy Joel or Queen because I'd never get anywhere writing my own stuff. So they decided to play a trick on me. They knew I'd come here looking for them, so they told you to pretend you'd never heard of these people—"

"You're going to have to trust me on this. If I still had the playbill of the concerts, I'd show it to you. But it said Elton John, and only Elton John. Not this Billy Joel or anyone else."

He scrutinized her face. There was not a hint of mirth or deception in it. If this was a joke, it was also on her.

Now he thought he knew what had happened. He didn't want to know, because it was impossible.

But hadn't he used that word to describe something else that had happened today? That hadn't kept it from happening.

"Do you..." His voice cracked. He cleared his throat and started again. "Do you like classical music?"

"Oh, yes! That's my favorite type of all!"

"Who...who's your favorite composer?"

"Ooh, that's a tough one. I'd say it's a tossup between Schubert and J. S. Bach. I like Haydn, too. And Handel, of course."

He swallowed. "What about Beethoven?"

Again the blank look. "Who?"

"Mozart?"

"Yes, I do know Mozart."

He wasn't sure whether to be relieved or disappointed.

155

"But I'm surprised you do. I'm not trying to be insulting, it's just that not many people who aren't serious violin students are familiar with Leopold Mozart."

He started to get dizzy, so he took some deep breaths. He had to compose himself before he could continue talking about composers.

"He never had a son?" He started to say the name Wolfgang Amadeus Mozart, but stopped himself. He wasn't sure why.

"No. His wife died in childbirth. That was common in those days."

Richard whistled the first ten bars of *Eine Kleine Nachtmusik* and asked her if she recognized it.

"No, but it's wonderful! Who wrote it?"

This was madness, so why not just go with it? "I did," he said. "Something I was tinkering with."

"Well, as a music lover, I can tell you we could use a lot more of that kind of tinkering. You should go home and write that down."

"Yeah, all right. I'll—oh! No! I can't!"

"What's wrong?" she asked.

"My friend's van's not in the parking lot. I don't know where they are—I'm not even sure where I am—but I don't have a way to get home. I'm stuck here!"

She leaned out of the booth, looked up one way, down the other.

"What are you looking for?"

"Somebody who looks like they'll care if I leave now. I don't see anyone like that."

"Huh?"

She left the booth and shuttered it. "Come on. I'll take you home."

"No! That's okay, you don't have to do that."

"Oh, really? Look, sometimes we all have to rely on the kindness of strangers. And I'd say that for you, this is one of those times. Am I wrong?"

"No," he had to admit.

"Come on then," she said. "I promise I don't bite. Not on the first date, anyway."

"That's good enough for me."

It might have been cute if she did bite, he thought. Everything about her was cute. Almost sickeningly so. But it worked for her. The girl was a life-sized pixie. All she needed was the bubble gum.

They walked to her car (an electric blue Beetle, which seemed fitting), got in, and drove away.

VI.

Claire emerged from the funhouse to find the fairway deserted. Wishing bitterly that they were doing whatever everyone else was doing, she went out to the parking lot, holding out a dim hope that one of the others had made it out and was waiting for the rest. She saw neither them nor Tom's van, but there was a cab idling in the first row of spaces. She jogged up to it.

"Excuse me?" she asked.

The driver looked up from his magazine. "Yes, ma'am?"

"Can you take me somewhere?"

"Well, if I can't, I'm in the wrong line of work! Hop in."

She did. "Thank you."

"So where we going?"

She gave him Tom's address, and they started off. He had given her an extra set of keys with the understanding that she would use them only in an emergency. This seemed to qualify. Also, her car was still there, so at least she would be mobile.

Lost in her own thoughts, she had no idea how much time had passed before the driver asked, "This it?"

She looked up. "Yes. What do I owe you?"

"I dunno. Meter conked out last night and they never got it fixed. You know what? Don't worry about it."

"I'm sorry?" She couldn't have heard that right.

"You heard right. It's your lucky day. So have a nice one."

"Well...thank you, sir! Thank you very much!"

He smiled and waved as she got out, then left her standing in front of the brownstone, wondering what to do next. Then the door opened and that one question was answered.

"Claire! You're here!"

She blinked slowly, not believing her eyes. She opened them and he was still there.

"Tom? Is that you?"

He looked at her curiously. "Who else would I be?"

"I...oh, never mind!" She leaped up the steps and threw her arms around him with such force that she almost knocked him over.

"Hey, easy there, kiddo, you'll hurt yourself!" he said, hugging her back. "Are you all right?"

"Yeah, I'm fine, but—what happened to you? I came around the mirror and you were gone, and then I walked around the fairway but I couldn't find you—"

"Hey. *Shhh*. You've had a long day, and you're a little punchy. Come inside and lie down. We'll talk after you've had some rest." He started to lead her to the bedroom.

"No, really, I'm fine. Listen, we have to go back. We have to find the others—"

"Don't worry about that. We'll go get them later. But first you have to recharge your batteries." He gently pushed her onto the bed.

"I...I guess you're right. I am starting to feel tired."

"Of course you are. It's all catching up to you. Just lie down and relax." She did, and he took off her shoes and tucked her in.

"Sleep now," he said. "Everything's going to be fine. I'll take care of you. I'm always here for you."

She was already sinking fast into sleep and wasn't sure if he really said that or if she just imagined it. She decided it didn't matter.

She had time to whisper "Love you" before she was out.

He stood there for some moments, watching her sleep, then he left the room.

VII.

Tom walked/ran around the fairgrounds, watching and listening for the slightest movement or sound. Nothing. No one else was there.

His van sat alone in the parking lot as if to ask, *Did I miss anything?*

He ran out to it, hoping the others were there waiting for him. They were not.

Maybe they had found another way home. Whatever had happened to them, he wasn't going to find out staying here. He got in the van and pulled out.

There was no one else on the highway, which was singularly odd, not to mention downright impossible—the running theme for the day—but it had two distinct advantages. He could make unbelievably good time, and since he didn't have to keep a wary eye on everyone around him, he could think as he drove, try to figure this out.

It now went very much without saying that they had not walked behind any ordinary mirror. But what *had* they done? He still had no idea, that was the maddening thing. He had to clear his mind. Emotions would cloud his reasoning.

Approach the problem logically. Break it down into its components. Seek out the hidden clues.

Richard and Jackie went through the mirror separately, and they both disappeared. He and Claire tried to go through together, but were separated. Once they were separated, he ended up here, and she disappeared to wherever she was now.

The inscription on the mirror had referred to wishes.

He could feel the pieces come together in his mind, and he smiled with the glow of understanding. This was so much easier without Claire here—

That was it!

He jerked in his seat, galvanized by this insight, and the van jerked with him. Now he felt even more fortunate no one was sharing the road with him.

Earlier this morning he had said it was his day off. That was true in more ways than one. He hadn't wanted to go to the carnival, but he knew Carrie would love it (was that her name? no, it was Claire), and with the rides and everything else to focus on, she would give the marriage talk a rest for the day. At least that had been his hope.

He did enjoy being with...what was her name again? Candace? Blair? No, something with six letters. Anyway, he enjoyed being with her. In small doses. She was extremely intelligent and well-educated, but did not feel the necessity of constantly reminding others of the fact. That alone made her worthwhile company.

But he could not tolerate being around other people for long periods of time, no matter how much he liked them. Richard understood this and let him have his space, which made him all right as a roommate. The few friends he did have were always after him not to be so antisocial. So he went on occasional outings, like this one, just enough to keep everyone off his back.

A few weeks ago the woman, whatever her name was, had started dropping hints. She never did anything so blatant as leave copies of *Bride* magazine around for him to find, but she had started talking more and more often about certain neighborhoods where it would be nice to settle down and raise a family, movies they both liked that included wedding scenes, that kind of thing. And she was always after him to invest himself more in their relationship. To be "more there for her," as those brainless daytime talk shows she sometimes watched put it.

He liked to think he was smart enough to solve most problems, but he hadn't yet figured out how to tell her that he didn't want to marry her, especially since the reason had nothing to do with her. Richard had once told him that any guy would be crazy not to want to marry her. All right, fine. He was crazy.

The reasonable hypothesis—if anything about this could be called reasonable—appeared to be that the mirror transported each person to a place corresponding to whatever their wish was. Granting their wishes, in a sense. They all wished for different things, which was why they could only go through one at a time.

He would never have admitted this; he had trouble admitting it to himself, but he often wondered how his life might have been if he had never met...never met...

Who was he thinking of? And why?

Oh well. Probably wasn't important.

VIII.

Jackie wandered aimlessly around the fairway. She had covered every square inch of the grounds at least three times and hadn't seen a sign of the others. She had nowhere else to look, but felt she had to keep moving or she would go nuts.

"Miss Crane?"

She whirled around and almost cried out in surprise. Although she had taken the day off from work so she wouldn't have to see the man who now stood a few feet from her, she had never been so glad to see anyone in her entire life.

"Mr. Weisbrod!" she said, rushing up to him. "Please help me, I don't know what's going on. I've lost my friends and—"

"Never mind that. Come with me."

He turned his back on her and strode to the parking lot, leaving her no choice but to fall in behind him. He pulled his keychain out of his pocket. Linked to it was an electronic doorlock. He pushed it and a sleek black Lexus whistled in response. He went to the driver's side and opened the door, indicating with an impatient nod that she was to get in also. She did, and only when they were on the highway did she ask where they were going.

"To the office."

His tone made it clear that he was not interested in conversation. Confused and more than a little frightened, she remained silent the rest of the way.

IX.

"We're here!" chirped Richard's benefactress. He now knew her name was Lisa. "Casa sweet casa."

He stepped out of the car, needing a moment to adjust to the quiet. She had chattered incessantly the whole way, and not only could he not get a word in edgewise (occasionally she would ask him a question but then answer it before he could), he was not even sure she had stopped to breathe. He seemed to remember that somewhere in there he'd been able to mention that his roommate had his keys. That would explain why they were at her house instead of his. Not that he had complained. Not that he could have. Something else he remembered, somewhere along the way, was her apologizing for not talking to him much at the carnival, but it took her a while to warm up to people. Then he told her not to worry about it, he was the same way...no, wait, he *wanted* to tell her that but didn't have the chance. Obviously she was comfortable with him now, and he wasn't certain whether to be flattered or to be afraid, very afraid.

Lisa's house was as relentlessly cheery as she was. There were pinks, purples, yellows, and blues everywhere, and he had to resist the temptation to look for a framed certificate naming her Pier 1's Customer of the Month. Fortunately, there were plenty of other things to look at. Each wall boasted at least one rendition of a painting by an artist of a certain style. Van Gogh to the left, Renoir to the right, here Chagall, there Dali, with some Pollack thrown in for good measure.

"Did you paint these?" he asked.

"Yeah, I did!" she answered brightly. "The Dali is my favorite, I figured you'd be looking at that one and you are, and that's cool 'cause he's my favorite painter, I just love surrealism, don't you? But of course it took the longest to paint, 'cause it's really hard to get everything just right when it's supposed to look all wrong, so I started with that one 'cause I figured after that the others would be really easy, and they were, pretty much, except that all Pollack did was lob paint on his canvas, at least that's what they say, and obviously I couldn't do that 'cause then it wouldn't be a Pollack, it would be a Lisa, actually I guess it would be a Reynolds, 'cause that's my last name and nobody buys a Jackson or a Vincent or a Salvador, I guess I can see their point, you can say 'and over there is my Monet' and sound like a connoisseur, but you couldn't really say 'and over there is my Claude,' that would just sound silly, especially if your husband or whatever's in the room and it sounds like you're calling him a clod, but anyway it had to be a Pollack, or at least look like a Pollack, so I had to spend a really long time making it look like it didn't take any time at all, isn't it weird how that works? And then I had to find a Van Gogh that I liked, I mean they're all really classic and everything, but one that wasn't a total

162

downer, you know? I wanted to do *Stars*, 'cause that one's like the best ever, but it would have taken forever to get everything, I mean it took him a majorly long time and it just came out of his head, so I did the sunflower one 'cause I really like sunflowers and that was the only one he ever sold so I figured it would be a good idea to have that one, and then of course I had to have a French painter, I figured that would be all chic or whatever, so I picked Renoir 'cause I just like saying his name, you know, like, 'and over there, that's my Ren-*wah*', makes me sound all sophisticated, don't you think? And then I had that whole other extra wall over there and of course I had to put something on it, and I was really into Chagall for a while, he sounds like he was French too but he wasn't, he was Russian, I'm not really sure how you get to be Russian with a name like Chagall, but anyway he was a terrific painter whatever else he was, and plus I had the summer off and I couldn't just watch TV all day, you know? Hey, are you thirsty? I think I still got some Sprite in the fridge. I'll be right back, okay? *Mi casa es su casa.* Make yourself at home."

X.

Mr. Weisbrod's parking space was the closest to the main entrance, indicating his position at the top of the pecking order.

"Come with me," he ordered.

Convinced that she was in very big trouble but with no idea why, Jackie scrambled out of the car and entered the lobby behind him. Inside, everyone was clacking on their keyboards or shuffling papers as usual. There was something different about them, though, and it wasn't just that they pointedly avoided her gaze. She knew the reason for that. The boss looked royally hacked off about something and they were just thankful it was her walking to the gallows instead of them. Something else wasn't right, but she couldn't pinpoint what it was. She was so nervous it was hard enough to keep walking.

He held his office door open so she could follow him in, shut it behind her, went to his desk, and flipped a switch. A small television over the door blinked on, and they saw everyone in the lobby.

"Notice anything?" he asked.

"Mr. Weisbrod, have...have I done something wrong?"

"I asked you a question. Do you notice anything?"

Jackie stared at the screen without blinking for several seconds, looking for the slightest sign that something was out of the ordinary. She saw none, and said so.

"No? Now that is odd, and I'll tell you why. Do you remember the three gentlemen who applied for employment here last month?"

"Um...yes, sir," she said in a shaking voice. Whatever this was about, it had something to do with them. But why didn't he say anything before?

"I asked you what was wrong with them, and you said they didn't look like they could do the job. I had hoped you would enlighten me further, but you never did. Do you remember that?"

"Yes, sir." She could barely manage a whisper.

He walked up next to her, looking at the screen as he spoke. "Think of this as an impromptu job performance evaluation."

She pressed her hands to her sides so he wouldn't see them tremble.

"I took the liberty of hiring them yesterday," Mr. Weisbrod said. "I was curious as to how keen these instincts of yours really are. So I'll tell you what. You tell me which of those people don't look as if they can do their jobs, and perhaps you'll get to keep yours."

Jackie stared at the screen for another full minute, then said in a small voice, "Mr. Weisbrod, the people I interviewed aren't here."

"Of course they are. I'm looking right at them. Don't imagine that you can trick me into telling you which ones they are. You're not smart enough."

"No, sir, really. They were...were..."

"Well?" he demanded. "They were what?"

That was it. That was what was different. She only associated with a few of the employees, those with whom she could "discuss" certain others without getting in trouble. That would not have been an issue today. There were as many employees in the lobby as there always were, but now...

"They're all white!" she blurted out.

"What are you talking about?"

164

For an instant she entertained the possibility that this was a joke. But she, along with most of her coworkers, believed that at some time in the past Mr. Weisbrod had had his funny bone surgically removed. He did not tolerate frivolity among the staff, and the notion that he would indulge in a practical joke himself was, well, laughable.

So this was real. But how...?

The mirror.

That had to be it. All this weirdness started after she walked around the mirror. And, she realized, it must have had something to do with the reason a man like Mr. Weisbrod would be at a carnival in the first place, and why he had said nothing about her somewhat unprofessional attire.

What had that inscription said?

May your wish not come to pass.

She had indeed wished for something, the thing she wished for more often than anything else. It was easier than either having to think about her racial myopia or moving to a place that would have been her version of paradise, like Sweden or Iceland. Those places had problems of their own, but it didn't do to think too much about that either. To speak plainly, she wanted to be in a place where there were no bleeding-hearts like Claire to tell her that looks didn't matter when they were all that mattered, whether you wanted to face it or not.

All things considered, it was easier just to wish.

And now, it seemed, her wish had been granted.

But how to even begin to explain this? For Mr. Weisbrod—this Mr. Weisbrod—this was how things were supposed to be, how they had always been. The reality she knew was different. And who was to say which reality was really *real*, if in fact either of them was?

She had to stop thinking. She was getting a headache.

No, she had to think fast. He was staring at her.

"I'm waiting, Miss Crane."

Helplessly she turned back to the screen and watched everyone as long as she could, grasping for the slightest sign that any of them were not up to their assigned tasks. Looks of confusion or uncertainty, slow response time, lack of attention to detail, anything. But everyone knew their jobs and did them well. There was no slacking off; they all knew

Big Brother was watching. What they didn't know was that someone else was watching, someone who was desperately hoping for one (or three) of them to mess up.

Or maybe they did know, because they seemed to be working even more efficiently than usual. No one especially liked Jackie, not even those who shared her ideology, and they would do nothing more than say the requisite words of sympathy if she got canned.

Mr. Weisbrod said nothing, merely watched her watching. Finally she lowered her head. She was beaten, and she knew it. There was no point in asking for mercy. That was not his policy. All she said, in a voice so low that even standing next to her he could barely hear, was "I'll have my desk cleared out by the end of the day."

He gave her a single brisk nod. "That will be all."

XI.

He collapsed onto the sofa, his mind still trying to absorb everything she had just said. He shook his head rapidly to clear it, and he realized he was breathing hard. It was tiring just listening to her.

There was a pile of books on the table, and Richard noticed that one of them was an encyclopedic biography of great composers. He snatched it up and opened to the Bs. Several Bachs...Bartok...Berlioz...Bizet.

No Beethoven.

He flipped to the Ms.

Mahler...Mendelssohn...Mussorgsky.

This is the coolest thing ever! I was thinking about what Claire said when I walked through the mirror, and now here I am, and it's real! These guys didn't exist here, and I can write their music and say it's mine, because it will be, and I'm gonna be the most famous guy on the planet! Yeah, and I wouldn't want that wish to come to pass! Stupid inscription. I gotta find a notebook. I'm already starting to think of stuff. I think I've got all of Eine Kleine Nachtmusik in my head. And it's mine, mine, mine, mine, mine! Just gotta write it down. Think I got a couple of symphonies in there too. Für Elise, Moonlight Sonata, Waltz of the Flowers...I can see all the notes. I know exactly what to write. The overture to The Marriage of Figaro...no, not just the overture, I've got the whole opera!

This is getting confusing. Just have to keep it together, get everything down on paper. Then I'll be okay. More important, I'll be famous. Even better, I'll be rich! Heck, I haven't even started yet and I've already got a groupie!

Lisa bounced back in, sat so close to him that their knees almost touched, and thrust a can of Sprite at him. She had started talking while still in the kitchen. "Here you go, it's the last one but I need to go shopping anyway, I am so stupid, I didn't even ask if you like Sprite, but I really hope you do 'cause it's all I have, I mean I could give you a glass of water but the water here tastes funny and one time I swear I saw things swimming around in it, how gross is that, is it cold enough?"

It took him a second to realize she was talking about the Sprite. "Oh! Yeah, it's fine. Thank you."

"Oh, my pleasure! Do you want anything else? Are you hungry? I make a mean bowl of Lucky Charms. The secret is the right proportion of marshmallows to cereal."

He had resolved not to encourage her further, hoping to leave with all the marbles he'd come in with (which admittedly wasn't saying much if you believed the rumors), but he laughed in spite of himself. Then someone shot a needle through his head.

"Richard! Are you all right?"

When he could open his eyes, he was doubled over, clawing at his hair, trying to mash his temples together. The pain had diminished somewhat, but this girl screaming diminished ninth fortissimos in his ear was not helping.

"Richard, what's wrong?"

What was wrong? Wasn't it obvious? The note of "Richard" was G, which was fine, but she went up to C on the "what's" and E-flat on the "wrong." She should have either completed the major chord or kept the same pitch for the second word and dropped to the next lower fifth to complete the...

What?

Since when did he think in musical terms? How did he have the slightest idea what any of that meant? Sure, he wrote music, or at least he scrawled words and notes on paper and called it music, but that was only because he wanted be a songwriter and tried to psyche himself into believing he was, not because...

"Richard! Please, talk to me!"

Good. That was the beginning of a duet. The spacing of notes was almost perfect. Now finish the aria. Her focal note was B-flat. Drop down to F.

"What shall I say to thee?"

Focus on tempo. Allegretto, six-eight time. Next lower D for the first three words, back up to F for the next three. Maintain pitch.

"I'm all right, as you see."

Last phrase. Stay on the F. Use it to carry the phrase to the last word, which should be B-natural.

"More than this I could not be!"

She was looking at him strangely. Had he done something wrong? Surely that was inconceivable, no fault was in his song. But now he should say something. He'd been silent for too long.

A-minor chord, I can afford notes of commiseration. She looks at me, and I can see much fear and consternation. In rapid time, maintain the rhyme, all is acceleration.

"I understand your feeling. It would not be appealing and would give me pause, were there no cause for all my senses reeling! If I could make you understand the energies at my command—"

The mental circuitry that had been glowing steadily brighter finally burned out and he slumped to the floor, unconscious.

XII.

Jackie left Mr. Weisbrod's office but did not go to her desk. She ran out of the building and made it to the parking lot before she was overcome by a fit of shivers that had little to do with the temperature.

She had to do something to keep her sanity, her grip on reality. But what?

Before she was fully aware of it, she started walking. As she crossed streets and intersections, having no idea where she was going but knowing only that she had to go somewhere, she realized she was doing the unthinkable: scanning the pedestrian traffic, actually *hoping* to see someone of another ethnicity. Any other would do. She had to find some link, however tenuous, to the world she knew. But no others were to be found. She supposed she had expected that.

As time passed and she saw face after face that looked like her own, she became less and less circumspect in her observations. These were the people that existed in her reality; some of them were just... bleached. She knew that because, not paying attention to where she was going, she walked past an intersection she normally avoided because of the deranged homeless man who had made it his center of operations. There he was, haranguing any and all passersby (who took care not to pass too close by) as he always did, warning them that the apocalypse was coming, and that instead of trying to kill cockroaches, we should form an alliance with them so that when nuclear winter came, we would be spared along with them.

It was the same sermon, but this time the man could not reinforce Jackie's opinions of blacks. He might have been Scandinavian from the look of him. As much as she wanted to try talking to him, she knew she would get nothing even approaching sense.

There had to be something, someone, somewhere. *One thing* she could point to, *some* kind of distinguishing factor, *something* distinctive to one race or another. It couldn't just be genetic roulette and nothing more. What she had believed all her life couldn't be wrong. More to the point, that insufferable know-it-all Claire couldn't be right. She would not allow it. She would find something to validate her belief, or she would die trying.

It could be anything, and time was limited. She stood against the wall and watched.

She had to remember anything she saw that might possibly have any significance, and she found it helped to say such things out loud. Not loudly, she didn't want to disturb anyone, so she muttered them to herself. Those who saw her found this disturbing enough, and they walked faster as they went by her. She couldn't worry about that. This was important.

No matter how long it took, she had to maintain her vigil.

XIII.

When Claire awoke, Tom was seated on the edge of the bed.

"Welcome back to the living," he said.

She rubbed her eyes. "What are you doing?"

"Watching you sleep."

"Why? I mean, I like it, it's just you never did that before."

"There are a lot of things I never did before that I should have. But I will now. You should always know how important you are to me."

She gaped at him a moment and said, "Okay. If I'm still dreaming, don't wake me."

He laughed. "No, you're not dreaming. And I promise, today is the start of a whole new reality for you. For us."

"Wow. This is all so...different."

"Is that good or bad?"

"Oh, it's good. It's very good."

But something was wrong. She couldn't pinpoint it at first, but then she had it. The light was different.

"How long was I asleep?"

"Whatever happened to you back there, it must have been a doozy. You were conked out all afternoon."

"What? Tom, we have to get back there! Richard and Jackie need our help!" Claire threw back the covers and started to get up.

"Whoa, whoa, whoa," Tom said, pushing her back down on the bed. "You're not going anywhere."

"But the others—"

"I don't care about the others. I care about you. You've been through a lot and you need to rest."

"Don't tell me what I need to do! I need to help my friends. You can come with me or stay here, but I'm going. Let me up."

"No."

"I said let me up."

"I said no. Claire, you've been saying you want me to be more attentive, haven't you? More there for you? So let me be what you want, all right?"

"Tom, we can talk about this later. Let go of me!"

He gripped her shoulders hard enough to hurt, and with knife-edge steel in his voice he said, "You're not going anywhere."

She didn't think about what she did next. She knew only that she had to get his eyes off her. There was not the slightest bit of affection in those eyes. There was something like psychosis in them.

So she jammed her thumbs in them. He screamed and jerked his hands up to his face. The instant her arms were free, she punched him in the stomach and knocked him to the floor. She leaped out of bed and sprinted out the front door, only to realize when she got outside that there was nowhere she could go. Tom's van was in the driveway, but he had the keys. Also, she was barefoot. Her shoes and her purse were still in the bedroom and she could not go back for them. Running would do no good, he would recover before long and he would have his van. Even if she stayed off the road, he could run much faster than she.

That's what first attracted me to him, she remembered. *Obviously I'm going to need better criteria in the future. Assuming I have a future.*

He was right about the time. The sun was already setting. She had to do something fast. But what?

The house next door. She would be safe there, at least for a while. She ran up to it and pounded on the door.

Footsteps. She glanced hurriedly over her shoulder. Tom had not come out yet, but he would at any time.

The door opened. Tom smiled when he saw who had come to visit him.

XIV.

Tom pulled up in his driveway, parked his van, and went inside. He wondered why he even had a van. The thing was a gas hog, and he didn't need all that space.

The place was a pit as usual. He supposed he should get a roommate. No, that was a stupid idea. Then it would be twice as much of a pit. Besides, this was his sanctuary, the place he came to get away from people. Having a person share it with him would kind of defeat the purpose.

He sat on the couch and tried to think of something to do. He could straighten up the place, he supposed, but why would he want to do that? He was bored with being here anyway. That was happening a lot lately, almost like he was getting sick of his own company, but that was silly. He was just stir crazy. Even though he had only been home for two minutes. Never mind. He would go for a walk, then he would feel better.

Or not.

All right, maybe he was crazy. He seemed to remember someone saying that to him once, and he thought of it now as he stood outside, looking around. But he was certain there were other houses here before. For that matter, he was reasonably sure he drove here on a paved road. He definitely would have noticed that his house stood alone, on empty, featureless prairieland. And yet, here it was.

Something felt wrong about this, but he wasn't sure why. It was supposed to be different, but he wasn't sure how. He was content...and that unsettled him. A paradox, yes, but the truth.

What was that?

He shielded his eyes and squinted. There was something on the horizon. He couldn't tell what it was, but it didn't seem to belong here

(any more than he did)

so it warranted looking into.

He had to drive slowly. His van was not designed for this kind of terrain.

So how did he get here?

Never mind that. Just get there.

Gradually, he did.

XV.

"Wh-what..."

Whipping her head back and forth between the house she had escaped and the house she stood in front of, Claire could only splutter the beginning of the question.

"It's all right, Claire," Tom said in what was meant to be a soothing voice. "I'm here for you. Why don't you come in?"

She shook her head in horror and backed away.

A car came up the street. She jumped out in front of it, screaming and frantically waving her arms. The car slowed, and she jerked open the passenger door and fell in.

"Please, you have to help me—"

She locked the door behind her, turned to face the driver, and could say nothing more.

"Of course I'll help you, Claire," said Tom. "I'm always here for you."

She lunged at him, clawed at his face and eyes. While he tried to defend himself, she stretched across the seat and opened his door. When he reached around to close it, she hammered a fist into his groin. He howled in pain and doubled over, and with muscles fueled by terror and adrenaline, she heaved him out the door, slammed and locked it, and clambered into the driver's seat. By the time he got to his feet and started yanking on the handle and pounding on the window, she had control of the machine and roared off, tires screaming.

Tom could only watch her go, and dream of what might have been. What was supposed to have been.

XVI.

The closer Tom got to the bright speck he'd seen from his house, the more details he could make out about it, and the more it seemed this was where he was supposed to be. When he got out of the van, he knew exactly where to go, although he was still a bit fuzzy on the why. There didn't seem to be anything special about the funhouse. In fact, he didn't want to go in there because it looked as though it might collapse on top of him. Still, he felt drawn by something inside, something he needed to see.

What he saw was himself, in front of a mirror. Big fat hairy deal.

This wasn't him, though. It was, but it wasn't. The person staring back at him was older than he knew himself to be. The difference was nothing definable. There were no lines on his face, and his hair was as thick and dark as ever. Something around the eyes, maybe? No, that wasn't it. No crow's feet, nothing.

That was it. There was nothing in his eyes. No joy, no sorrow, no hope, no life.

Visually, his eyes were brown. Emotionally, they were gray. Flat. Expressionless. Dead.

Why should it be otherwise? He had no reason to feel anything or do anything. He was alone. He was free to do anything or nothing. He could live however he wished.

However he wished...

Something about a wish. A distant, nebulous memory tantalizing his brain. There was something he had thought he wanted, but he was wrong. He was here now because this mirror could somehow fix it.

Had there been something written on top of it?

No, there was nothing, but he knew what he had to do.

He started to cross behind the mirror on the left. He seemed to remember doing that before...so why should he do it this time? Walking around the mirror that way had brought him into a world that, for all he knew, was now empty except for him. Not much point in doing the same thing. Maybe it wouldn't make a difference, but that one tiny bit of variety in this static life might be his only way out.

He moved to the right of the mirror and walked behind it.

XVII.

Claire knew this area so well that she could navigate on autopilot, which was fortunate because her overloaded brain was trying to shut down and reboot itself. She just had to keep it working long enough to get back to the carnival, and to that devil-crafted mirror.

In a few minutes she reached the front entrance. Then she drove through the front entrance. There was still no one at the carnival, but if there had been, they would have had to look out for themselves. She screeched to a stop in front of the funhouse, flung open the door, and hit the ground running.

The mirror was to her left. She started to run behind it, but felt a sharp pain in her leg and crumpled to the floor. Slowly she got up, tested her leg to make sure she hadn't sprained anything, and it was then that she remembered the inscription:

Make a wish, but do not talk,
Then once around the mirror walk...

Walk. She had to *walk* or it wouldn't work. Fine. The method of locomotion didn't matter as long as it got her out of this place and away from this version of Tom.

She walked behind the mirror.

XVIII.

"Richard?"

He felt a hand gently stroking the side of his face. Slowly, painfully, he opened his eyes, expecting to be sprawled out on Lisa's floor, looking up at her. Instead, he was buckled in the passenger seat of her car, looking at the entrance to the carnival.

"What..." he croaked.

"Shhh. Don't talk. You were moaning something about having to get back to the mirror, and since this is where I met you, and you were spared the sight of my bathroom, I figured you meant the funhouse mirror, right?" He nodded weakly.

"Yeah. So I brought you back here. I didn't know what else to do. I wasn't sure I'd be able to move you because you're so tall. It's a good thing you're so skinny."

"Thank you." He gave her a tremulous smile and fumbled with his seat belt.

Lisa got out, ran around to his side, and opened the door. He had managed to release the latch and was trying to get out.

"Easy," she said. "Let me help you." He accepted wordlessly but gladly.

The carnival was still deserted. Ordinarily that would have been worrisome, but they were grateful not to have to answer any bothersome questions. They walked into the funhouse, arms around each other for support, and she led him up to the mirror. He started for the left side, as he had before, and stopped.

"Harmony and counterpoint."

She looked at him, frightened. "Oh, no—"

"No, it's all right. I think I just figured this out. I walked behind the mirror from this side and it brought me here. Wherever 'here' is. So if I walk behind it from the other side—"

"Then it will send you back to...wherever you came from. Counterpoint. I get it. What I don't get is why I get any of this."

"It was great meeting you, Lisa. Please don't take this the wrong way, but I hope I never see you again."

Her laughter was musical but mercifully brief. She put her hands on his shoulders, stretched up, and kissed him, half on the cheek and half on the mouth.

"Take care of yourself, Richard."

"You too."

There wasn't much space behind the mirror. That made it marginally easier not to look back.

XIX.

He almost collided with Claire, who had almost collided with Tom. They came back at almost exactly the same time.

After many exclamations and embracings, they linked arms—they were taking no chances—and exited the funhouse at a rapid clip. It was still midmorning, and a few people were now milling around. There was a scattering of vehicles in the parking lot. Their van was one of them.

They could not recount their adventures without the risk that they would be overheard and probably taken to some nice men in white coats for a nice little chat, so they focused on making certain they were none the worse for their experiences. Then they wondered about Jackie. She should have come back with the rest of them, but she had not.

After ten minutes, there was still no sign of her. And they knew— they weren't entirely sure how they knew, but they knew—that there never would be. Wherever she was, she was staying there.

She would not be greatly missed.

Claire smiled at Richard. "This time, try to pick someone worthy of you, huh?"

He couldn't help smiling back. "Guess I should get started, huh? Right back on the horse and all that. Let's get out of here."

They all started for the van, but Richard walked faster by default because his legs were so long. When he was a few meters ahead, Claire and Tom looked at each other. They were thinking the same thing and said it at the same time.

"I don't think we should see each other anymore."

That was that, perhaps the first truly mutual breakup. The first credible one, anyway.

Scant seconds later, as if to finalize the deal, they heard the first of several loud cracks as supporting beams gave way. They turned just in time to see the funhouse call it a life and collapse in a pile of kindling.

The other patrons rushed over to oooh and aaah at the destruction. Two older men, apparently the carnival's proprietors, started screaming at each other, gesticulating furiously, and exchanging progressively harsher invective to denounce their respective incompetence.

With muffled laughter, the survivors turned away and walked on. They were now saved the trouble of figuring out how to warn the management about the funhouse without ending up in the nuthouse. Besides, there were other things to consider.

They would all think of the future, just as before. But for the first time since she had met him, Claire was perfectly content to imagine a future without Tom, just as he had always been (though he guarded the secret well) to imagine one without her.

The carnival was soon shrinking in the rearview mirror. There hadn't been much to see, but that was all right. They had seen as much as they ever wanted to.

Unexpected Guest

It is said of certain towns: "It's not the end of the world, but you can see it from here." Many residents of Perpignan, France considered that an accurate description of their lonely coastal town.

The saying had a special potency on winter nights, if you were unlucky enough to find yourself among the dense, swirling mists that coated the cold and desolate moors. Then it was very easy to imagine that you were not only at the edge of the world, but at the edge of time. You tried not to look down, since you would not be able to see anything below your knees. And you tried not to allow yourself to imagine that at any moment the ground you were walking on would end, and you would tumble off the Earth altogether and into the void.

For that reason, visitors to these moors were few. That was just the way Adelie Lacoste liked it.

She lived alone here, in a house that was even more ancient than she was. Her mother had died the previous summer and left her this immense domicile that, although slowly succumbing to the elements, still evoked much of the awe it had once commanded. If there were such a thing as a house you could get lost in, this was the one. Boasting long hallways lined with a multitude of rooms, vaulted ceilings, and high, winding staircases, this house was constructed to have a personality. It was built, or so it seemed, for the express purpose of making anyone inside it feel puny and insignificant. The architect, whose name is lost to the mists, did his job well.

Even from a hundred meters away the house was intimidating. It was slate-grey and adorned with crenellated buttresses and soaring spires more suited to a Gothic cathedral. Children would dare each other just to walk up to the front door. More often than not, these challenges went unanswered.

This, too, was just the way Adelie Lacoste liked it.

She was as frail as her residence was implacable. Her white hair was like straw, her skin was translucent and papery, and hers was the halting tread of someone who had a great many miles to walk and did not especially want to walk them.

Yet she was at home in this hulking manor. It was her bulwark against the hostile world with its masses of people, those who were visible and those who were not.

However much you kept to yourself, in small towns you were never really alone. Perhaps you were not visited by the living, but you often kept company with the dead.

Signs of the dead were everywhere, kept alive in the long memories peculiar to small towns. In the course of your normal errands, you were certain to run across someone you knew, and you were equally certain to hear of those you would have run across in ages past. You heard of them through memories, anecdotes, and legends.

Adelie was well acquainted with one legend in particular, which was not a story but a set of proscriptions. Three, to be exact, which could perhaps be ignored the rest of the year but had to be kept faithfully during the winter.

Never read by candlelight.

Never go out after midnight.

Never adopt a wild animal.

She ridiculed such things as foolish old wives' tales. She might be old, but she was not a wife—had never seen a reason to marry, to the regret of the many men who had pursued her in her time—and she was most certainly not foolish. Or so she believed.

Thus it was that on this twenty-second night in December, she was in her library. This was not unusual in itself; reading had always been her one great passion in life. Reading about the lives of others helped her forget, for a while, the unalloyed misery that was her own, and learning interesting facts helped her forget the bleak realities. So she had spent most of her life avidly collecting books of every kind, and now, when her life was near its end (a lot nearer than she knew), she had assembled a library that few universities would not have envied.

It is the curse of aging that the more rest you need, the less you tend to get. Adelie was always tired now, but her endless search for the arms of Morpheus was often a futile one. The ceaseless din of the roiling, frothy sea of her thoughts would keep even the god of sleep awake.

When she was younger and serving her sentence for committing the unpardonable crime of having been born female, her restless mind had been a useful ally and a source of comfort. Now it was the bane of her existence. Night after night, sleep eluded her. Night after night, since lying awake in bed had become intolerable, she passed the hours in her library, sharing the dreams of others since she would have none of her own.

She selected a book to read. Normally this was a painstaking process, but this time she simply plucked from its shelf the first book that caught her eye. Tonight she was not interested in reading for its own sake, but only in proving the legend just related for the stuff and nonsense she knew it to be, especially since its creator hadn't bothered to mention what would happen if you broke the rules.

She began with the easiest of the rules to break, that of reading by candlelight.

Just as she had collected books, so her mother, God rest that hateful miser's soul, had collected candles. Her mother apparently believed electricity was the tool of the devil, so great was her aversion to leaving even a single light on anywhere in this cavernous house. Therefore, when Adelie hosted the old woman's wake, she had the house lit up like the Las Vegas Strip, so great was her aversion to her mother. She received the endless stream of compliments on how beautiful the house looked, and on how much trouble she had obviously gone to in order to honor her beloved mother, with a mien somewhere between amused disbelief and barely suppressed glee.

Now the house was dark again, except the library, which was ablaze with candlelight. Lighting all the candles took a long time, but during the night she always had time in abundance.

Gingerly, her chosen book in one arthritic hand, she lowered herself into an overstuffed chair, opened the book, and began to read.

As she did so, she realized that this book had belonged to her mother, who was a schoolteacher. The title was "Practical Methods for Solving Ordinary Differential Equations," and the title was the only part of the book she could understand. But what God had not seen fit to grant her in intelligence, he more than made up for in stubborn, intractable pride, and so the fact that she was going to spend hours reading a text that was incomprehensible to her was of no importance. She had a point to make, and that was all that mattered.

As soon as she finished the first page, every candle in the room blew out.

Being plunged into darkness put her out of countenance only for an instant. Adelie and fear had never been well acquainted, and she was not about to stop and chat with it now. She put her book on the armrest, got up, and made her way to the light switch.

The library was large but sparsely furnished, so she didn't have to worry about tripping over anything. Soon she found the switch and flipped it on. She hadn't really been afraid, but the light given off by the three hundred-watt bulbs set high above her had never seemed quite so comforting as it did then.

She started back to her chair, intending to relight the candles and resume reading her book, but stopped.

She could not make herself do it.

She remonstrated furiously with herself. How she could give any credence to the mindless superstitions of these mindless townsfolk? No answer. Self-flagellation was all very well, but in this case it could not contradict the simple fact. And the simple fact was that every candle in the room—and they numbered in the dozens—blew out at exactly the same time. Exactly. Even if the windows were open, which they were not, a wind strong enough to do that would have sent her sprawling.

So then, how...?

Before she could finish asking herself this question, the answer rose unbidden. She had invoked the wrath of whoever—or whatever—had inspired the legend.

That is ludicrous.

Of course it was. But what other explanation was there?

She had none and had no wish to ponder it further, which she knew she would do if she stayed here. Instead, she decided to go to the kitchen and fix something to eat. She was not hungry, but she had read enough stories about the paranormal to know that nothing could ward off the specter of the macabre as well as the semblance of mundanity. The paranormal was a crock, but even the most outlandish tales usually had a grain of truth to them. Indeed, during the time it took her to light the candles, she had not thought much at all about the reason for that little exercise.

Laboriously she started for the kitchen. She had no idea what to make, but felt much better having simply decided to make something.

What was the perfect thing to sustain a good mood? Ice cream, what else? The gallon of chocolate mocha she bought four days ago would hit the spot nicely. She hefted the box out of the freezer onto the counter and was hunting for the scooper when she heard a sound coming from outside.

A high, keening, ululating cry that shriveled the skin on her bones.

The cry itself was mercifully brief, but it reverberated through her head like a tennis ball careening off the walls of a small room. By degrees this too died down, but she stood there for some minutes, unable to move or even think of how to respond.

There were not many animals adventurous enough, or antisocial enough, to make their home in these moors, and she knew all the ones that did. None of them made a sound even remotely like that.

A person? She supposed that was possible, but only if the person was in mortal agony. A cry like that would have ruptured human vocal cords, and one did not do that for the sake of giving a shout to his neighbor.

If it was neither human nor animal, what was it?

She didn't know. But she did know that she had reached her limit of questions for one night and was now determined to get some answers. The logical place to start was to find out what could have made that sound. She knew, on a level more primal than intellectual knowledge, that it would give her some understanding, even if it was not something that could express that understanding in words. Even if...

She saw where this line of thought was going and choked it off. Moving as quickly as she was able, she went to her room, put on her shoes and overcoat, and headed out the front door. She squinted against the fierce coastal winds and headed cautiously out into the frigid night.

As far from the house as she cared to go, which was not more than fifteen feet from the door, she stopped and looked in all directions. Fortunately (or not) there was a full moon tonight, so she could see a fair distance. Because there were no other lights to get in the way, the sky was filled with stars.

From her earliest childhood, she had always enjoyed looking at the stars. Earthly beauty was fleeting. Buildings crumbled, plants withered, trinkets rotted. People, who defined themselves and others by their standards of beauty, did all three. But the stars were eternal, or close enough, so their beauty was something she could allow herself to appreciate. And when, as a little girl, she got lost exploring the moors—a very easy thing to do—she used the stars to get her bearings, and they never failed to lead her home. There were few if any people about whom she could have said the same.

The immensity the stars bespoke made others feel insignificant, but for her it had the opposite effect. It gave her the feeling of being part of some grand and benevolent design, one that had deigned to share itself with her. She looked up out of habit, and then did something she had never done before. She looked down again almost at once.

Even the stars seemed different this strange night. Instead of the friendly guiding lights they had always been, now they were hard, cold eyes glaring down at her from the measureless dark, like a celestial tribunal sitting in judgment of her.

She looked all around her, but saw nothing that could have made the sound she had heard. Saw nothing at all, in fact, aside from the capering grass and the churning sea.

Not knowing which would be worse, to find nothing or to find something, she hurried back into the house and slammed the door. She had just about recovered her breath when she saw something that took it away again. She stood just inside the door, and her gaze happened to fall at the grandfather clock that stood in front of the opposite wall. Unbidden and unwelcome, the second rule of the legend rushed to the front of her mind.

She had just been outside, and it was five minutes past midnight.

She felt herself start to lapse into hysteria when her mind delivered the equivalent of a slap across the face.

Get a hold of yourself, you stupid old woman! it hissed at her. *How dare you allow yourself to behave this way! A few unusual happenings, a few disturbances in your tranquil life, and you are reduced to a frightened child, jumping at shadows and looking in the corners for ghosts! If your mother were alive to see the spectacle you are making of yourself, she would die of shame. Now pull yourself together. Go wash up and go to bed. Put this night behind you before you disgrace yourself any further.*

Forced to admit that this was eminently sage advice, she decided to follow it. Her bedroom was off to her right, very close by, and just the sight of it comforted her. She made a beeline for it.

She almost made it.

As if on cue, the wind began to howl again, and it carried another noise with it. A cry.

But it was not, thank goodness, like the one she had heard before. A repeat performance of that might have blown every working circuit she had left. In any event, the spokesperson for her higher thought processes, the one that so stridently rebuked her a moment ago, had nothing to say now.

This time the sound was soft, gentle, almost melancholy. It came from just outside the front door, along with the sound of...scratching?

She listened hard. Yes, a feeble but insistent scratching. She was not stirred by the insensate wail of the wind, since she had heard it countless times before, but the scratching, the soft, steady scratching, seemed to be summoning her.

Having resigned herself to the fact that it was useless to resist whatever forces were at work this night—forces she had awakened from their uneasy slumber into malevolent life—she walked to the door. A dispassionate observer would have noticed that she walked more fluidly than she had in years, but she herself did not realize this and would not have cared if she had.

She opened the door.

Nothing was there.

Normally she would have been relieved, or at least perplexed. But she had bid normality a final *adieu*, so instead of either of those, she was disappointed. She peered into the darkness, searching for any sign of life, when she felt one.

Something nuzzled against her leg. She looked down into the upturned face of a brown fox.

Foxes were once plentiful here, but it was hard for her to remember the last time one had graced the moors with its presence. Now, here it was. Cute as foxes were, they were not affectionate with other animals. This one, however, rubbed against her as if it were a long-lost pet.

She tried to persuade herself that it was the humane thing to do.

She tried to bear in mind that the fox was unlikely to survive such a night without shelter.

She tried to convince herself that she would take it to a veterinarian in the morning, so it could be properly cared for.

She tried, most of all, not to realize that she was about to break the third and final commandment of the legend.

All these things proved amazingly easy to do. Having done them, she stepped aside to let the fox enter.

Like most small mammals, foxes have an acute sense of smell, and right away it smelled the ice cream she had left on the kitchen counter five minutes and a hundred years ago. Very hungry and not impressed in the slightest by its new surroundings, it scampered to the kitchen.

When it got there, it stopped, uncertain how to proceed. It could smell where the ice cream was, and thus could tell it was inaccessible. Adelie at once understood the problem and also knew that ice cream was not the best way to solve it. She opened the refrigerator, took out what remained of a chicken she had prepared earlier that week, and placed it on the floor. In a bound, the fox was at the chicken. It examined the meat eagerly, but did not touch it. Instead it looked plaintively up at her.

She looked back at it, trying to guess what it wanted. It shifted its gaze back and forth between her and the chicken, then stood on its hind legs for a moment. Then she understood. It wanted her to feed it.

To kneel or squat might have been within the realm of possibility fifteen years ago. Now the attempt would have been futile, not to mention painful. She picked up the platter and went to the nearby table, with the fox close behind. She put the chicken on the table and sat in one of the chairs. Immediately the fox hopped onto the other chair. She tore off small pieces of meat and gave them to the fox, which wolfed them down in succession until most of the bird was gone. It licked her hand in gratitude, then curled up on the chair and went to sleep.

She watched the fox for a long time, envying how peaceful it looked. She could still remember being able to sleep through the night, but as the years rolled on, those memories became more distant. One might even say more dreamlike.

Since she was still not even drowsy, she sat and kept watch over the slumbering fox, wishing she could do as it was doing one last time...

She was not even aware she had fallen asleep. But she was disoriented, which she never was on waking, and looked around for some clue as to what time it was. She felt like she had slept a long time, so surely it must be morning. Perhaps it was technically morning, but it was still dark outside.

Her eyes were drawn back to the fox. At a loss for what else to do, she resumed watching it.

At that moment its eyes flew open and fastened on hers.

It started whimpering, so softly that she didn't hear it right away. She tore off another piece of chicken and held it up to the fox's mouth. But it ignored this morsel and continued to stare at her, its whimpers louder now.

Then she understood. It wanted her to hold it.

Adelie was childless, by choice. She had never cared much for children. In fact, she always considered them something of a nuisance. On rare occasions, when she observed mothers cuddling their children, she felt a pang, a momentary stirring, but always so faint it could be, and was, ignored. The sum total of these pangs hit her all at once as she looked at this fox, this helpless little fox, which was alone in the world, like her. It wanted to be cuddled, as if it were her child.

Would it be so hard now, at the end of her life, to be a mother just this once?

She picked up the fox and held it close to her. It buried its head under her chin. This felt so nice, so natural, that she did not even mind when it buried its teeth in her throat.

The darkness she had kept outside for so long finally found its way in. Had she been able, she would have asked what took it so long. For she did not recognize that she was dying. She knew only what she no longer knew.

Seven decades of memories, regrets, feelings from the past, forebodings of the future...the constant roar in her mind was silent at last. She could see nothing. Had there ever really been anything to see? What was here was all that mattered.

There was herself. There was her child.

And after a lifetime, there was peace.

GARDEN VARIETY MYSTERY

Beverly's eyes flicked again to the time display on her car stereo. 7:48. *It's a Wonderful Life* was coming on in twelve minutes and she was still several miles from home, so she eased the car up to fifty, as fast as she dared to go. This was a shortcut she hadn't used in years, because it was rare she had to be anywhere in a hurry. But time was not her ally tonight.

Northampton was a picturesque little Massachusetts town with one main road and a serpentine network of back roads. The police seldom had much to worry about from the locals, but it seemed that every week some fool tourist overestimated how fast he could take a blind curve and spun off into a ditch or someone's back yard. In the latter case, some unfortunate trooper was called out to mediate between the homeowner demanding restitution for the damage to his property, and the driver rattling off the litany of people he was going to sue. The trooper reasonably pointed out to the driver that the speed limit and approaching curve were clearly marked. If reasoning failed, as it usually did, the irritated expression on the trooper's face, his size (which seemed to be one of the factors involved in selecting rural New England cops), the sight of his gun or of the landowner's gun, or some combination thereof was enough to persuade the unlucky motorist that it wasn't that big a deal after all, accidents did happen, and he really should be more careful in the future.

There was no chance of that happening to Beverly, who was driving an Escalade and was acutely aware of how big it was and how small this road was. She had hoped to buy her mother's Volkswagen Jetta, but her mother traded that in the day after they returned from a jaunt to Maine.

They had made the colossal (but hilarious, to anyone else who heard the story) mistake of going up there in a small car during rutting season. They stopped in a rest area just for a minute, because they were behind schedule, and came back to find that they were going to need a new schedule. Probably a new car too, by the looks of the moose trying to mate with this one.

They flagged down a passing state trooper. After he stopped laughing, he assured them this was nothing to worry about. Their car would be fine.

"Well, how long is he going to..." Beverly's mother started to ask, but couldn't finish the question.

The trooper shrugged. "He's bound to get tired eventually."

"*Eventually?* Officer, you don't understand. We're on our way to the hospital. My sister is having a baby, and she's due any time now. Isn't there some way to—"

"No," he said flatly. "You try to stop a moose from doing what that one's doing, all you'll do is annoy him. When moose get annoyed, they have a nasty habit of trampling you to death."

They both recoiled. He nodded slowly, to make sure they got it. "Take my advice, folks, and just let him wind down on his own. Who knows, lady? You just might be an aunt twice."

She didn't think that was very funny. Fortunately he thought it was funny enough for both of them. He was still laughing as he drove off.

Beverly looked again at the clock. 7:54. One more sharp curve, and only a straight shot would be left.

She rounded the bend and came face to face with the most hideous scarecrow she had ever seen.

Its face was shriveled and contorted in a grimace of unknowable despair. Instead of a hat it had long, dark, mangy, mold-encrusted hair. Its clothes were rotted. It looked as if it had dug its way out of its grave to stand watch on this lonely road.

Beverly screamed, jerked the wheel to the right, crashed through a fence, narrowly missed a tree just beyond it, and bounced across a field and into a muddy bog, where she was dragged to a stop.

She quickly checked herself for injuries, felt none, and gunned the engine. It whined as the wheels spun uselessly in the mud. She shifted from forward to reverse to forward, but it was no use.

After three minutes of this, she shut off the engine and considered her options. She really didn't want to get out of the car. It was pitch dark, there were no houses she could see, and this road was not a popular one. It could easily be hours before someone else came by. This had been a routine visit to her sister, so she hadn't brought her phone.

She contemplated spending the night in the car and setting out on foot in the morning. That was a possibility; the car had plenty of room and she was petite. The problem was that she was almost out of gas, and once the engine stopped, so would the heater. Without the heater, she would freeze to death. It was the night before the first day of spring, but it was not uncommon for New England winters to deliver a bitingly cold parting shot.

Then she saw something. Could it be...?

Yes! It was a light. She couldn't see the house from here, but someone must have heard the noise and wondered what had happened.

She stepped out into ankle-deep mud and trudged toward the light, taking the utmost care not to let that horrible apparition by the road wander into her line of sight.

A few minutes' walk brought her to a ramshackle little house. The front door was flung open before she could knock, but this was not what made her jump back. The owner of the house kept three enormous dogs in an enclosure adjoining the house. They charged the fence that had been built to hold them, and it just barely did.

Only when they quieted down did she notice the open door and the wizened old man who had come out to the porch. He wore horn-rimmed glasses and a terry cloth robe that dragged on the floor. A corncob pipe dangled from a corner of his mouth. The dogs' barking and growling had drowned out her screaming, but their absolute silence now was almost worse. At least they were well trained, right?

"Well," he drawled around his pipe, "ain't you jest the cutest little thing!"

"Um...thank you," she said nervously. Ordinarily she would have appreciated the compliment, but the way he said it implied either that he hated cute little things or that he could have just eaten her up. With some fava beans and a nice chianti.

"I hate to bother you, but could I use your phone? My car is stuck in the mud, and I need to call a tow truck."

"Ayuh. I heard."

He said this as if it happened every day, and that was all he said. He did not even invite her inside, just stood there staring at her. Her skin erupted in goosebumps. Not from the cold.

"Sooo...may I use your phone?"

"Nuh."

She waited for a reason. None was forthcoming.

Just my luck, she thought. There were not many dyed-in-the-wool Yankees in these parts, but she managed to find one.

"I can't?"

"Ain't got a phone."

"You're kidding," she said, but knew he wasn't. Yankee men didn't talk much and they joked even less.

"Got a truck though."

She couldn't have heard that right. "I beg your pardon?"

"Round back."

She paused to be certain he wasn't telling her that something was wrong with his back, and asked if she could see it.

"Ayuh. That's the best thing."

Not about to argue with this logic, she walked around to the back of the house.

It was too good to be true. There, big as life, was a tow truck.

Ready to weep with joy, she started back to the house to thank the man. But that wasn't necessary. He was standing behind her, holding a flashlight. It was turned off and raised above his head.

He brought it down hard.

And her with it.

New England springs are beautiful, especially for the residents, after the long winter. But for the people in rural towns like Northampton, the coming of spring meant there was a lot of work to be done. Roof tiles had to be replaced, gutters fixed, fences mended, fallow ground tilled.

For one man, on the first day of this particular spring, much more was involved.

A scarecrow had to be taken down and put away.

A car had to be towed into the garage and disassembled.

A corpse had to be cut open, and its innards eviscerated and fed to three hungry, growing dogs.

Then the skin of the corpse had to be cured, dried, and fastened to a makeshift cross, with its clothing properly arranged. Although the skin's former occupant would not have minded, it wouldn't do to be immodest.

When his new scarecrow was ready, he had to take it out and put it in just the right spot. He was proud of his work and felt that it deserved to be seen.

He made sure it faced the right direction, so it would be the first thing a driver saw when he rounded the bend. It was those special little touches that made all the difference. But his crowning achievement was for his eyes only.

After all the work was done, he went down to the root cellar to have a special moment with his wife.

She was just as he had arranged her, in her favorite rocking chair. He didn't dare move her. It had been years since the accident and her bones would soon crumble to dust. He had to make good use of the time they had left.

"Made you another one, Nora," he said, sitting on the floor next to her. "Course, not a one of em's as good as the one you seen, almost right out there in the road, that made you spin out n hit that tree. You went quick. But the owner didn't, no sir, I made right sure o' that. Nobody said anythin when I moved into his house and took his land. Good thing about folks in these parts, they mind their own business. Thought about cuttin that tree down a time or two, but it didn't seem right. That tree's seen a lot, it has. Makes me look like a young'un, and that ain't no easy thing. It's keepin watch over the new scarecrow now. Figured the fella owned this house before us should be the first one, cause I knew it'd be sloppy. But you'd like this one. She was easy, not much on her. I think they get better every time. Soon I'll get it jest right. You wait n see."

He went upstairs and stood on his porch just in time to see a car round the bend. It fishtailed, regained its moorings, and continued on.

"Don't work s'well in the daytime," he muttered with a crooked little smile. "But one o' these times I'll get it right. Man oughta have somethin he can be proud of. Somethin to show for his life. Like somebody else's life."

He nodded, approving of what he'd said.

"Ayuh. That's the best thing."

Moving Day

Trent had no idea why the strange little man was so interested in their house. It was all right as houses went, but it was aging and the foundation was beginning to make strange noises at night. Not that these sounds didn't have their uses. He often used them to prove to his sister that the trolls had finally tracked her down and had come to take her back to the center of the Earth so she could reign as their queen. Leigh's reactions to these stories always made the effort he put into inventing them worthwhile. Aside from that, though, this house had no great value that he could see.

So when his parents put it on the market, he wondered out loud who would be stupid enough to buy it. That won him an all-expenses-paid trip to his room for the rest of the evening, with a great periodic view of Leigh sticking out her tongue at him. He couldn't figure out why he was the one being punished, since she was the reason they were selling the house.

They lived on the Texas coastline, in a small town a stone's throw from the Gulf of Mexico. But the sea air wreaked havoc on her sinuses, so it was decided (by his parents, he had not been consulted) that they would pack up and move in with their cousins in West Texas until they could find a house in that area.

West Texas! That was a fate worse than death. Texas City was such a loser town that the local Whataburger was actually the Saturday night hangout. But at least there were things to do, lame as they were. So what were they doing? They were moving to the middle of the for-crying-out-loud *desert,* where the height of fun was watching the tumbleweeds blow around. His cousins also lived there, and if the choice was between hanging out with them and hanging out with a cactus, a cactus was only torture if you got stuck with the needles.

He couldn't see why they didn't just go with his idea of shipping her off to West Texas—or better yet, Neptune—and the rest of them would stay where they were. But *noooo*. What did he get for trying to be helpful? He had to help his father paint the garage.

What a life this was. When his parents put the "For Sale" sign up in the front yard, he decided that as soon as the dump was sold, he was moving out. He was fed up with Texas City anyway, and there was no way in perdition he was going to have a home where the buffalo roam. He had no idea where he would go, but anything was better than this.

Still, he wasn't holding his breath that the house would sell anytime soon, or at all. Even in the best of times, which these certainly were not, the Texas City real estate market might rise to the level of dismal, so he had lots of time to consider his options. Or so he thought.

The sign had not even been out for two days when there came a knock at the door. Trent was sprawled on a couch in the living room, but before he could get up (not that he was going to), Leigh bounded out of her room. She opened the door to a short, wiry, immaculately dressed man who clutched an expensive-looking burgundy briefcase in his left hand. As soon as he saw her, he grinned effusively and shot out his right hand. Reflexively she took it, and he pumped her hand four times, so hard that she bounced.

He had a shock of blond hair, and he wore a black shirt, dark red silk tie, purple suit, and black wingtips. Trent thought he looked like the Mad Hatter. Leigh didn't seem to know what to think. She didn't say anything, just stood there staring at him.

"Ah!" he cried, making her jump. "Forgive my impertinence, my dear. Morrison is the name. At your service." He bowed with a flourish. Before she could stop him, he came in and started looking around, examining things seemingly at random but in minute detail.

"Mom? Dad?" Leigh yelled. She looked at Trent and motioned at the stranger. *Do something, will you?*

But he was as disconcerted by this bizarre visitor, who now seemed oblivious to their presence, as she was. He stayed where he was and watched the man from the couch.

Their parents came in but stopped short at the sight of the apparition who was now busily tapping the walls.

"Excuse me? Can we help you?"

The stranger's face lit up as though he had never been so pleased to see anyone in his life.

"Begging your pardon, sir," he said, walking rapidly over to them, "but it is I who can help you. I have been admiring your quaint little domicile, and would like to purchase it."

They looked at him blankly for a moment, then they both said, "What?"

Trent, who couldn't believe what just happened, took it upon himself to act as translator. "He wants to buy the house." He looked at his watch and made a mental note of what time it was when he uttered these miraculous words. 11:07.

His father shot him a look and turned back to the stranger.

"Ah...well, Mister..."

"Morrison, sir." Again he bowed.

"Mr. Morrison...you are aware that our asking price is ninety thousand dollars?"

Morrison walked—almost skipped—to the table, set his briefcase on top of it, and opened it. Inside were neatly bound stacks of hundred-dollar bills.

"You may count it if you wish. But you will find it's all there."

They crowded around the briefcase, and each of them picked up one of the stacks and ruffled through it. Morrison stood off to the side, watching them in silence but with obvious pleasure. They were all mesmerized by the contents of the briefcase: eighteen bound stacks of fifty hundred-dollar bills, every bill so crisp it might have been delivered hot off the presses of the mint.

"Mr. Morrison," said the father, "I'm sorry, but you understand, I have to ask—"

"Of course, sir. Allow me to assuage your concerns. Not a single one of those bills is counterfeit. As you can see, each one possesses its authentic Treasury watermark. You are welcome to inspect them as closely as you like."

"I'm not calling you a liar, sir, it's just that...well, most people don't walk around carrying ninety thousand dollars in cash."

"Especially in this neighborhood," Trent muttered.

His parents glared at him but, wanting to avoid a fight today of all days, said nothing.

"You are quite correct, sir," Morrison replied. "But I find all the paperwork associated with purchasing a home to be an awful tedium. I haven't the patience for it, and paying upfront in cash expedites matters greatly. Wouldn't you agree, sir?"

"Yeah. Yeah, it sure does."

"Splendid! To business, then. As I said, your home meets with my approval. Am I correct in assuming my money meets with yours?"

Still examining the money, they all nodded.

"In that case, all that remains is your signature on the dotted line." Morrison produced a pen and a deed transfer and held them under the father's nose. He reached for them, but his wife stopped him.

"Mr. Morrison," she said, "would you please excuse us for just a moment?"

"But of course, dear lady. I can avail myself of the opportunity to explore the grounds." Morrison left and closed the door behind him.

"You're just going to sign the first thing he shoves at you?" she said.

"No," he said. "That wasn't the first thing he shoved at me. This is." He held up one of the stacks of money. "He was telling the truth. This is all real."

"Okay, so he's not a counterfeiter. Maybe he's a drug dealer. Did you think of that?"

"Who cares what he is?" Trent said. "You want to sell the house, he wants to buy it. And he's already paid for it. What's the problem?"

"The jerkwad's right," said Leigh. "This might be the only buyer we get."

"I just don't know...Bryan, there's something wrong about this. Who comes to a house he's never seen with the cash and the papers to buy it? I think we ought to tell him thanks but no thanks."

"And then do what? What everyone selling a house here does? Wait five or six months and then have to take an offer that's maybe half of what we hoped for? Janet, the kids are right and you know

197

it. This guy wants the house, and he's put down the money. Let's just take it so we don't have to worry."

Seeing she was the lone dissenter, she gave in.

Bryan opened the door to see Morrison inspecting the shrubbery.

"Have you decided, sir?" Morrison asked.

"Yes. We accept your offer."

"Splendid, sir!" Morrison clapped his hands. For an instant it was easy to imagine him as a ten-year-old, especially since he wasn't much bigger than one.

He returned to the living room and they gathered around the table. Bryan signed the deed transfer, and Morrison witnessed it. As soon as Morrison lifted his pen from the paper, a slight tremor ran through the house.

"What was that?" asked Janet, alarmed.

"You know these old houses," Morrison said. "It was just settling a little."

Janet offered a slight, embarrassed smile. "Yes, of course."

"When do you want us to move out?" Leigh asked.

"Oh, there's no rush, child. Take all the time you need."

"Really? Thanks!"

"Not at all. And now I bid you all farewell." He said this with a final bow.

Janet started to ask if he would like some coffee, but the door was already shut behind him.

"Well," Leigh said, "*that* wasn't weird or anything."

"Can you believe our luck?" Bryan asked. "Wait until I tell Gunderson about this. That blowhard told me I'd be lucky to get forty."

"Still," Janet said, "this whole thing is very odd, don't you think?"

"No, what this whole thing is," Bryan said, "is a done deal. Now if you'll excuse me, I'm going to count this money again."

"Can I help?" Leigh asked.

"Sure, why not? Janet?"

"Sure, why not?"

"Trent?"

Trent was nowhere to be seen.

"He must have gone out," Janet said.

Bryan shook his head. "Just as well. Sometimes I wonder about that boy."

Leigh had a smart remark ready, but decided to restrain herself this once. She was in high spirits, and thinking about her gnome of a brother wouldn't help.

Speaking of help, Trent could have used some just then.

He had gone to the window to get a look at what kind of car a man like Morrison would drive. But there were no cars anywhere along the street, and no Morrison anywhere in sight. That shouldn't have been possible. Even at a sprint, he couldn't have made it across their huge front yard before Trent got to the window. Had he walked around to the back of the house? Maybe, but if he had pulled into their driveway—which a first-time visitor would hardly have done—they would have heard his car.

The only explanation was that he had walked. But from where? And why would anyone be walking around dressed like that? Carrying a fortune in cash, no less?

His curiosity piqued, Trent went outside to see if he could spot the guy. He glanced at his parents and sister, but they were still whooping over their good fortune. He shrugged and left. Once outside, he started to break into a run, but screeched to a halt and looked around.

There was a strange tint to everything. The grass, the trees, and the houses across the street looked the same as they always had, yet they looked different, somehow. He looked up and saw why.

He was looking at an overcast, yellowish-green sky.

He looked down, closed his eyes, shook his head, opened his eyes, and looked up into the same yellowish-green sky.

Okay. He knew he'd had a lot to drink at the party he went to last night. He always drank a lot at parties. But nothing like this had ever happened. Had somebody slipped him something? No, that couldn't be it. He could still think straight, and if he were under the influence of something strong enough to make him see what he was seeing, he wouldn't be thinking much at all.

Looking up was a bad idea, so he looked down one side of the street, then the other, looking for Morrison. Not a sign of him. By now he was probably long gone. Weird, but whatever. Trent didn't know what he would have done if he had caught him. He turned back to the house, but couldn't make himself go in.

His own house seemed different now. It looked dark, sinister...it looked *alive*, pulsing with a primitive sentience. The blinds had been open a moment ago, but now they were all closed. Looking through the small windows in the door, he saw that no lights were on inside.

What was all this? Had he gone crazy?

Granted, it would have been a short trip—Leigh had told him that enough times—but he kind of doubted he could have taken a trip like this in the last few minutes. Something was going on, and he had to find out what. But he would need help. His legs refused to take him inside his house, so he set off to find someone who could confirm what he was seeing, recommend a good nut hut for him, or check into one with him.

Something else was different across the neighborhood, but he couldn't put his finger on it. After he walked two blocks, he realized what it was.

There were no cars. None parked in driveways, none along the curbs, none on the streets. He was the only person outside, but he had the sensation of being watched from the other houses—all of which, like his, were dark. He looked apprehensively at the houses as he walked past, but saw no curtains opening or closing.

It's not people in the houses watching you. It's the houses *watching you.*

That thought flashed across his brain like the come-on of a scrolling Web banner, but unlike those, he couldn't ignore this one. It made a weird kind of sense, because all the houses now seemed to have some kind of primal consciousness.

He slapped himself across the face. Twice. Hard.

"Cut it out," he said to himself. "Quit trying to scare me."

Sure, no problem! replied a jovial inner voice. *I can quit scaring you anytime I want. I won't even think about houses coming to life anymore. That big one's kind of spooky, though, isn't it? Looks prettier and more kept up than it usually does. Almost like it wants you to come over and look at it so it can eat you up! And the houses next to it? They're just waiting. Got ringside seats. Boy, I'm glad you told me not to think about possessed houses. Sure gives a guy the creeps, all right.*

He forced himself to look straight ahead, to think of nothing but walking, picking them up and setting them down. He had to get to a place where there were people. But where?

Of course! Like all summer days here, today was humid and blisteringly hot, so there would certainly have been people at the town pool when they had the...the...

Right. Feeling better just to have a place to go, he ran as fast as he could to the Lowry Center.

There was indeed life at the pool. If you wanted to call it that.

Half a dozen children sat around the edge of the pool. But there was no laughing or running or splashing here. These children looked like survivors of Buchenwald. Their skin was stretched tightly over their faces, and their limbs were so woefully thin and weak they shouldn't have been able to move at all. Their eyes were large and haunted. They appeared to be miniature zombies.

Trent shuffled in tiny steps to the edge of the pool. The possibility that these...children, or whatever they really were, might be able to tell him what had happened was remote, but he had to try.

They turned listlessly to look at him. One look at their faces was enough to tell him that even if they had answers, none would be forthcoming. Like the windows of the houses he passed, there was nothing behind these eyes. Their expressions were blank, beyond caring who he was or why he was there.

His own eyes were drawn to the pool.

Two children were in the pool, but what they were doing could not properly be called wading. The water was sludgy and brackish, as though the pool had been emptied and refilled with toxic waste. Which would be just about right, Trent thought.

Swamp gas rose off the surface, obscuring the children for brief intervals. Then he saw that it had obscured something else.

Creatures that vaguely resembled sharks swam lazily around the pool, but gave the children a wide berth. Their fins sliced the surface of the water, but their bodies were shriveled and mutated, as if whatever they were swimming in was slowly dissolving them. With a sort of horrified fascination, Trent watched them swim around.

Abruptly, as if they knew they were being watched, two of the shark-things changed course and swam toward where he stood. Trent did not run, but he backed up a few giant paces. They reached the edge of the pool and lifted their flippers over the side. The flippers had small, underdeveloped appendages that looked something like human fingers. They were using these to hoist themselves out of the water.

His next lucid memory was of being in somebody's front yard about two miles away, with screaming legs and burning lungs. As he started to get himself under control, he heard a ripping noise behind him. He didn't want to know what it was, but not knowing would be worse, so he turned to look.

The house behind him was made of wood planking. Two of the planks were pulling away from each other, the upper one pushing up the planks over it, the lower pushing down the planks under it, making a hole that looked distinctly like a mouth, with nails for teeth.

He took off again, but his energy was almost gone. He got as far as the street before he had to stop. Fortunately the street was wide, so he just had to stay in the middle of it. That was the safest place from carnivorous houses. He laughed nervously at this thought, but his laughter rang out in the funereal quiet, so he choked it off, hoping that he hadn't attracted anyone's—or anything's—attention.

Also, there was something in his laugh he didn't like. It was too high and brassy.

He was starting to lose it. He couldn't let that happen, no matter what.

Then he noticed it was getting darker and looked up, hoping the sun was not setting. He didn't even want to think about being in this hellish place at night. This once, fortune was with him. It was darker because of storm clouds. A minute or so later, it started to rain. It was only a sprinkle, but he would have kept walking even if it had been a downpour. How bad could rain be?

He felt a weird tickling sensation on his skin. He looked down at himself and saw that the raindrops were not leaving water trails. This was because they were not sliding down his arms and face, but running down them on tiny legs. There were thousands of these water-bugs all over him. They seemed harmless, but he wasn't about to take the chance. He ducked under a nearby tree to slap them all off and wait out the storm.

No sooner had he taken shelter under the tree than the rain stopped. He stayed a moment longer, just to make sure there were no water-bugs left on him. But then he heard a faint rustling noise above him.

He didn't even look up to see what it was. He forced his legs into a jog until he got back out to the middle of the street, where he stopped and almost fell. He was exhausted, but he had to keep moving.

Where? he thought wearily, and it was a good question. Where could he go?

The answer was obvious. There was only one place he could go. He could run no farther, and so, walking as fast as he could and trying to block out the searing pain in his legs, he set off for home.

He didn't know what he would find when he got there, but he didn't care. He would have his family, and they would face this bizarre horror together. As he walked he whispered a prayer, swearing to whomever might be listening that if he got out of this, he would never again backtalk his parents and he would always be nice to his sister. Even one of her insults would be music to his ears.

Soon he was walking up his front yard, knowing that he couldn't stop or slow down or he would lose his nerve.

Left, right, left, right. Pick 'em up and set 'em down.

He remembered these words of his father's from three years ago, when they went for a hike in the woods. Bryan was on a fitness kick then, and had decided that Saturday mornings were to be their time to get pumped up.

They were coming to the end of a five-mile walk, and Trent had sat under a tree and refused to walk another step. His mother tried to reassure him that they were almost there, but he didn't believe her. She'd been saying that for the last two miles. Leigh tried to haul him up, but he wrenched his arm away and then kicked at her so she couldn't get close enough to try again.

"If you want to stay here, fine," his father said. "Come on, girls, let's go." They walked on without looking back.

A few minutes later, he lost sight of them. A few minutes after that, they still hadn't come back. He got up and chased after them, and found them waiting just over the crest of a hill.

"Now march," Bryan commanded. "Left, right, left, right. Pick 'em up and set 'em down. Look down at your feet and don't think about anything else." So he did, and no one said anything else until Janet said brightly, "We're here!" When Trent looked up, there was their Ford Explorer.

On the way home Leigh said, "See, that wasn't so bad, was it?"

He made a face at her but said nothing, because she was right. By the time his father's fitness craze wore off, he was actually starting to enjoy the walks. Although neither he nor anyone else ever suggested they resume this activity, it served him well now.

He looked down at his feet until they were right in front of the door. Without pausing, he looked up, turned the knob, and went inside. The house was dark, so he called out.

"Dad? Mom? Leigh?"

No one was home. He searched every room of the house, but only confirmed that he was its sole occupant. He flipped the light switch in the living room, but the lights did not come on. Flipping every other switch in the house yielded the same result, even after he changed a few bulbs and flipped the breakers.

Now what was he supposed to do?

Obviously he had to go out and look for them. But he had to rest first. He sat on the living room couch, leaned back, and closed his eyes.

He jerked awake. How long had he been asleep? He looked at his watch, which told him it was 11:07. But that was impossible. That was the time it had been when...

When Morrison came to the house.

He stared at his watch for three full minutes, counting the seconds in his head, but the minute hand did not move. It had stopped. Every clock in the house had also stopped.

That was something to add to his growing list of things he couldn't figure out. But it was useless to focus on the things he couldn't do. He had to focus on what he could do. And what he could do—*all* he could do—was look for his family.

Fine. Knowing that was all very well, but what he didn't know was where he would even begin to look. A house-to-house search would take weeks, and was exceedingly unlikely to do any good.

This was all academic, of course. He knew where he had to go, even if he didn't want to face the truth. Back to the only other place he had seen life, such as it was. He inhaled deeply, exhaled quickly, left the house, and set off again for the pool.

The sky was still overcast, so he couldn't tell where the sun was or how close it was to setting. That was bad. Very bad. Whatever time it was, time was most definitely running out. His legs were still sore, but he managed to coax them into a run.

By the time he got to the pool, he was still jogging, but it was hardly faster than a leisurely walk.

Death's children were still there.

His family was not.

His lower lip started to quiver, and he squeezed his eyes shut and clenched his fists. He was not going to start bawling like a baby. He was *not*. That wouldn't help anything and would waste precious time.

He opened his eyes, took a step forward, stumbled, almost fell. His legs had gone rubbery. It seemed like a hundred years since he had last eaten, and this place had been one horror after another. Being so scared for so long had drained all the strength out of him. He couldn't run at all, he could only walk a little, and he wasn't even sure how much longer he would be able to stand. He had to sit down. Naturally there were no chairs.

Not knowing where else to look, he looked at the children. They were all sitting exactly where they had been, joined by the ones who had been in the pool the last time, looking back at him.

One of them made a gesture that would have been sweet under other circumstances but was grotesque under these. The child (he couldn't tell if they were boys or girls) lightly patted the ground next to him/her. The meaning was unmistakable. It wanted him to sit there.

The shark-things were still swimming around, but they showed no interest in him. Now desperate for companionship of any kind—even this—he did as the child indicated and sat on the edge of the pool.

In abject helplessness and frustration, Trent screamed.

He was still there when Leigh came.

She had no idea how much time had passed, and he, like the children, no longer cared.

"Trent!" she cried and rushed over to him. "It's really you! Thank God! Are you all right?"

She knelt down and threw her arms around him. "I got so worried when you didn't come back! I went out to look for you, and I didn't find you, so I went back to the house because I thought you might be there but you weren't, the truck's still in the driveway but Mom and Dad are gone, so I was just trying to find you, and...and...Trent?"

She drew back and looked at him. If he was listening to any of this, or even knew she was there, he gave no sign. His eyes were wide but unseeing, his expression vacant.

"*Trent!*" she shouted. She turned his face to hers, grabbed his shoulders and shook him. "Trent, snap out of it! Come back to me!"

Nothing. His body was here, but he was gone.

"Trent, please! Let's just go home, okay? And we'll do whatever you want. You can tell me about the trolls who want to make me their queen! You remember how you wanted to ship me off to Neptune? Go ahead! I'll even pay for the postage! Trent!" She alternately hugged and shook him. "Anything you want, just tell me and I'll do it! Just come back to me!"

No use. There was no more recognition of her, or of anything, in his face than in the faces of the other children. Whatever they were, he was one of them now.

Leigh screamed.

Definitive Therapy

Kevin Gray was a man with a problem.

With many problems, in fact.

So many, if the truth be known, that he was the only person his therapist had ever encountered whose identity seemed to be no more than the sum of his problems. That was the last thing she said to him before she stopped taking his calls.

That was one more problem.

Kevin was always ready to talk about his problems. This was itself yet another problem, not so much for him as for anyone who had to interact with him on any level for any reason. No one willingly did this, because he would launch into detailed descriptions and analyses of his problems whether anyone asked him to or not. Nobody ever asked him to do this more than once.

That led to, or stemmed from, still another problem: he was screamingly lonely, and had little to no opportunity to develop his social skills, which could charitably be described as nonexistent. Two problems there, for the price of one, and one of the many chicken-and-egg scenarios he tried to work through during those endless hours in the dark. He was not an insomniac, but he routinely made himself stay up as late as he could. His dreams only reflected his waking hours, and so he couldn't escape the tragedy that was his life even when he was asleep. As a result he was always fatigued and lethargic at work, but it wasn't as though his job required a nimble mind. In context, it wasn't so clear whether this was a problem or an advantage, but since he didn't know how to handle advantages, he looked at it as another problem.

He would even have welcomed a few nightmares. At least they would provide an illusion of the change of scenery that he couldn't afford to give himself, and wasn't sure he would if he could. He had never been outside of Houston and didn't know anyone anywhere else. Also, if he did go on a vacation and by some complete accident managed to have a good time, that would rob him of a week or two of problems to complain about. And he *needed* his problems. The one simple joy of his life was railing about the compounded misery of his life.

Even his name was fodder for the angst mill. Gray. Never was the name a more accurate descriptor of the man. He was only moody in the sense that his moods alternated between gray and black.

His wardrobe was as drab as his personality. What hair he had left was almost entirely gray. Both of those follicular maladies tended to strike early in his family. Woo-hoo. He had been an average student in high school, a so-so student in community college, and had spent the seventeen years since then toiling in obscurity as a nameless cipher in one of a hundred identical cubicles in a company not many people had ever heard of. For thirteen of those years he'd smoked three packs a day, so even his skin had a sickly grayish tinge.

His other addiction was comfort food. It did not comfort him in the least, though not for lack of trying. All he had to show for it was the additional problem of being seventy pounds overweight. So much mass on his six-foot-six frame might have been imposing on someone else. On him it was comical, and not in a good way. He had always been self-conscious about his height and started walking with a slouch at an early age. Now it was the only way he knew how to walk. If anyone cared enough to say anything to him, they might have said he would become a hunchback if he kept it up. He was not unaware of the possibility, but he looked on the bright side. If that happened, it would be another problem he could grouse about.

That was Kevin Gray. A man with no mission, a life with no meaning, a problem with no solution.

On a night that was otherwise just like any night, he was at last presented with a sliver of…well, he couldn't call it hope. That state of being was foreign to him. It was something worth pursuing, however, and that was a novelty in itself.

He was on his computer, browsing websites advertising prescription drugs that would be delivered to your home in a plain brown wrapper with no questions asked, looking specifically for ones that would bring a quick and painless death if he happened to miscalculate the dosage and upend the bottle into his mouth. Just to kill time. Maybe. He had the television on for background noise, and a commercial came on with this opening line.

"Would you like to erase your problems?"

Kevin stopped what he was doing and shifted in his chair. A dark-haired man, probably in his early forties, dressed in a white mock turtleneck, sweater vest, and blue jeans, was strolling through a litter-free park on a cloudless day. Birdsong was in the background.

"I'm not talking about 'solving' your problems. That's a word even traditional psychotherapists have grown uncomfortable with. If you ask them, and if they have the courage to be honest with you, they'll tell you that you can't 'solve' a mental imbalance the way you would solve a math problem. The mind is far too complex, far too intricate, and far too delicate to go in with a hammer and start swinging, hoping you'll get lucky and knock something back into place."

Without taking his eyes off the screen, Kevin felt around for his remote and turned up the volume. He wasn't sure yet what to make of this man, but the fellow had his attention.

"My system of psychotherapy," the man went on, "has nothing to do with drugs."

What's the sense of it then? Kevin wondered.

"Drugs invariably do more harm than good, whatever their intended purpose. I don't even take aspirin."

Now Kevin had this guy's number. He went back to his computer. As if reading his mind, the man then said, "And my system also has nothing to do with holistic, New Age 'healing,' 'integration,' or any of those buzzwords..."

The computer was forgotten again.

"...of an approach which I believe to be well-meant but ultimately misguided. No. Behaviorism is the school of psychological thought which teaches that every person is the sum of his or her experiences."

Kevin's eyes widened. Those were almost the exact words his therapist had used. Was this man a colleague of hers? Maybe he should call her and ask...oh, right. He couldn't.

"And our behaviors, or lack thereof, are the single most important factor in determining how closely the way our lives are match the way we think they should be. We program ourselves as we would program a computer. And when a computer has an anomalous or destructive piece of code that causes it to do the wrong things, does the programmer help the computer come to terms with it? No. He *erases* it!"

That, Kevin decided, made a lot of sense.

"So if you would like to know more about what I humbly refer to as my revolutionary techniques—"

Oh, yeah. So revolutionary you have to shill them at two in the morning.

"—then why not call my office and set up an appointment?"

Kevin snatched up a pen and wrote down the doctor's name and number on the back of the envelope his cable bill came in. Maybe this would turn out to be worth the expense after all.

If nothing else, it would be one more thing to complain about, so it wouldn't be a total loss.

The next afternoon found him in an unremarkable waiting room. The same tastefully bland décor seen in any waiting room, same sign-in window, same comfortable couch, same outdated magazines.

But there was one difference. As a new patient, he expected to have to fill out a bunch of paperwork, including a section where he had to describe the problems that led him to seek therapy. This was the only part of the process he enjoyed. He especially liked seeing the look on the receptionist's face when he asked for an extra sheet of paper because he had run out of room. Come to think of it, that was the second difference. There was no receptionist here. There was only the sheet, and a bell that dinged softly when he had opened the door.

He had spoken to no human when he called the office. His only interaction was with that calm, friendly, professional recorded voice that asked him to speak his name, slowly and clearly, and the date and time he would like to come in.

Morning appointments were too disruptive to his wonderfully hateful routine, and he didn't want to come in at the end of the day and be stuck in rush-hour traffic on the way home. He lived just off Interstate 10 in the northwest part of Houston, so rush-hour traffic was largely unavoidable, but being alone with himself in the confines of his car for any longer than absolutely necessary was to be avoided at all costs. Therefore he decided on midafternoon that same day, knowing there would be a collective sigh of relief at his job that he was knocking off early. One stroke of luck was that the doctor's office was within walking distance of where he worked.

"Your appointment is confirmed," the voice had said.

That was all. No "thank you," no "goodbye," no "have a nice day." That bothered him. Even if those phrases meant nothing to machines and very little to humans, they were still supposed to be said, right?

No sooner had he written his name—in space number one, even though he had a one-thirty appointment—than a door opened and Dr. James Jackson gestured for Kevin to follow him to his office. There was no 'Nice to meet you.' No trying to put him at ease. Kevin had assumed that was one of the rules, not that it would have worked. No 'Just call me Jim' either, but there wasn't much indication that the doctor cared what his patients called him as long as their checks cleared.

He had on another mock turtleneck, this one black. The sweater vest was gone, replaced with a tan suit. He ushered Kevin into his office and shut the door behind him. Then the weirdness began.

Kevin knew the routine. He could not sit down until the therapist sat and invited him to do the same. But Dr. Jackson did neither. Instead, he slipped off his Gucci loafers, stepped onto his leather chair, and from there onto his cedar desk. There he stood, staring down at a confused patient.

"Come here," he said. "Let me get a look at you."

Kevin shuffled over in his patented slouch, arms down at his sides. Had he been looking higher than the doctor's ankles, he might have seen it coming. The backhand slap to the forehead sent him reeling backward, pinwheeling his arms for balance. Now he wasn't just looking at Dr. Jackson, he was goggling at him.

"That's a little better. Now perhaps you can tell me what it was about my socks that you found so interesting. Or perhaps you have a foot fetish? That's not my area, but I can recommend someone."

Kevin went on staring at him, with no idea what to say.

"Well? What's the matter with you?"

Something in Kevin's brain tripped over and lit up. No matter how strange the circumstances, he was always in his element with that question. With the ease of long practice he launched into his litany, stopping only at the sound Dr. Jackson filling his lungs and letting out the air in a huge yawn. He didn't even bother to cover his mouth.

"Oh, I'm so sorry," said Kevin. He tried to sound sarcastic, but didn't make it far out of woe-is-me mode. "Do my problems bore you?"

"Yes, they do."

Kevin wasn't sure why he took such offense. Every single person he knew, when asked that question, would have given that answer, and that was if they were feeling polite. But a therapist wasn't supposed to say things like that.

"But...but a...a therapist isn't supposed to say things like that. Aren't you supposed to...you know, to..."

"Validate your existence?" the doctor asked, in a way that suggested the expression might make a good one-liner but nothing more.

"Yes! Yes, you're supposed to—"

"Oh, I am? Is that what you want me to do? All right, I can do that. In your case, it will be easy."

Dr. Jackson jumped off his desk, opened the center drawer, pulled out a handgun, and leveled it at Kevin.

"Wha—hey! What are you doing? Are you crazy?"

"Of course I am," Dr. Jackson said in a conversational tone, as though he weren't holding anything more dangerous than a cell phone. "Why do you think I got into this line of work? But never mind that. You wanted me to validate your existence, and the only way to do that is to end it. It will help if you hold still."

Kevin backed away to the far wall, hands and mouth trembling. "No...you can't...Help! Somebody help me!"

"There's no one here, Kevin," said Dr. Jackson. He closed the gap with a casual stride, pointing the gun at Kevin's chest. "Besides, you can't tell me this isn't what you want. What you've been wanting for a long time. You've just never had the nerve to take that step. Just as with all the other miserable problems that define your miserable life, you want someone to take pity on you and solve this one for you too. Isn't that right?"

The barrel pressed into his ribcage. Kevin's eyes flitted between the undeniable reality of the gun and the unreadable eyes of its owner, while he frantically tried to come up with something, anything, to say or do. Would this maniac actually pull the trigger? If Kevin just stood there, he might. If he tried to make a run for it, he might. Maybe he could reason with him. Maybe offer him a bribe? *Yeah, right. His suit's probably worth more than my car.*

Still, he had to say *something*. Yell, scream, squawk his outrage.

But he said nothing. Because there was no outrage to squawk.

Because Dr. Jackson was right.

As if he saw the truth of his statement reflected in Kevin's eyes, Dr. Jackson lowered the gun and took a step back.

The door was to Kevin's right. Maybe this was some extreme way of getting him to take control of some aspect of his life, no matter how small, even if it was just leaving this office alive. He ran at the door. Actually, he ran into the door. It was locked from the outside.

Dr. Jackson hadn't moved, and the gun now rested on a lower shelf of a nearby bookcase.

"Why don't you sit down, Kevin?"

Kevin moved on numbed legs and sat at one end of the couch. Dr. Jackson moved to retrieve his shoes, and he had to pass by Kevin to do so. Kevin kept his eyes riveted on him, but did not shrink away. For the moment, his fear reflex had been overloaded.

Dr. Jackson sat on the edge of his chair, laced his fingers on the desk, and looked at Kevin in silence for a moment before continuing the session.

"How did that feel, Kevin?"

Kevin's mouth labored to dredge up a few intelligible sounds, but the well had run dry. Finally a trickle broke through. The trickle became a stream, and the stream became a flood. He declared that never in all his life had he *ever* witnessed such dangerously irresponsible behavior from a man who was supposed to be a professional. He asserted that Dr. Jackson ought to be locked away someplace where he could never harm anyone, pumped full of the drugs he didn't believe in. He avowed that the second he was allowed to leave, he was going straight home to write to the American Psychiatric Association and have his license revoked. He informed the good doctor that it was fortunate for him that he, Kevin, was not a violent man, or he would knock out several of those capped teeth. And he swore that if the man made a move for his gun, or for any other weapon, or for anything in here that could be used as a weapon, then he was going to let loose with a little therapy of his own, and how did he like them apples?

If he was hoping for Dr. Jackson to be scared, or impressed, or moved, or to have any visible reaction, he was hoping in vain. The doctor only sat and waited until he was sure Kevin had wound down. Then came his next question.

"Is it fair to say, Kevin, that this is the longest you've ever spoken to anyone without mentioning one of your problems?"

Kevin opened his mouth. Closed it again. He had to chew on that one a bit. No, that wasn't quite right. What he had to do was search his memory for one instance, just one, that would allow him to answer that question in the negative. But he could not. Again Dr. Jackson surmised as much from his silence.

"Once more: how do you feel? Right now? Don't think. Answer! How do you feel?"

"I feel confused."

"What else? Don't think! Answer!"

"I'm angry!"

"What else?"

"Alive!"

He was so stunned that it took him a moment to remember to close his mouth. Did that word really come out of it?

Whether or not that was the answer Dr. Jackson expected, he took the snap and ran with it. "Of course you do. Because for the first time in who knows how long, your consciousness had something new to examine. Something outside yourself to think about. A part of you that's nearly atrophied from lack of use was put through its paces, and it felt good. Didn't it?"

"Yes." Whatever Kevin thought of this person's methods, he could not deny the truth of his statements. "Yes, it did."

Dr. Jackson pushed back from his desk and got to his feet. "Stand up," he commanded, and Kevin did. Dr. Jackson came out from behind his desk to stand in front of him. Kevin did not recoil, but he tensed up. His breathing became rapid and shallow.

"What do you see?"

Kevin didn't understand the question, but did not want to admit it. "I see you." That was all he could think of to say.

"Precisely. I'm not as tall as you, so you have to bend your head down to look at me. But that's all you're doing. You're so wary of what I might do next that you're looking me in the eye. I'm willing to bet you're not accustomed to doing that. And you've forgotten you have to slouch."

Kevin noticed an odd sensation in his back. Sure enough, he was standing up straight.

"So," Dr. Jackson said, "this is your homework until our next session. First, focus on your posture. There's nothing on the ground worth looking at, so concentrate on looking straight ahead of you. Second, do not speak to anyone except in answer to a question. If you are asked for information of some kind, confine your response to providing that information. Do not speak of your personal life at all. I can just about guarantee that no one will ask you about it. The key word is *focus*. Do you understand?"

"Yes, sir," he said at once, because he *did* understand. This man had him pegged like a croquet stake from the moment he walked in his office. As much as Kevin wanted to hate him for that, however dim a view he held of his technique, he had to acknowledge that there was something to it, and maybe, just maybe, that something was the key to remaking who and what he was. Speaking of which...

"But...isn't there something I'm supposed to do along with that? Some kind of meditation, or affirmation, or—"

"Sure. If you want to put on a robe and go sit on a mountaintop somewhere. But since there are no mountains around here, and you would look really stupid dressed as a yogi, and I'm assuming you do want to live in the real world since you wouldn't stand still and let me pull the trigger, just focus on those two steps for now. That will get you far enough down the road that you'll be able to see the next steps. We're called shrinks because we help to shrink the road ahead of you, to make the journey manageable enough that you can get to where you want to be. That's how it works. You see?"

"Yes, sir." Somewhat less clear was how the doctor could hold such a low opinion of systems of thought he was supposed to revere as gospel. One day, if he really wanted to know, he might ask.

"Good. Come back one week from today, same time, and we'll analyze your progress."

Kevin knew it was no good even pretending he had to check his schedule in case he had a conflict. "Okay. But, look…next time, would you mind leaving the gun at your house?"

"Not at all. It's a movie prop anyway."

Dr. Jackson pressed a button under his desk, and the lock on the door clicked open.

Kevin soon settled into another routine, radically different from the one he had known and loathed lo these many years. Instead of going home from work and eating himself into a caloric stupor, he parked his car in his driveway and went for a walk. Late into the evening he walked, while he practiced his new posture and the newfound art of *not* complaining about anything and everything. When he returned home sometime after nine, he was amazed to find that the only feeling he had was one of exhilarated exhaustion. He'd never had any desire to exercise and had hardly any muscle tone, yet his legs were not howling in pain, were not sore, were not even stiff.

This would have been impossible, except that for years it had been his custom to pace his apartment for hours at a time, forcing himself to stay awake, so his legs were used to the activity. Drat. He had expected, although not with his usual masochistic hope, that his walking would lead to another problem or three.

Oh well, he thought, *you can't have everything.*

His workmates had perfected the art of diving into their cubicles and melding with their computers at a moment's notice when they saw him coming. But now, instead of seeking out someone—anyone—to whine and moan to, he breezed by everyone and went right to his cubicle to become one with his own workstation. Even the quality of his work improved.

After several days of this, those people whose cubicles abutted his began to say (to each other, never to him) that he seemed to have a new lease on life, or some such hoary old chestnut. It was not enough to get him interested in his work—no power on Earth could do that—but it was, as Dr. Jackson would say at their next session, a definitive step in the right direction.

A certain word was an entrenched part of Dr. Jackson's lexicon, and it became a more important part of Kevin's own. In the office, Dr. Jackson said the same things again and again. Out of the office, Kevin said them, to himself if he was in public, out loud if he was not.

The word was *definition*, and it rapidly came to form the core of his new religion, what Dr. Jackson called *definitive therapy*. It was called that because the key was not just to identify your problems, it was to define them. Give something a name, and you take away its mystique. With its mystique goes its power over your life. With its power goes the thing itself. You have erased it from your consciousness like erasing a line of text from a screen. The funny thing about problems was that they fed on themselves, but the process required a conscious effort to nurture and sustain it. As with any organism, stop feeding it and it starves, withers, and dies. The effect was cumulative, but it worked both ways, as Dr. Jackson promised Kevin he would soon discover. The next few months proved him correct.

Had Kevin known that 'definitive therapy' was a euphemism once applied to prefrontal lobotomization, he might have been worried. But he did not, and he was not. Dr. Jackson never saw fit to share that piece of information with him. He simply liked the term, and Kevin loved it, perhaps because up to this point so little in his life had been definitive.

His evening walks consumed the time he would normally have spent eating foods loaded with fat and sugar, so his excess weight, concentrated mostly in his bulging stomach, began to disappear. He was always so tired when he returned home that he went right to bed and sank into a deep, dreamless sleep. Because he was always well-rested, he stopped dragging himself around at work. And now that his eyes were wide open, he could really see how depressing his wardrobe was. That, coupled with the fact that most of his clothes were now too big for him, prompted him to splurge on an upgrade. And he soon found that he was so much more relaxed, about himself and about life in general, that he no longer felt the need for a calming smoke.

So it was that one Monday morning, when he strolled into the office sporting a smart blue suit, white shirt, and beige tie, instead of scurrying out of the way, everyone stared at him as he passed, still certain they were risking a catalog of ills but unable to help themselves. One young woman who was five cubicles down from him said "Good morning, Kevin" before she could stop herself.

There were nearly audible groans. Now she'd done it.

Except she hadn't. He looked at her, smiled, said "Good morning, Danielle," and went on his way.

Everyone who heard was thunderstruck. That was it. Not a kvetch, not a sigh, not even a "What's so good about it?" They would even compare notes later to be sure they hadn't imagined it, but there was no mistake. The man had actually *smiled*, and they would have sworn that any attempt at a smile would crack the lower half of his face like a clay pigeon at a skeet shoot.

Around 11:30, the inconceivable happened.

Danielle, a cute brunette who had started working there a year and a half earlier but had soon learned to avoid Kevin like everyone else, wandered by his cubicle and looked in. Kevin looked up from his work to see her standing there. Again he smiled and said, "Hi, Danielle."

She smiled back. "Hi, Kevin. Am I disturbing you?"

"No, not at all." He swiveled his chair to face her. "What can I do for you?"

"I just wanted to say that...wow. You..." She fluttered with her hands as if trying to conjure up the right words. "You really look good."

"Thank you. So do you. That dress flatters you."

"Oh, thank you!" She shifted her weight and smoothed out her skirt. "So, listen, I was wondering...do you have any plans for lunch?"

Two cubicles up and one over, a man shrieked in pain. He overheard the invitation, mostly because he was eavesdropping, was so flabbergasted that he forgot to pay attention to the envelopes he was opening, and sliced his finger with the letter opener. He sprang up from his chair, right hand tightly curled around left index finger, and raced to the bathroom.

Kevin turned back to Danielle as if nothing had happened and said, "Wouldn't you know, I was supposed to meet the Sultan of Brunei for lunch on his private plane, but he just called to cancel, so I can pencil you in."

Danielle laughed. Everyone within a three-cubicle radius tried to suppress chuckles with varying degrees of success, abject incredulity vying with long-honed caution. Kevin Gray had told a *joke*. And it was *funny*.

"Well, then," said Danielle, "I know a good Mexican buffet not far from here. It's probably not up to the Sultan's standards, but since he won't be there…?"

"I'd like that. Let me finish this up and I'll meet you in the lobby. Twenty minutes?"

"It's a date." She flashed him another smile and was gone.

But she only got halfway back to her own cubicle before she was pulled into the cubicle of a man she might have looked at directly five or six times during her employment there.

"What are you doing?" he hissed.

"What am *I* doing? You want to get your hand off me and try again?"

He was still holding her arm where he had hooked it. He released it and backed away, but leaned in so he could whisper.

"Are you out of your mind? You just asked the Gray Ghoul out to lunch!"

"He's not like that anymore. You can see how much he's changed. I want to find out what's behind it."

"Bad idea, Dani. Okay, yeah, he's totally not like he usually is, but I still think you're courting death by terminal boredom by going off alone with him."

"Opinion noted. Can I go now?"

"Yeah. Yeah." He waved a resigned hand, because he wasn't really thinking that Kevin would bore her to death. He was thinking *I've got a Mercedes, I can bench two-forty, and I've been after her since she got here, and all that guy has to do is lose some weight and show up in a new suit and she's all into him, what's the world coming to,* but he hoped that what he said sounded more gracious than what he thought.

While Danielle's hapless suitor was being rebuffed, Kevin headed off to the bathroom in search of the man who would be more selective with his nosiness in the future. The man gave a start of surprise when he saw Kevin, who did not come in but held the door open.

"Are you all right?" Kevin asked.

"Uh...yeah. Yeah, I'm fine," the man said, and offered a tentative smile to prove it.

Kevin backed out the door without further comment.

A few minutes later, the man left the bathroom. Shortly after that, another man came to the injured man's cubicle to get the story.

"What did he want?"

"Just wanted to know if I was okay. I said yeah, and he left."

"This is too weird. I say he's on something. Gotta be."

"Yeah, well, whatever's up with him, it's major."

Exactly twenty minutes after he'd spoken to Danielle, Kevin walked into the lobby. She was waiting for him.

Again she offered him a smile, and again he returned it. Now feeling rather jaunty, he extended the crook of his arm. She smiled at him yet again and threaded her arm through his.

Neither of them spoke on the way. He was content to enjoy the marvelous day and the marvelous company. He couldn't resist sneaking a peek at her, just to convince himself he was actually here with her. At once she turned a dazzling smile up to him and, just for a moment, squeezed his arm to her side.

Could all this really have stemmed from Dr. Jackson's therapy? Kevin could scarcely believe he wasn't the most famous psychotherapist on the planet. But he wouldn't be confined to late-night commercials for much longer, not if Kevin had anything to say about it. He still didn't really understand the doctor's techniques, but he knew the entire world could benefit from them. He was living proof. Definitive proof.

He had been about as far gone as anyone could be who still had a pulse. And now...and now. Where to begin? Just having these few minutes with Danielle was more than enough to focus on now. And she was all he did want to focus on. Even though he had more than a foot on her, for the first time since high school he was not uncomfortably aware of his height.

They got to the restaurant, he opened the door for her, and she went in. He moved to follow, thinking to make a grand entrance, but stumbled on something. He couldn't see what it was. Oh well. If the day had been entirely perfect, he would have been tempted to think it was an extended daydream.

"Oh, be careful!" Danielle shot out her arms and caught him around the midsection. "Are you okay?"

"Yeah, I think so." He wouldn't have lost his balance, but she didn't need to know that. Not right then.

It was while he was studying the buffet selections that he noticed she was studying him.

"Danielle? Is something wrong?"

"What? No. No, I'm sorry. I didn't mean to stare, it's just that…"

"What?"

"I don't know if it's the lighting in here, but you look…shorter."

Kevin caught his reflection in the sneeze guard covering the pastas and sauces. He did look shorter. When they left the office, the top of her head came only up to his chest. Now it was almost level with his shoulder. He would swear to it.

Oh come on. That was too weird. It had to be what Danielle said, just a trick of the light or something. And the sneeze guard was hardly a perfect mirror. For once, he didn't need to turn an observation into a problem. They were here and they were hungry, so they would just enjoy a leisurely lunch.

He had to remind himself that his next appointment was that afternoon. Was Dr. Jackson going to love this!

They finished eating at quarter past twelve, but Danielle made no move to get up. He had told her he was going to his therapy appointment after lunch, so she asked him to tell her about Dr. Jackson.

He didn't just talk about him, he gushed about him. When he finished, she said, "You make him sound like a miracle worker."

"That's because he is. You remember the way I was before. What you see now? It's his work."

"No, Kevin." She reached across the table and took his hands in hers. "You've always had this in you. Maybe he helped you bring it out, and for that he does deserve your gratitude. But give yourself a little credit, too." She accentuated her point by squeezing his hands.

221

"Yes, dear," he said, and she laughed. Then she looked at her watch and sighed. "I guess I better get back to the grind."

"Yeah." He started to stand, but she pulled him back down.

"Hang on a sec." Danielle rummaged through her purse and found a pencil, scribbled on a clean napkin, and handed it to him.

"I'm usually home by six," she said. "If you're not entertaining the Duchess of York, why don't you call me?"

"Heck with it," he said, tucking the napkin into his pocket. "Fergie can wait."

Just inside the door, she turned him to face her, stood on her tiptoes, pecked him on the lips, then hurried back to the office. He stood there for a moment, savoring what had just happened, then left the restaurant. Again he stumbled on the doorstep. This time he stopped to examine the ground, but saw only flat tile that turned into flat sidewalk.

He shrugged, hitched up his trouser legs, and sprinted up the sidewalk in the opposite direction.

An hour later, Dr. Jackson said, "Well, that was probably the easiest hundred dollars I've ever made."

Kevin had to laugh. It was true. He didn't even wait for Dr. Jackson to come out and get him. He just went in, saw the doctor sitting on the sofa, plopped himself down on the other end, and launched into a near-monologue about the pronounced changes in his life. Mostly he talked about Danielle. Dr. Jackson seemed almost as happy about her giving him her phone number as he himself was.

"As Obi-Wan Kenobi might say: You've taken your first steps into a larger world."

Kevin nodded. "Yeah. Yeah, I have. I know I have."

He removed a hundred-dollar bill from his wallet. Dr. Jackson took it and thanked him.

"So, same time next week?"

Dr. Jackson didn't answer right away. When he did, what he said surely broke some cardinal rule of the psychologists' code.

"You don't need me anymore, Kevin."

That was the last thing Kevin would have expected to hear from a therapist. The sentence, so succinctly spoken, knocked him for a loop.

He was silent for several seconds, and when he found his voice, the only word he could make with it was "What?"

"Did Danielle make any comments about your height?"

He liked the word so much he decided to use it again. "What?"

"You heard me. Did Danielle make any comments about your height?"

"Uh...yeah. In the restaurant. She said she didn't know if it was a trick of the light in there, but I looked shorter. But how did you—"

"Look at your suit."

Kevin looked. And looked.

When he bought the suit, maybe a week ago, it had been a good fit. Now he looked like a boy playing dress-up in his father's clothes.

"Wh... how..."

"Do you remember what I told you is the essence of what a 'shrink' does, Kevin? Answer me!" Dr. Jackson barked, snapping Kevin's floundering mind back to the present.

"Shrinks don't stop at analyzing problems. They shrink the sources away to nothing, and the problems wither and die." His voice was as mechanical as Dr. Jackson's recording.

"Close enough. How did your last therapist describe you?"

"As the only person she had ever encountered who was the sum of their problems. But what—"

He did not have to finish the question. Like a flash of heat lightning in a hazy sky, he saw what Dr. Jackson was getting at. And it was, to employ the clinical term, looney-tunes.

"Are you saying," he asked with an unbelieving laugh, "that my identity, the essence of what I am, was defined by my problems, and now that my problems are disappearing, I'm disappearing with them?"

"I'm not saying that," Dr. Jackson said quietly. "You are."

"Then I'm stark raving nuts!" Kevin stood up and started to pace in his agitation. "You're saying it wasn't just the lighting in the restaurant, that I actually am shorter, that I'm *shrinking*, for pity's sake, but this isn't a Rick Moranis movie, this isn't *Fantastic Voyage*, people don't just shrink away, they—"

He paced to the bookcase at the other end of the office. As soon as he turned back, he stopped. Dr. Jackson had stood up also and was walking toward him. Kevin backed up, trying to disallow what he could no longer ignore. When his back was against the bookcase, he closed his eyes.

Dr. Jackson brought his hands up next to Kevin's right ear and clapped. Kevin's eyes flew open. It was too late to close them again. There were few possible explanations for what they were showing him, and in short order he rejected them all.

Dr. Jackson stood five-eleven, give or take. Until now he had taken care not to stand too close to Kevin because if he did, looking into his eyes meant looking straight up. Now Kevin had to look up at him.

"You don't need me anymore, Kevin. Now do you understand why?"

Unable to speak, Kevin tried to nod his head, but it did a loopy circular motion instead. He admitted the truth and shook it.

"You will. Very soon, you will. Now go home. And be careful."

Kevin didn't have to ask what he meant by that.

While he was deciding whether to eat anything for dinner the following evening, he heard the knock on the door that part of him had hoped for, part of him had dreaded, and all of him had expected.

He had taken a cab home from Dr. Jackson's office, with only one detour: to go through his bank's drive-through window and close out his account. He had not called Danielle. He had not gone to work the next day. When the phone rang, he let it. So Danielle came looking for him.

"Kevin? Are you there?"

He walked to the door but didn't open it.

"I know you're in there. I can hear you. I was worried because you weren't at work today and you never called me. Are you sick?"

"No," Kevin said. "In fact, I've never felt better in my life. But that's exactly the problem, as you can tell."

What she could tell, he knew, was that he no longer sounded like himself. His vocal cords had shrunk with the rest of him. The result was that the voice on the other side of the door, the one that spoke as Kevin, was the high, reedy voice of a prepubescent boy.

She was quiet for a while. He expected that. He also expected her to leave in confusion and fear, but she did not.

"Please open the door," she said.

"You don't want to see me, Danielle."

"Yes I do, Kevin. Maybe…maybe I can help you."

"I'm beyond help. You know that."

"I don't know any such thing, Kevin! But I do know we can figure something out if we talk about this. Open the door. Please."

"I can't, Danielle. Please go."

"No. Not until you let me see you."

"Danielle—"

"I mean it, Kevin. Either let me in or have me arrested for loitering. You're not getting rid of me any other way."

He heard the caring for him, the desire to do whatever she could for him, in her words, and he tried to quash the surge of happiness it gave him. He couldn't, and found he didn't really want to. A shudder ran through him and the floor seemed to rush up to meet him. But it wasn't the floor.

Might as well get it over with, he told himself.

He unlocked the door. Almost immediately the handle turned and the door opened.

Danielle gasped when she saw him, but she didn't scream. She didn't run away. She didn't even back away. He stepped aside to let her enter, and she did. She even retained the presence of mind to close the door behind her. She dropped to one knee and took in her hands what was still more or less the face of Kevin Gray, except that it was now on the body of an eight-year-old that had a towel cinched around it. None of his clothes came close to fitting him now.

"You know why this is happening, don't you?" she asked.

"Yes."

"Tell me."

"There's nothing you can—"

"I know. Tell me anyway." She sat on the floor, expecting sensibly enough that it was going to be a long story.

He sat next to her and told her everything, beginning with the late-night commercial and ending with what Dr. Jackson said to him at the end of their final session. Having had all this time to think about it, he could now add to it.

"My old therapist was right. I really was the sum of my problems. They were all I could think about, all I could talk about. Complaining about them was the only thing I ever had to look forward to. How pathetic is that? They were fundamental parts of me. As each one was erased, part of me was erased with it. Now I'm cured—therapists never use that word, and now I guess I know why—so I'm going to disappear."

Danielle listened to his story in silence, her face a mask of other-worldly serenity.

Some things are too big for the conscious mind to process. Perhaps sometimes, by some mechanism psychologists have managed to fool themselves into believing they understand, these things get shunted in their entirety to the subconscious, the wilderness of the mind where the sun of what we call reason never shines, where all the monsters and fairy queens live out their impossible existences in the eternal dark of the inviolate unknown.

The subconscious mind loved the unexplained. The stranger, the better. Danielle's subconscious not only held her together in the face of Kevin's unimaginable fate, it even formed the words of her next sentence.

"I'll stay here with you."

"No." Not because he didn't want that. He couldn't think of anything he would like better than for Danielle's face to be the last thing he saw before he…what would he do? Die? Flip into some other dimension? He couldn't even guess until it happened. It was pointless to try.

"I don't know what will happen," he said, "but it could be dangerous for you."

"I don't care."

"I do. There's something I need you to do for me."

"Of course. Anything."

"On the dining room table there's an envelope, a set of keys, and my wallet. My car's on the roof of the parking garage next to the office. It's yours if you want it, or the junkyard might give you enough for it that you could splurge at Fuddrucker's." She smiled; she had seen his car. He smiled too. It had gotten really easy to do. "Inside the envelope is all the money that was in my bank account. Three thousand and change. I want you to keep some for yourself and give the rest to Dr. Jackson. His number's in my wallet. He'll know what it's for."

She knew as well. "For curing you."

"Yes. Oh—I know this is doubtful, but if anyone asks—"

"I'll tell them you got a better job at another company. It's not like that would be hard to do."

He stared at her, to burn the image of her into his brain for however long he still had it.

"Thank you, Danielle."

"You're welcome, Kevin."

She leaned forward and hugged him for a long time, and did not flinch when she felt his body shrink in her arms. Then she got up, took the money, keys, and wallet off the table, and started for the door. She stopped with her hand on the knob.

"Take care of yourself, Kevin."

He had expected "goodbye," but that was better. "You too."

When she was gone, he climbed up on the couch and turned on the television. He did not want to watch the news. Nothing but problems. Luckily a rerun of *Seinfeld* was on.

It was too bad Jerry, George, Elaine, and Kramer weren't real, he thought. Dr. Jackson could make a career out of them.

PICTURE IMPERFECT

In the rural community of Cascade Locks, Oregon, another hard year was winding down. For the congregation of Cascade Christian Church, it was time to enjoy the fruits of their labor and let their hair down—well, for those members who still had hair. This was a small but multigenerational church, as the graying faithful proved.

The pastor had called a planning meeting to discuss the end-of-year social. Nobody knew why he even bothered; what they would plan to do this year what was they did every year. They would meet in one of the older couples' homes for a potluck dinner, indulge in some light conversation (but never on subjects that were not discussed in polite company, which meant that pretty much the only things they could talk about were the weather, the county fair, the prices at the supermarkets along Route 26 and the progress of Mrs. Denton's chemotherapy), and call it an early night.

He announced the meeting in church the previous Sunday, after his sermon. Nobody really knew why he bothered with this either. They knew what the Bible said and were perfectly capable of reading it in their homes. They went to church faithfully because it was their Christian duty, but that didn't mean he had to stand up there and prattle on and on.

Especially lately. For some reason he had a bee in his bonnet about how Jesus taught his followers to have the right hearts, not just the right actions. He had preached on that for three Sundays in a row now. Or was it four? It didn't matter. They didn't listen to the sermons anyway. Many of them had attended this church since the day it was founded. Nobody was going to tell them how to worship in it, and nobody was going to tell them how to plan their social events.

The church had a few young people, but they never attended the year-end social. Although this tiny community boasted some of the best cooks in the region, the younger crowd always elected to skip the social in favor of something more fun. Like keeping a running tally of which items got the most orders on the Home Shopping Network.

That was the way of life here. Nothing much ever happened, and nothing much ever would.

This year the young people got emails inviting them to the planning meeting for this year's social. Who knew the geezers even knew how to use email, let alone would use it for this? They were never asked why they did not attend the previous meetings. It intrigued them that the pastor would go out of his way to invite them this time, and it didn't take them long to decide they would all go.

On December fourteenth, just before the meeting was scheduled to start, the young people were gathered in the Taylors' living room with the rest of the congregation, but they neither spoke nor were spoken to.

At 7:30 sharp, Pastor Jeremiah Rice, a skeletally thin man who was so old some of the children joked among themselves that he might have been the Prophet Jeremiah, shuffled in, accompanied by a man in his late twenties.

"This is my grandson, Lawrence," Jeremiah said. "He's visiting from Los Angeles."

The younger people raised their hands in greeting. The older ones offered strained smiles. Those smiles said that they understood why the pastor had never mentioned he had a grandson. The boy lived in Los Angeles, and they all knew what kind of place that was, and they all knew what kinds of people lived in those kinds of places. True, his hair wasn't long like a girl's, and he didn't have any metal on his face like a freak, and he was dressed in sensibly plain clothes. In fact, he almost looked respectable. But they all knew the wickedest hearts often hid beneath the most innocuous exteriors, and looking at this boy reminded them to be grateful they had kept their own hearts pure in this fallen world.

Then Jeremiah dropped the bombshell. He had nothing to say tonight. This meeting was Lawrence's idea.

There were surprised looks and stifled gasps. Jeremiah had expected that. He had just broken three of the innumerable unwritten rules of congregational conduct. Not only was he not leading the meeting, but he had surrendered that responsibility to someone who was not a member of the church, without consulting those in the church. No one said anything to him directly (that was another of the rules), but they would have plenty to say to each other after the meeting was over, you could be sure of *that*.

But for now this was the pastor's show, and the pastor, Heaven only knew why, said it was Lawrence's show. That meant they all had to do their Christian duty and listen to him with the respect he had been accorded. Maybe that wouldn't be so bad. Whatever he said would be the subject of their conversations at least through New Year's, so they hoped he would at least be interesting.

Lawrence looked around to be sure he had everyone's attention. This was wholly unnecessary. He had everyone's attention the second he walked in the door. Satisfied on this score, he said, "I don't have much to say, so this meeting will be brief."

Furtive glances were exchanged. They weren't sure whether to be relieved or disappointed.

"You're probably wondering," he went on, "why my grandfather let me call a meeting of your church. Well, I had a great idea for your party, and since I thought of it, he thought I should share it with you."

The oldtimers' gaze flitted between him and Jeremiah, hoping to catch the pastor's eyes and see something in them that would explain just what in tarnation this was all about. First of all, if there were any ideas to be shared, the pastor did the sharing. That was how it worked. Second, this young fool even got his events wrong. This was not a *party*, it was a *social*. They *never* had parties. Only drunkards and trollops and no-accounts had parties, and they had no doubt he was at least one of those.

Lawrence was not privy to any of these thoughts, so he kept talking. "What I was thinking you should do is something you've never done before."

This was what they were afraid of. They could just imagine what someone who made his home in *Los Angeles* would think was fun. What could possibly have made the old man agree to this? Did the boy have something on him? Oooh, yes, that was probably it. Now they had to figure out what that might be. That meant they were going to have to watch him extra closely for a while. They might even end up having to vote him out. Never could tell how these things might end up.

"I was thinking about a slide show."

The young people perked up. That wasn't a bad idea. It was even something they could get excited about. Who would have thought that would ever happen in burg like this? The older ones were confused. That was it? That was his idea? Why, there was nothing wicked about that at all. How many rumors could they make out of the boy suggesting a slide show? Still, the young people looked excited about it. That had to count for something.

Lawrence would be staying with his grandfather for a week, he said, so if anyone had any pictures they wanted included, they were welcome to drop them off. While he was here, he wouldn't have much else to do, so he would handle all the organizational work.

Most of the young people had camera phones, and now they had an excuse to take candid photos of the other members of the congregation. That was normally not allowed, of course—there was no rule against it, it was just not allowed. And delivery would be easy, because everyone knew where the pastor lived. In a town as small as Cascade Locks, there wasn't much everyone didn't know about everyone else.

Not that the pastor got a lot of visitors. It was rare that anyone had reason or inclination to see him outside of church. He was nice enough, they supposed, but those books he had on his shelves, talking about theology and mythology and all those other —ologies that didn't belong in a decent Christian home...well, it gave them the willies.

They just weren't at all sure what to make of him. That was another reason they took care not to listen too closely to his sermons. He might try to slip in some of those funny ideas he got from reading those books. Lots of pastors were doing that now, and they couldn't understand why, but they were disturbed by the trend. Ideas had no place in church.

Hood River was a beautiful place in winter, ideal for nature photos. The girls took most of the pictures and were always agreeable to dropping them off. A boy always insisted on going with her to see Lawrence, to make certain their pictures were all they would give him. Big-city sinner or not, he was a good-looking man. Being the proper young ladies they were, they took offense at the implication, but always acquiesced. They did have their reputations to consider.

Most of the photos were taken on Sunday. Jeremiah even posed for a few shots. Apart from a generous helping of dirty looks, there was nothing the old folks could do about it, since the oldest one of them all was so thoroughly enjoying himself.

Lawrence spent most of that evening arranging the photos according to who was in them and where they were taken. Shortly after ten, he decided he had done a fair night's work and went to bed.

Shortly before midnight, Jeremiah crept into the study and sat at the table where the photos lay. He picked out the ones of the elderly people (himself excluded), took them to the fireplace, knelt before it, mumbled a litany that was not exactly a prayer (but he was not exactly talking to God), and dropped them into the crackling flames.

The next morning the police were swamped with frantic calls, all for the same thing. "I'll swear on Judgment Day," the sheriff would later say, "that I never saw anything like this."

Those people taking care of elderly parents had noticed they were sleeping in far longer than they usually did, and knocked on their bedroom doors to make sure they were all right. When they got no answer, they knocked louder. When they still got no answer, they pounded and shouted. And when they *still* got no answer, they opened the door and found cadavers that had once been their parents.

Those whose parents were night owls had a more shocking tale to relate. Their parents had stopped whatever they were doing and stared into space, mouths hanging open. Before the horrified eyes of their children, their eyes melted into their sockets, their skin decayed and sloughed off their bones, and their clothes rotted on their bodies. They died in their La-Z-Boy recliners and then did about a year's worth of decomposing in the space of a few minutes. In every house where this happened, it happened right around midnight.

This was not the way it was told to the police. It was all they could do to get the hysterical callers calm enough to be able to recognize their voices. That was all they needed; it was not necessary to ask for their addresses.

The only person with an elderly relative who did not call the police was Lawrence. When a police officer went to Jeremiah's house to check on him, he found that the pastor was just fine, but Lawrence was gone. He had an emergency back home, Jeremiah explained, and he had to take the red-eye to LAX. No, he hadn't heard about what had happened to some of the old people in town. He had no idea what could have caused it, but anything he could do, he was happy to help.

The funerals were perfunctory affairs. Jeremiah was master of ceremonies, and he played the part masterfully. He relished the role he played in their funerals nearly as much as he relished the role he had played in their deaths, but that was a snippet of information he would take to his own grave.

There was nothing for the morticians to do. The bodies were far beyond the scope of their tender ministrations. The deceased had always been the ones to arrange the wakes when someone in town died, and no one who was left felt the need to do so.

Jeremiah's flock was of course much smaller after that, but it was also much livelier, you should excuse the pun. He had come to believe that the spiritual and temporal realms were symbiotic, that physical life and spiritual life should be linked, as should physical death and spiritual death, and that life, both physical and spiritual, was for the living. By those definitions, people such as these, who physically were alive but spiritually were rotted corpses, were an abomination that could not be allowed to continue. He had to give them physical death to match their spiritual death if he were to restore the natural order of things in his little corner of the cosmos.

He had not been entirely truthful with them. The idea for the planning meeting was his. Lawrence merely went along with it for the price of a plane ticket away from the sewer that was Los Angeles and the shrew that was his wife, to anyplace he wanted to go. He wasn't sure where that was yet, but he was sure that he was weary of life in the big city and wanted to settle down and raise a family someplace in the country. Someplace with clean air and snowy winters. Someplace peaceful.

Maybe even someplace like Cascade Locks, Oregon.

THE WIZARD AND THE WONK

If Mitchell Corvin kept running, he believed his heart would explode.

If he stopped running, he knew his heart would be torn out of him. And it would be devoured before he had time to fall to the ground.

He kept running.

Not much farther, surely, and he would be safe. The clornblech could go only so far from its summoner before the Perceptigone enchantment wore off and it became visible to anyone else. He had a fairly good idea of how far away he had to get before the wizard was forced to call it off, and he was almost far enough.

There was always the chance that the wizard had gotten an upgrade and expanded the Perceptigone radius. Or that the wizard could teleport, radius and all. Or something else just as bad. If so, Mitchell would be dead in seconds anyway, so there wasn't much point worrying about it, was there?

He kept running.

He shot past someone on the sidewalk who watched him go. The watcher pressed a button on something that looked like an iPhone, except it had a few apps Apple wouldn't be coming out with anytime soon.

"Now I've got you," the watcher whispered.

Seconds later, Mitchell heard the crackle and hum behind him. The enchantment was failing. They were moving out of the wizard's range.

But the clornblech was right on his heels. He would have heard it breathing if it had a respiratory system. Its arms were long and its claws could cut him in half. All it needed was one good swipe.

He kept running.

Until he felt the faint *pop* in his ears. Air rushing in to fill the space a seven-foot insanity had occupied an instant before.

It was gone now. So was the last of Mitchell's strength. He collapsed to the sidewalk, gasping for breath, his thin chest heaving with the effort.

All anyone else had seen was a man running until he dropped. True, the man was wearing an ill-fitting suit and vinaigrette-stained tie, but at this time of night it would take something a lot weirder than that to get anybody worked up. The pedestrians went on pedestrianing, stepping around, over, and occasionally on him. In this city, no one would take pity on him. The best he could hope for was that no one would take his wallet.

Even if that happens, so what? You're alive. That's what counts.

Count was the operative word. The language of magic had its own rules, like any other language. One of them was that once the clornblech had been called out of wherever it came from, it could not be summoned again for fourteen days. He now had a reprieve for at least that long. Assuming he didn't drown.

It always "happened" to be raining when the clornblech showed up. But the best magic looked like, or could blend into, natural occurrences. First-tier wizards were not stupid. The period between manifestations was never shorter than two weeks, and it was often much longer. And it rained a lot here. Most of the time it meant nothing.

Slowly, shakily, Mitchell sat up, then stood on rubbery legs that tingled with promises of the pain soon to come. No matter. All he needed was an anesthetic. He had bottles of those in his apartment. Bourbon and beer, whiskey and wine, mix them right and all is fine.

He shivered and almost told himself out loud to knock that off. It sounded too much like an incantation. Spells did not have to rhyme, but usually they did. They just sounded cooler that way. Mitchell was no wizard—these days he barely felt human—but one of the few things that remained within his power was not to tempt fate.

An inexhaustible topic of discussion was what was different about the handful of normals who became wizards. Mutation? Meteorite dust? Midichlorians? Nobody knew. Nothing out of the ordinary showed up in medical exams. Nor was there anything special about puberty or any other age; it had happened to people as young as six and as old as eighty-three. You simply woke up one morning able to do things you couldn't do the night before. As a result, it was common to hear people spouting nonsensical quatrains just to see if something would happen. Most people *liked* magic, even if they knew—or believed they knew—how dangerous it could be.

Then again, most people had not made a mortal enemy of one of the most powerful magicians known to exist. As far as Mitchell knew, only he had earned that distinction. What he still did not know was how he'd earned it.

There were clues. Things he inexplicably knew about the wizard, though neither had ever invited the other over for tea.

Third-tier wizards loved to talk about their condition, show off what they could do. Magic was a fickle and demanding mistress, but it was so popular that TTs could spend an entire reality show babbling and waving their hands around, and whatever happened, which was often nothing, the audience ate it up.

First-tiers were a different breed, aloft and aloof. They were the masters of magic and guarded their secrets well. No one even knew how many of them existed. The only one Mitchell had ever encountered was the one trying to kill him.

However, maybe they had chinks in their armor, points of vulnerability through which hints of their nature could seep out. Mitchell might have blundered onto one of these weak spots and thus committed what amounted to a capital offense.

There were certain things he knew about the wizard, but that was one thing he would *like* to know. It remained speculation. He had to get facts. Find out exactly how he had offended the wizard and how he could fix it. Preferably in a manner that did not involve him being turned inside out.

That was not likely to happen standing here in the slackening rain. He had to get home and get on his computer.

He still had his wallet. Thank goodness for small comforts.

And he still had his life. What was left of it. For at least two more weeks. This time.

He hailed a taxi.

The next afternoon, when his hangover had faded to a dull

background agony, he tried again to find out what specific thing he'd done to get on Dalton Smith's bad side.

That was what the wizard called himself. Mitchell somehow knew that too, just as he knew the limitations of the spell used to conjure the clornblech. It was probably not the wizard's true name, but nobody ever checked his ID.

Mitchell could work a sort of magic with computers, but the magic now routinely used to enhance natural abilities had made his abilities obsolete. Why hire a hacker to enhance your company's security when a complex encryption algorithm might keep out other hackers but was worthless against a wizard? It was much better to go to a second-tier and buy a spell that made your systems impervious not only to hackers but to other wizards except first-tiers, who never bothered with such minor incursions. This took only a fraction of the time a normal like Mitchell would need.

Specialists in scientific disciplines were sometimes called wonks. The word was apt. It was a wonky world in which no one could function without computers, yet a computer programmer was unemployable.

Still, Mitchell's hacking skills had not deserted him. They hadn't saved his livelihood, but he had to hope they would save his life. He had no choice but to dig in the dark—Dalton probably did not do anything a normal would recognize as blogging—but now and then he struck gold. At these times he always found, not necessarily what he was looking for, but exactly what he needed. Whether this was through skill or serendipity, he neither knew nor cared.

The mystery began with why he could see the clornblech in the first place. His giant nerd brain had figured out that much right away. Even though he didn't have a magical bone in his body, he could see it, but not clearly. It was an image not quite there, that wavered and rippled like something seen at the bottom of a pond at dusk.

There were two reasons for this. One, his human eyes and mind rebelled at the sight of the thing. Not its hideousness, he'd seen uglier creatures depicted in paintings, but its *wrongness*. It was a creature that had no place on this planet or in any part of a universe that made sense. His senses were unwilling to grasp the reality of it.

The second reason he couldn't see it clearly? It's hard to get a good look at something while you're running away from it.

All the same, he could see it. Perhaps this was only because Dalton wanted him to see his death coming, but he doubted that. First-tiers were not big on melodrama.

But so far he'd been the only one who needed to see it. It always came for him, and always at night. Sunlight, he'd learned in his delvings, had no weakening effect on either the creature or the enchantment that kept it hidden. It was simply easier to chase him through the streets after hours, when it didn't have to shove anyone out of its way to get to him. Your perceptions would register that just fine, and not seeing what had flung you aside would only add to the complications. Any FT could alter or erase memories, but the spell only worked effectively on one person at a time. If it was cast on a crowd, each person's memories were blurred at most, no more than a few shots of tequila would do, and even that wore off after a while.

There again the storms came in handy, as did the town Mitchell lived in. Any damage the thing did do could be chalked up to lightning or vandals.

With the memory spell there was another small oddity. Wielded by a powerful enough wizard, it worked even on a lesser wizard. But for some reason it did not work on him.

He'd done everything he could think of to eliminate the possibility that either he really was a wizard and just hadn't been initiated, or whatever was done with newly minted magic-makers, or that he had some latent psychic ability.

Sometimes, just for something to do, he would visit a storefront psychic or tarot-card reader. They were as plentiful and as phony as they'd been before the advent of the wizards, but they could still be good for a laugh. Laughter was in short supply in his life.

Every psychic he consulted told him he was a second-tier wizard (sometimes he'd even been a first-tier in a previous life), but his magical abilities were being suppressed on a metaconscious level. This was instantly obvious from his Kirlian aura, or from how he interpreted some version of a Rorschach test, or from the geometric patterns that could be seen in his beard stubble.

It was important to understand, he was earnestly told, that no spirit has an innate capacity for evil. They inhabit a higher plane, above all concepts of human weakness and depravity. However, the spirit tormenting him has been enslaved by a powerful and evil wizard who forces it to do his bidding. *(Wow, ya think?)* But as incredible good fortune would have it, whichever psychic he happened to be talking to just happened to have an inside line to the invisible powers who control and call forth the wizard-spark that resides within all of us. For what was admittedly a steep price, but necessary given the strain involved, this psychic would speed-dial these powers and persuade them to cast restraining spells strong enough to bind even a first-tier.

It also had to be understood, of course, that there was no guarantee of when this would happen. As well as being above human conceptions of malice, the spirits are above human conceptions of time. Therefore it might happen tomorrow, or three years from tomorrow.

"In other words," Mitchell would say, "they might not get around to it until after he kills me."

Regrettably, that was a possibility. But willful murder adds a terrible surcharge to a wizard's account in the Bank of Karma. He would have his reckoning that much sooner. As for Mitchell, his soul would earn a place on the tribunal that would render final judgment upon the wizard.

At this point he would thank the psychic, pay the consultation fee, and leave. The sheer absurdity of these pitches put him in a better mood for a short time, and that alone was worth the money. He was grateful they didn't say much about Dalton's misuse of his power, because that would almost certainly have led to saying something like "With great power comes great responsibility." Mitchell had not yet made an enemy of Spider-Man.

Books that told how to cast spells could be found almost anywhere. Ninety-nine percent of them were worth buying only if you were out of kindling or toilet paper, but *supposedly*, genuine occult lore did exist. Mitchell had spent most of his meager savings buying a random selection of spellbooks from every store within reasonable driving distance and ordering them online from every English-speaking country. Running a text through a translating website would only get him to more or less the same place and would waste precious time getting there.

He now owned more than a hundred of these books and had tried everything on every page of every one. Nothing. Zeroes all the way down. He'd not so much as levitated a glass, made his MasterCard bill spontaneously combust, or caused a certain former colleague to fall hopelessly in love with him. This former colleague had once seen him making peculiar gestures and understood what he was trying to do because he hadn't been the first to try it on her. Her answering gesture, an uppercut to his solar plexus, needed no magic to make it work.

Many of these tomes were written by third-tiers who were unemployed and needed the money. Making the boss's pants disappear in the middle of a meeting was not all that difficult. Hiding the fact that you were the one who did it was a lot trickier.

There were reasons the wizards who really had something to teach seldom did so. One of these was another quirk of magic: once a particular spell had been cast by a particular wizard, that spell became that wizard's property and would work for no one else. That fact had been hidden in a website Mitchell hadn't even meant to go to, but it explained why spells so often failed. He wished he'd found that out before he'd bought all those books, but nobody else seemed to know it either. If someone was chanting from a spellbook but wasn't alone, someone else in the group would get impatient and snatch it away. "You're doing it wrong, lemme try." Or "Okay, you've tried it. You're not a wizard. But I bet I am."

Many bets were lost that way.

Mitchell thought of this limitation as the Intellectual Property rule. Its real name, according to the site, was in an extinct language that seemed to have little use for vowels. Whatever it was called, it did not apply to FTs. Not many rules applied to them. They could even have made this one themselves, to keep random spellcasting in check.

It was rare for a third-tier to become a second-tier, but it was possible. Not so with first-tiers. They were born, never made. Also, they kept out of normal sight. They had no great love for normals, but they had no problem with them either. Normally.

So what's Dalton's problem with me? What could I possibly have done to a wizard who can control the weather that would make him want me dead? And why does he keep sending his special friend after me? He knows where I live, for crying out loud. Why doesn't he just show up here with a gun? Bang, problem solved. Not like I'd be missed.

He kept a journal on his computer of everything he had learned and theorized about the wizard. It helped him sort out his thoughts, and he believed it was helping him inch toward an answer.

The first time he remembered meeting Dalton was three years ago, the pilot episode of the *Clornblech Variety Hour.* It was entirely possible he'd seen him a dozen times before that but hadn't yet done anything to set him off.

First-tiers were protected by different types of mind foozlers. Dalton used one to ward off curiosity. He was an attractive man of, um, indeterminate age. He was not muscular, but he was well-proportioned. Sometimes his hair was silvered, sometimes it wasn't, according to his whim. Not a wrinkle, mole, or liver spot was to be seen anywhere on his face, neck, or hands, and yet the effect was not such that you would ever think he'd had aesthetic surgery or was taking HGH. Mitchell could not have said what color his eyes were, but he had never seen him in a suit that cost less than a thousand dollars. The women who frequented the galas where he always saw him should have been drawn to him like moths to a flame, but they were not. On the contrary, Mitchell had noticed that when Dalton moved through a room, people instinctively moved away from him. No one ever spoke to or about him. No one ever breathed a sigh of relief when he left. He was there, or he was not. That was it.

And that was how he seemed to like it. Mitchell had never seen him ask a woman to dance. It would be interesting to see how she would react if he did.

What would be funny under other circumstances was that Mitchell kept running into Dalton at these black-tie affairs because he kept getting invited to them. The first one was a $100-a-plate fundraiser. His bank balance had been roughly that, but with a minus sign in front of it.

He threw these gilt-edged RSVPs in the trash, at first because he thought he was being played, and later because he knew better. Didn't matter. A chauffeur—a very large chauffeur—always showed up to get him no matter where he was. Once he crossed the state line into a big city, drove aimlessly around all day, then went to see a movie at a thirty-screen multiplex. In the middle of the feature, he heard the door open, turned, and saw a man in a cap and uniform come in. He snapped his head back to the screen and scrunched down in his seat, but knew it would make no difference. The man was not checking faces row by row. He knew exactly where Mitchell was.

When he got to the sixth row from the front, he edged between the seats until he came to Mitchell's. He touched his cap and said, "Good evening, Mr. Corvin. Are you ready?" He did not whisper. No one shushed him. If they even knew he was there, they might have assumed he was Mr. Corvin's bodyguard.

Mitchell got up and followed the man out.

A Bentley Mulsanne was parked in the fire lane. The security guards ignored it.

The evening's gala was due to start in less than an hour and was at least five hundred miles away. They made it in plenty of time. When Mitchell got back to his apartment building later that evening, his own car, not the Bentley, was parked out front. Just as well, he told himself. The Bentley would have been stolen before daybreak.

Dalton could not have made it plainer that he was sending the invitations and the drivers. Why? What did it matter to him?

It was not for the pleasure of his company. The wizard never spoke to him or anyone else at these gatherings, which were never more than ten miles from Mitchell's home. That in itself was apparently a sign that the wizard wanted him to have something approaching a chance. His wallet was never suddenly stuffed with cash, so if he didn't have enough for a cab, he could take a bus, or in the last extremity he could walk home. He was left to do this more than once, but even if it rained on him the entire way, he never got sick from it. Wouldn't have been sporting.

At any rate it didn't take him long to figure out that, while Dalton could send a driver after him anywhere, he had to be able to see him in order to send the clornblech after him. He never did this until the guests had been seated and were well into the meal. At least Mitchell got that much out of it. Sometimes he didn't do it at all. He would grease the wheels so Mitchell had no problem getting into some formal do, hang around for two or three hours, then get up and leave, leaving his victim to wonder why the second shoe did not drop this time. Was he just toying with him? Trying to keep him off-balance? Keep him scared? It didn't make sense. Why would a first-tier wizard feel the need or desire to play such games with a normal?

These free passes were the exception. What typically happened was that at some point during the keynote speech, Dalton began mumbling into his plate and fingerpainting in the air. This was always Mitchell's cue to get up and start edging toward the door. Whichever driver had fetched him made sure he stuck around that long, but never made a move to stop him then.

One might think seeing a spell being woven with such confidence, without a spellbook, would make everyone at the table lean in, listen to the words and memorize what they could of the intricate gestures, so they could later try to replicate what this wizard was doing. It wouldn't work for them, thankfully, but they wouldn't know that.

But no one ever noticed anything. They couldn't see or hear what was done to summon the clornblech any more than they could see or hear the clornblech. Another foozler that for whatever reason did not work on Mitchell.

Maybe there's some other rule, unique to FTs, he typed in his journal. *Maybe if one of them wants to take out a normal, he can't do it the way a normal would. Maybe he has to use magic. Maybe it even has to be the kind of magic only an FT can do. That would explain why he never just dumps a vial of strychnine into my wine glass when I'm not looking. Be easy for him to fix it so nobody else could see him do it. Or why he doesn't make a steak knife fly across the room and stab me in the chest. STs have done things like that by accident, and there are always a couple of them at those fancy parties. Be just as easy for him to make it look like they did it, if he wanted. But no. Always the junkyard dog from Hell, and I mean that literally. Is that because of some rule he has to play by? Why would there be a rule like that? Don't ask me, I'm not a wizard.*

He sat for several minutes brooding over what he'd just written. As theories went, he'd had worse. No other ideas were forthcoming, so he saved the entry, shut down his computer, sank into his chair, and shut his eyes. Perhaps he would take a nap. He was psychologically exhausted, and his head still hurt from the bender the night before.

The knock on the door was not loud, but it made him leap up as though he'd sat on a joy-buzzer.

"No cause for alarm," he whispered, trying to slow his jackhammering heart. From everything he had figured out, he could be reasonably sure it wasn't Dalton or one of his minions. Whatever the reason anyone else would come calling, it might be interesting, even if it was a woman selling Avon. Shoot, he'd buy some perfume from her if she was pretty enough.

He opened the door.

"Interesting" did not begin to describe the person standing there.

"Hello, Mr. Corvin," she said. "Remember me?"

He would not have thought it possible, but the question made him laugh.

"I've only been punched in the stomach one other time in my life," he replied, "and lunch money was involved."

"Yeah. Well, I didn't come over to apologize for that, but as long as I'm here...sorry."

He shrugged. "Forget it. Maybe I had it coming. I don't think so, but maybe I did. Not like the love spell would've worked anyway."

"That's actually along the lines of what we need to talk about. Can I come in?" She brushed past him before he could answer.

"Where are my manners?" he asked the empty hallway. "Come in. Make yourself at home." By the time he said this, she was perched on an arm of his sofa. That was as close as she wished to come to sitting on any of his furniture. He couldn't blame her.

She waited for him to follow her into what passed for his living room and said, "I do owe you an apology for something else. It's long overdue, but I couldn't say anything until I was ready."

Mitchell blinked at her, trying to take that in. Had a gorgeous woman, who first of all had come to his apartment unannounced, just told him she'd been trying to work up the nerve to apologize to him for something? He must have misunderstood, but whatever she wanted to say was cool with him. The more she talked, the longer she would stay.

"O...kay..."

"First off, the best news for you: I can't be absolutely certain—that word doesn't exist when dealing with a first-tier—but I don't think you'll have any more trouble with the clornblech. Not much more, anyway."

His mouth fell open. He clacked it shut. Opened it again to state the obvious.

"You're a wizard."

"Mm-hmm. Second-tier. That's why I've been having to use you as a buffer. Long story, but Reader's Digest version, Dalton's gone off the rails. I'm guessing you figured that much out already."

"Uh..." That was the closest he got to a witty comeback.

"We've been looking for a way to rein him in," she said. "We came up with a plan, but it only had a chance with one person doing the trench work alone, everybody else watching from the bunker. I drew the short straw. Thing is, Dalton might've lost his marbles, but not his mojo. We can't match his power—he'd crush the lot of us if we tried—but we can work around the edges of it."

"Can I ask who the 'we'—"

"Sorry. If you knew, he would know. The only reason I'm telling you anything now is we're ready to take him out, or at least try, but we need your help."

"So he can read minds? Doesn't that include your mind?"

"Wizards can't read minds. That's one of the absolute limits, but I can't think of a better way to describe what FTs do. They just look at you and *know* things. But they have to be looking at you, or one of their familiars has to be looking at you."

Dalton could easily have had a familiar stationed outside his apartment, in the guise of a homeless man or stray dog. Nobody gave them a second look. But if it had seen her come here...no, second-tiers were smarter than that. They had to be to get to second-tier. She would have some kind of early warning system that tipped her off to the presence of anything unnatural lurking nearby before it could spot her.

With this assurance, Mitchell regained his minuscule powers of seduction. "So that means you're not risking an instant smackdown with him if you tell me your name."

"Samantha S. Maguire."

"Your folks too?"

"Yeah. Lucky it worked out for them."

In late eighteenth-century Europe, parents who wanted to raise great composers sometimes named their newborn sons Wolfgang or Ludwig. It was believed that doing so would infuse the musical genius of Mozart or Beethoven into their namesakes. That was serious magic. Good thing it didn't work that way.

That did not stop fans of the 1960s sitcom *Bewitched*, about the everyday misadventures of beautiful sorceress Samantha Stevens and her hapless mortal husband, from trying the same trick. Endora, Serena, and Maurice were also common names.

Hmm...her name is Samantha Stevens, and I'm a hapless mortal. This Samantha's mortal too, but maybe...

Never mind that. He could ask her out later. There were slightly more important things to ask her now.

"You can see the clornblech too?"

Samantha fished a gadget that looked like an iPhone out of her pocket. "With this I can. When Dalton invites you to a black-tie, I find out where it's going to be, and I go there and wait for you to come running out. I figure that'll be because there's something chasing you, so I take a picture of whatever's right behind you. Even with the camera's enhancements, it doesn't come out as much more than a blur, so we needed lots of pictures to figure out what the range of his Perceptigone spell is. And from that, we could put other pieces together. We knew it was going to take a while, the way we had to do it, so we were hoping that we could help you stay alive long enough to give us the time we needed."

A light bulb finally flickered on in Mitchell's head.

"That's how I know what I know about him and his pet. You've been finding it out and feeding it to me."

"Sort of like a satellite router. The kind of thing they use in spy movies to keep the Feds from tracing a phone call."

"You and your people are the reason his spells haven't worked on me. You shield me from them or deflect them or something."

"Yeah. Or something."

"And you were guiding me to those websites."

"Your fingers make certain keystrokes in place of others, while your eyes see the ones you think you're typing," she explained. "That way you can't find a certain website again unless we need you to. I hate to tell you this, Mr. Corvin, but on this subject you're not quite as good a hacker or theoretician as you think."

"You know what?" Mitchell said. "I can live with that. The key word here is *live*, right?"

"That's the plan."

"So you're also the reason I can see the clornblech."

"Taking its picture with this takes away its cloak. Not all the way, but a little. If you can see it coming, you've got a fighting chance. Why do you call it a 'clornblech' anyway? It doesn't even have a name as far as I know."

"*Clorn*, because it's all claws and horns. *Blech*, because...well, you've seen it."

"Yeah," Samantha said. "Can't argue with that."

"So Dalton Smith is his real name?"

"No idea. Does it matter?"

"Not in the least," Mitchell said. "He puts out some kind of vibe that makes it so I can't even talk to him—"

"They like their privacy. Maybe to a fault."

"Yeah, I got that. But it's not like I'm looking to write an unauthorized biography. There's only one other thing I want to know about him."

"Think I can guess," Samantha said. "Why he's after you."

"Any ideas?"

"Actually...that might be our fault."

Mitchell fell silent. In his mind he was still asking her out when this was over (yes, he *was* that infatuated with her, and was not ashamed to admit it), but Olive Garden was being replaced with Chick-Fil-A.

"Come again?" he said.

"I told you that we've been using you as a buffer. More like a reflector, or maybe a funhouse mirror. When we first picked up on his condition, we needed to calibrate it, find out just how much of a danger he might represent, and how he might be contained if it came to that. The problem is, he's...prickly. He would have sensed anything coming at him directly, traced it back to its source, and unpleasant things would have happened. So we thought if we took some intricate precautions, picked someone at random who was unremarkable even among normals, and bounced our questing spells off that person, that would make them unnoticeable."

"But something went wrong, like it always does. All you've managed to do is get a psychotic first-tier torqued off at me—"

"He's not psychotic—"

"Shut up, I'm ranting here."

"Sorry. Rant on."

"'Thanks a lot' doesn't begin to say it. On top of that, now he thinks a normal's got some kind of defense against him, and he's got no idea how that's possible, which makes it even worse. I bet that's the reason he keeps sending his clornblech after me. He doesn't just want to kill me, he wants to cut me open and study me!"

"Mr. Corvin...Mitchell...I know 'I'm sorry' doesn't begin to say it either—"

Mitchell slumped in his chair. "Never mind. You had a bad scene brewing, you tried something that would've been a genius move if it had worked, it didn't, so here we are. Just have to deal. Story of my life. But I never heard of a wizard going nutso. Didn't think that was possible. What happened to him?"

"We don't know very much about first-tiers, but we do know he's not an isolated case," Samantha said. "You know first-tiers are born that way."

"Yeah."

"Well, the problem is it takes two first-tiers to make a baby first-tier, and even then it's not guaranteed. There have never been all that many of them, and they're doing whatever they can to keep from dying out. Sometimes 'whatever they can' includes inbreeding. Same as they used to do to preserve royal bloodlines."

"Yet there are no royal bloodlines left, at least none that are worth anything," Mitchell said.

"That's what happening to the first-tiers. It's only a matter of time until there aren't any left. At least none who are worth anything."

"So Dalton's the product of incest, huh?"

"I'm sure of it. But in a weird way, we caught a break on that one. The same thing that unhinged him might also make him vulnerable."

"How so?"

"Why do most cultures frown on sleeping with a close relative?" Samantha asked.

"Because it's icky."

"Besides that."

"Because it brings out all kinds of recessive genes in the offspring. The royal families, back in the day, sometimes a king would marry his sister to keep the dynasty going, and maybe they would have a son, but they'd have to lock him away because he was microcephalic or born with hooves or something."

"Exactly. Lots of bad things can come out of inbreeding. One of the most common is hemophilia. Something like that can happen on a magical level. The available evidence indicates that's what happened to Dalton."

Mitchell didn't grasp the importance. "So all I have to do is stick him with a needle and he'll bleed to death? I don't think he'll let me get close enough."

"No, listen. He doesn't have it the way normals do. He has it the way wizards do. Meaning, he 'bleeds out' part of the essence of himself. Or maybe 'leaks out' is a better way to put it. Not enough to weaken him to any real extent, but enough to track and analyze."

Now Mitchell got it. "How'd you figure all this out? I always thought Seconds were basically Thirds on steroids. No offense."

"None taken. You're right. We can do a few more things, and we're better at them, but that's about it."

"So how do you get that kind of info about a First?"

"From another First."

"You've got a First helping you? I never heard of them helping anybody."

"Because you've never heard of a case like this," Samantha pointed out. "He's become an embarrassment to them. But first-tiers don't act against their own unless they absolutely have to, and in their view it hasn't gotten to that point yet. He's only fixated on you, after all, and you're nobody. No offense."

"None taken."

"But it's gotten bad enough that one of them has been dropping hints for us, the same way we've been dropping hints for you. Enough to point us in the right direction."

"So you can do the dirty work," Mitchell said.

"Right."

"So what's the plan?"

"Sooner or later he'll sic the clornblech on you again. We wait for that to happen."

"Not loving the plan."

"It's our best shot," Samantha said. "Summoning on that level draws out a first-tier more than almost anything else, because it takes so much power to maintain the spell. While he's focused on you, if we're right, we'll be able to use what we've learned about him and turn it back on him. Basically it should neuter him."

"It *should* neuter him," Mitchell echoed, still nonplussed. "*If* you're right. And if you're wrong?"

"He'll probably kill us all."

"And the other first-tiers won't lift a finger to stop him."

"I doubt it," Samantha said. "I may be a slightly bigger insect to them than you are, but if I get swatted, so what?"

Mitchell decided to look on the bright side. "Oh well. Maybe at the next fundraiser they'll have filet mignon. That's what I'd want for my last meal if I ever went to Death Row, and now it looks like that's where I'm going."

Samantha grimaced. "Don't get all dramatic on me. That's exactly what we're trying to avoid, remember?"

"I have not yet begun to get all dramatic," Mitchell said. "When the clornblech shows up again, sure, do whatever you're gonna do to it. Use it to put Dalton in a wizard straitjacket. But just so you know, I'm not going to spend the rest of my life running from this thing. Every time I do, I ask myself later why I'm trying so hard to stay alive. Why I don't just let it rip me open and be done with it. Every time, that question gets harder to answer. So whatever you plan on doing, just make sure you get it right, okay?"

"That was the idea anyway," Samantha said. "But while we're at it, we'll also try to keep you from committing suicide. Anything else?"

"How do I contact you when the next invite comes in the mail?"

"Don't worry about that. What we need to know, we'll know."

"Of course you will. So is that everything?"

"I believe so. I'll show myself out," she added before he could offer to escort her to the door and accidentally feel her up while reaching for the security chain. Not that he would ever do such a thing.

The next twelve days passed without incident. Then he saw an envelope in his mailbox. It had no return address. No sending address either. It was blank. Yet there it was with the usual assortment of junk.

No use pretending he didn't know what it was—they always came in blank envelopes—but out of morbid curiosity he opened it anyway.

Even if he had anywhere to go, he had been taught in many ways that it did no good to run. So after he saw that he had been cordially invited to his grisly death...uh, to a $1000-a-plate political fundraiser at 8:00 tomorrow night (which made him wonder idly who Dalton was going to vote for), he tossed the card in the trash and plopped back down in his armchair. He had no real errands to run, nobody he wanted or needed to see, and no possessions anyone would want to be bequeathed in a will, so he merely settled in to wait.

Despite Samantha's assurances, Mitchell was certain he had just been informed of the hour of his demise. Not because he intended to make good on his half-threat and let the clornblech have him, but because she'd said it herself: insane hemophiliac inbred or not, Dalton Smith was still a first-tier wizard, and first-tiers were close enough to omnipotent that the smattering of churches that worshipped them did not raise many eyebrows.

Like the gods of old, they also kept themselves removed from the tiny affairs of tiny humankind. The first-tier providing Samantha with intel—and doing that much only out of the direst necessity—would not intervene regardless of what Dalton ultimately did, and no matter how many other second-tiers Samantha had in her corner, how much could they reasonably hope to do against him?

He would find out in thirty-two hours.

When the chauffeur knocked on his door the next night at 7:15, he was ready. He had even put on his finest suit for the occasion, but "finest" was a relative term. The only reason he would not be thrown out on his ear the moment he walked in the door was that Dalton would not permit it. Mitchell was the star of this long-running play, and one way or another, the curtain was coming down tonight.

It had been raining since midafternoon.

The chauffeur touched his cap in greeting when Mitchell opened the door. None of Dalton's drivers had been puny, but this was the largest of them all. Between him and the clornblech, it would be a fair fight.

"Good evening, Mr. Corvin. Are you ready?"

Mitchell nodded. "Yeah. For once, I am."

"Very good, sir. If you'll follow me?" As if the man wouldn't haul him down the stairs like a sack of laundry if he said no.

An Aston Martin V12 awaited him this time, but no one walking past it even seemed to know it was there. Pity. If nothing else, climbing out of a car like that at the gala would silence any inquiries as to what he was doing there. Except of course that there would be no inquiries.

He waited in line while everyone's invitations were scrupulously checked. When he got to the front, the doorkeeper did what they always did. His eyes glided over the place where Mitchell was standing and refocused on the person behind him. Just for a lark, he decided to see if he could get the doorkeeper's attention. Wave his hands in front of his face, yell in his ear, something. However, his chauffeur/minder, standing beside him and also unnoticed despite his size, hooked a paw around his arm and propelled him to the center of the ballroom before he could do anything.

Dalton stood there, alone. The crowd flowed around him. This one time, Mitchell was not just going to wait until it was time to run away. Whether or not he was going to die tonight, he would find out once and for all why he was supposed to. Samantha had given him an idea, but maybe if he could get Dalton to say it in his own words, he would realize how ridiculous they sounded and forget his grudge.

Yeah. And maybe when the clornblech showed up, Mitchell could just sprinkle pixie dust on himself and float out of its reach.

He knew all about the privacy spell encircling Dalton, the one that kept anyone from wanting to speak to him or even acknowledge his presence. But a spell did not stop working on you once you recognized it for what it was, and Mitchell felt his desire to approach Dalton fade with every step. No, it was more than that. He could feel something repelling him from his adversary, and when he closed the distance to about ten feet, his legs would not take another step in that direction.

That was fine. Ten feet was close enough to say what he had to say.

But he couldn't say it. His jaws had locked up. Opening his mouth required an effort akin to lifting a barbell, and he could force not one syllable out of it. Dalton apparently didn't feel like answering questions.

Until now, Samantha and her people had managed to blunt the effects of Dalton's spells on Mitchell. Either they were no longer extending him that protection or—far more likely—Dalton was overloading it.

The wizard had done nothing outwardly. At most, all anyone else could see was a staring contest. Yet for the first time, Mitchell *felt* himself to be as helpless in Dalton's power as any normal. That was scarier than facing the clornblech. For all its obvious strength and terrifying appearance, it was a known quantity. If he could not confront it, at least he could run from it. But here, now, he could do nothing that Dalton did not want him to do.

Nor did it help that, though he must have looked as though he were in the initial stages of a seizure, no one paid him any attention. Because they were not meant to.

Dalton just stood there, detached and imperturbable, regarding Mitchell with what might have been amusement. This did not last. The expression on his face did not change, but his lips began to move and his hands began to flutter.

Oh come on! They haven't even served dinner yet! Mitchell screamed inside his head. He had glanced at the menu on the way in. No filet mignon, so at least he wasn't missing that. The main course was saltimbocca alla romana, whatever that was. He wouldn't even get to find out.

Whatever. I'm not running.

Something flickered across Dalton's face. Puzzlement, maybe? Mitchell hoped the wizard could pick up the thoughts he wouldn't let him speak aloud.

That's right. You want to send your interdimensional beastie after me? Do it in this room, no rain or darkness. Let's see how big your wand really is.

Having decided to make a stand, he turned and sprinted out of the building.

It should have been difficult for him to weave around the people between him and the door, but just like that there was no one in his way. His path was clear. No one turned to watch him go. As soon as he got outside and the first drops of rain hit him, he tried to stop or at least slow down. He was incapable of either.

Dalton wanted him to run, so by golly he was going to run.

Soon enough he heard the thunderous tread of the clornblech right behind him. Samantha was nowhere in sight. The few people out and about glanced at him as he ran past, but none of them seemed to be expecting him to run past.

And he was running faster than he would have believed possible. He was largely resigned to his fate, so he knew it was not fear that drove him. Nor had he consumed an inordinate amount of carbohydrates that day. His muscles were being fueled by nothing inside him but by some kind of stimulator spell.

Another of Dalton's games. But why? *Why?*

Duh, because he was insane. Why else would he send an extra-dimensional instrument of death after him and then give him the means to outrun it?

Except he wasn't outrunning it. Slowly but inexorably, the clornblech was gaining on him. He could hear its pounding steps over the pounding rain.

Then came the lance of pain. Mitchell screamed and dropped to his knees.

The claws had raked his back. His jacket and his skin hung off him in strips.

He pitched forward onto his stomach. Wherever Samantha was, whatever she was trying to do, he didn't care anymore. Had he been able, he might have croaked out a prayer. Maybe even to Dalton.

Finish it already. Make it quick.

Something pressed into his back. Not claws. A hand. A human hand.

A flash of searing heat, enough to make him cry out in his abject exhaustion...and then nothing. The pain was gone. Even before he brought a trembling hand up to his back, he knew his grievous injuries were healed as if they'd never happened.

He wasn't even going to try to guess. Shakily he rose to his hands and knees, and there he might have remained for a little while had the *other* hand not caught him under his arm and pulled him to his feet.

People continued to scurry past, anxious to get to shelter. They had not seen or heard anything out of the ordinary. Nor did Mitchell, not anymore. The clornblech was gone. He was alone with the wizard.

"It's over now," Samantha said.

It was? That was it? No titanic mystical duel? No impossibly loud voice chanting words of ultimate doom in the ancient vowelless language used on that website Mitchell "accidentally" visited? Not so much as a *You'll never take me alive*?

She did not elaborate. He supposed he should have figured it out sooner.

"You were the one," he said. "All along, you were the one. The only one. Only first-tiers have that kind of healing magic."

"Yes," she said simply.

That explained it, sort of. There were reasons first-tiers left everyone alone, including each other. Not the least of these was that a brawl between them had the potential to leave a smoking crater where the greater metropolitan area used to be. They preferred to avoid things like that when possible.

"*You* made me run," he surmised. "And you made me run fast. That way he had to give the clornblech more juice so it could keep up. That's how you drew him out enough so you could do whatever you did."

"Yes," she said again.

"Don't suppose I can ask what that was? Even if I wanted to put it in a spellbook, it's not like it would do anyone else any good."

"It isn't necessary for you to know."

"Classified. Got it. Where is he?"

"We will look after him now. He will cause you no more trouble."

The soft note of sadness that crept into her voice told him what her words did not.

"He's someone special to you. That's why you got involved. Not because you cared what might've happened to me but because you care about him."

She did not answer that, so he knew he'd guessed correctly. All the more reason neither of them would have wished to fight the other. There was another possible reason, but he decided it would be inadvisable to ask her if they practiced safe sex. Instead he asked, "What do I do now?"

"Go home."

"Right. Thanks for that."

"And call the number written on the back of the business card in your pocket."

"Huh?" Nobody had given him any business cards.

"A software company executive was at the party you attended two weeks ago," Samantha said. "He's interested in offering you a job."

So that was how it worked. No one had given him a business card two weeks ago, either. After all this, she was throwing him a bone. Did she think he was just going to take it, thank her for it, and go on his way?

Darn right he was. "Thank you. But...this guy knows I'm a normal, right?"

"You needn't worry about that. Ours is a world in flux. It still needs wonks as much as it needs wizards."

Mitchell had his doubts about that but was not about to argue the point.

"In fact," she continued, "you don't even have to wait until morning to call him. He's at home now with nothing to do."

"And he won't wonder how I got his home number." It was a confirmation, not a question. Of course he wouldn't.

"Keep faith, Mr. Corvin. Don't forget your wallet." She pointed at a spot on the ground beside him.

In the time it took him to glance at the sidewalk and look back, she had vanished. Once again she had shown herself out. Only then did he notice it had stopped raining and his clothes were dry.

He patted his back pocket. His wallet was there. It felt fatter now, and a quick check showed why. It had a thousand dollars in it. Payment for whatever help she believed he'd given her. He could go back to the fundraiser if he wanted, explain to anyone who asked that he'd felt the need for a breath of air, sit down and eat the salty-who-all-the-what, and...

Yeah, right. But he did return to the building, just to take a look.

The Aston Martin was gone. He'd expected as much, but it was worth a shot.

He still had his wallet. And he had his life. What was left of it might even be worth living now.

He hailed a taxi.

THE DINNER PARTY

Once upon a time, an upheaval took place in the Kingdom of Winstonville.

The events that transpired are not recorded in any history book, and the kingdom does not appear on any map. This is because Winstonville was a kingdom in name only, and the name was created by two of its princesses, who were royalty only to themselves. The third princess did not consider the name worthy of comment.

Actually, there was very little the third princess did consider worthy of comment, a fact that made her the subject of many comments and much speculation far beyond the borders of the Kingdom of Winstonville. This was not terribly surprising, since said borders were defined by the walls of a single house. Had you walked past this house one overcast morning, you might have heard the opening salvo of the revolution that is the reason for this tale.

"Cynthia Ashleigh Winston!"

Having been so imperiously summoned, Cindy responded in a manner befitting the solemnity of the occasion. Stretched out on her bed, dressed in a ripped black t-shirt and red boxer shorts, reading the collected works of Spinoza, she yelled, "What?"

The door was flung open. There stood her mother and her fourteen-year-old sister Courtney.

"Would you care to explain this?" Mrs. Winston asked.

"A biology experiment gone cataclysmically wrong?" Cindy said. "That's the only explanation I can think of."

"She means my shirt, you freak!" Courtney shouted.

Courtney was wearing a yellow halter with the word "Spoiled" across the chest in glittering black letters. When they purchased the shirt, it had no other decoration. Now, under the word "spoiled" was a drawing of a piece of meat, colored a sickeningly convincing shade of grayish-green and covered with squirming maggots.

"How could you do this?" Mrs. Winston demanded.

"It wasn't hard," Cindy said. "I knew crayons wouldn't work well on that material, so I took some colored markers and—"

"Don't you smart-mouth me, young lady. You're in enough trouble as it is. Why would you do something like this?"

"I wasn't sure Courtney was aware of the intended meaning of the word 'spoiled.' I didn't feel like sitting her down and explaining it to her, so I thought an artistic representation would do the trick."

Mrs. Winston heaved a theatrical, long-suffering sigh, honed from years of practice to an edge that would have impressed anyone else.

"Courtney, wait for me downstairs," she said. "I'll take you shopping later."

Courtney crossed behind her and shot Cindy an obscene gesture.

"I saw that," Mrs. Winston said without anger.

When Courtney was gone, Mrs. Winston said to her other daughter, "You are going to pay for this. And I'm going to tell you how."

"I'm tingling with anticipation."

"If you don't watch it, your backside's going to be tingling."

"What exactly is to be the mode of my restitution?"

"Go into Courtney's room and open her closet door."

"What?"

"Do it."

With her own sigh, this one of mingled boredom and exasperation, Cindy got up. She crossed the hall to her sister's room, which she had never entered and never wanted to, went to the closet, opened the door, and slammed it shut.

"Okay, she got a new dress. What's that got to do with me?"

"Everything, dear. That dress isn't for her. It's for you."

Cindy's mouth dropped open. "No."

"Yes."

She opened the door again. Hanging on the inside of it was the most beautiful dress she had ever seen. It was pale blue silk, with small gems woven into the bodice. The skirt was floor-length and nearly as wide as the skirt on Princess Diana's wedding dress.

Cindy slammed the door shut again and whirled to face her mother. "Is this some kind of sick joke?"

"Do you know how many girls would give everything they owned to have a dress like that?" Mrs. Winston asked.

"No, but any of them is welcome to this one," Cindy said. "In fact, just give me an address and I'll take it to her myself."

"Sorry. You're wearing the dress tonight, for my dinner party."

"I'm afraid you've been misinformed."

"I have?"

"You have. First, I'm not going to be within ten miles of the house tonight. Second, even if I'd been lobotomized and actually wanted to be here, I'd sit at the table naked before I'd wear...*this*. Why don't you just give it to Courtney? It's already in her closet."

"Who do you think picked it out for you?" Mrs. Winston said.

"I should've known. She would be telling the story for the rest of her life. Well, forget it. I'm not wearing this obscenity."

"Your grandmother will be here. She paid for the dress, and she told me just last week that her life's dream is to see you dressed like a princess in a fairy tale."

"Her life's dream since *way* before last week was to be marooned on a desert island with Charlton Heston," Cindy said. "She was sadder when he died than when Grandpa did, remember?"

"Cynthia, please. It would mean so much to her."

"In what universe? The only reason she ever talks to me is to insult me. She knows how I feel about the mindless image obsession that a dress like this stands for, and if she does want me to wear it, it's only so she can humiliate me. Well, yeah, I can see how that would mean a lot to her. But I'm sure you'll understand if I don't share her enthusiasm."

"Cynthia—"

"I am not wearing this thing, tonight or ever. Subject closed."

"Okay," her mother said and turned to leave. "Have it your way. Oberlin will be disappointed, though."

She had barely stepped into the hall before Cindy asked, "What about Oberlin?"

Her mother allowed herself a small smile before turning back to face her with an expression of utmost seriousness.

"Oberlin was your first choice for college in the fall, wasn't it?"

"You know it is. And you know I've been accepted there."

"I also know you weren't able to get a full scholarship."

Cindy connected the dots at once. "You wouldn't."

"After you've spent the last two years systematically making it impossible for me to have any sympathy for you about anything? You'd better believe I would."

Cindy scowled, but knew the battle was lost. For as long as she could remember, she had wanted to study music. Oberlin was her dream school, the only one that would do. She had framed their acceptance letter and hung it over her bed.

The problem was tuition. Her grades were good enough for a partial scholarship, but not good enough for a free ride. Getting a job would only help a little. Her mother had graciously offered to make up the difference, but from the day she made the offer, Cindy had suspected that her help came with a price.

This, she saw, was the price.

"All right." She was choking on her anger and could barely get the words out. To her mother, that alone made the argument worthwhile. "You win."

"Not yet I haven't," Mrs. Winston said.

"What?"

"There are certain things I'll expect you to do to contribute to the evening's success. Wearing the dress is only one of them."

"It's not enough you have to stab me through the heart?" Cindy yelled. "You have to twist the knife and break it off?"

"Yes. And leave it there to rust. There are three other things. Ready to hear what they are?"

Cindy leaned against the wall and tried to resume her former pose of world-weary cynicism. "By all means. The suspense is boring me."

The darker Cindy's mood, the brighter her mother's. Mrs. Winston was almost singing now. "All righty. One: you will tidy up downstairs. That means dust the dining room table, vacuum the carpet, mop the kitchen floor, wipe down the counter, and wash the dishes. The dishwasher's still broken, so I'm afraid you'll have to wash them by hand. Two: your grandmother is coming over this afternoon. You will make her as comfortable as possible for the duration of her visit. Three: you will transform yourself into a human being. That means wash and comb your hair, remove the metal from your face, and take off all that disgusting Goth makeup. From the moment my first guest arrives until the last one leaves, you will be wearing that dress, acting every inch the refined young lady. Do I make myself clear?"

"Aren't you just giving this party so you can schmooze some rapacious corporate bigwig? Why do you even need me here? Why do you even *want* me here?"

Her mother smiled with what seemed to be genuine tenderness. That only infuriated Cindy more, which was probably the point.

"Tell me honestly, Cynthia, is there any way I could answer those questions that would make the evening any more palatable to you?"

"Not really, no."

"I didn't think so. Get cracking."

Cindy had put all the cups, bowls, and plates in the drying rack and was working her way through the silverware when the doorbell rang. She opened the door to a woman in her mid-seventies.

"Hello, dear," the woman said with a radiant smile. "I'm your fairy godmother."

Right away Cindy knew something was wrong. Her grandmother's clothing was usually austere but perfectly coordinated. Now she wore a garishly colored shawl over a haphazard ensemble. Her white hair, always tied back in a bun, was loose and matted.

"Gramma," she whispered, "did you go off your meds again?"

The woman's face clouded over and her smile faltered. Almost before Cindy could register this, her expression cleared again and her smile was back, brighter than before. She stepped into the dining room and asked, "Would you like to go to the ball tonight?"

"The what?" Cindy knew it was unlikely they would be able to have a conversation in the regular sense, but decided she had earned the right to have a little fun.

"The queen is having a ball tonight, isn't she? You can't possibly go dressed like that."

Cindy knew her sisters sometimes referred to their mother as "the queen" when she wasn't around. Apparently their grandmother was in on the joke. There was little love lost between generations.

"I'm not. I'm wearing the dress you bought me." Cindy somehow managed not to say it through clenched teeth.

"Oh, but that's not enough! You should ride to the ball in a gilded carriage, pulled by six white horses!"

Oh man. She's really stepped off the dock this time. "Yeah, well, as much fun as that would be, the dinn—uh, the ball's going to be here, so—"

"I'll use my magic to help you. All you have to do is find six mice—"

"Mice?! *Ugh!* As *if!*" Cindy recoiled as if she had just seen one skittering across the kitchen floor, and abruptly decided she was tired of this game. "Look, Gramma, it was nice to see you, but I've got work to do, so—"

Her grandmother plowed on as if she hadn't said anything. "Then you must go out to the garden—"

"We don't have a garden."

"—harvest the biggest pumpkin you can find—"

"So it follows we don't have any pumpkins."

"—and make sure..." Her grandmother lowered her voice and looked around. "...that your two wicked stepsisters know nothing of this!"

That one Cindy was reluctant to correct, but she didn't want to feed her grandmother's delusions. "They're my sisters. Unfortunately. And they're not wicked, they're just lame." In Cindy's circle, "wicked" was a compliment, but she wasn't even going to try to explain that. "Besides, they're not here. Mom took Courtney shopping, so of course Cameron had to go too. But they'll be back soon. I'll tell them you were here."

It was a longshot. Even when she was lucid, her grandmother was not good at taking a hint. This time, though, she surprised her.

"Right!" exclaimed the old woman. "I must be off now. The magic will take effect when you need it, but it will wear off at the stroke of midnight, so you must leave the ball before then. Bippity-boppity-boo!" She used her right hand to wave an imaginary wand and was gone.

Cindy went to the window and watched her grandmother walk swiftly up the street. She lived half a mile away and liked to walk when she didn't have anything to carry. When she was around the corner and out of sight, Cindy smiled with something close to affection and went back to the dishes.

Mrs. Winston maxed out one of her credit cards to buy an ornate grandfather clock that would, she hoped, impress her guests. The dinner party was in full swing when this clock chimed eight. All the guests had arrived and were clustered in groups of three or four, discussing various arcana about the stock market and the Federal Reserve. The clock got only generic compliments, and those only in response to her not-so-subtle promptings.

Courtney and Cameron worked the room, keeping everyone's wine and champagne glasses full, taking sips from the bottles when they weren't being watched, and accepting everyone's compliments on how beautiful they looked with all the proper humility. Their mother had attached herself to an executive of the company that was in merger talks with hers. While trying to monopolize him, she also cast vexed glances around the room. Cindy had not yet seen fit to grace them with her presence.

When she could stand it no longer, she disengaged herself from the executive, much to his thinly-disguised relief. She beckoned Cameron over and whispered in her ear.

"Get your sister down here. Now."

Cameron rolled her eyes—the party *was* going so well—but went upstairs and pounded on Cindy's door.

No answer.

"Hey, zombie-brain! Mom wants you downstairs!"

Still no answer. But before Cameron could think of another suitably derogatory remark, the door opened, and there Cindy stood.

Cameron's mouth dropped open. She backed away, turned, and ran.

A few seconds later, Cindy glided down the stairs. All conversations stopped in mid-sentence, some in mid-syllable. Every eye fastened on her.

As she had promised, she was wearing the dress. But she thought she deserved to be comfortable while wearing it, so she had made some slight alterations. While everyone else was out, she had her best friend come over, tie the dress to the back of her car, and take it for a little drive. After a while they stopped to rotate the dress. It wouldn't do to be mismatched.

She had removed her earrings, lip rings, nose ring, eyebrow ring, and makeup. She had combed her hair. And she had donned a once-exquisite dress that was now shredded and filthy.

"Good evening, everyone," she said with a smile.

No one responded.

"I'm so glad all of you could come," she went on. "My mother asked me to wear this dress so that you all would know what kind of impression she wanted this dinner party to make."

Everyone turned to stare at Mrs. Winston, who was turning purple with rage. Cindy saw this and decided to carry out her instructions to the letter. "May I get anyone anything? Courtney, dear, I think the gentleman in the corner needs more wine."

Mouth still wide open, moving as if pulled by strings, Courtney stumbled over to the man and took her eyes off Cindy only long enough to fill his glass. With his own eyes locked on Cindy, he emptied it in one gulp.

"I hope you all will excuse me," Cindy went on, "but I feel a bit faint, so I believe I'll go outside for a breath of air. Unless of course you need me to stay, Mother."

Again everyone looked at her mother, as if daring her to say something. She couldn't. Her jaw was clenched so tightly it might have been wired shut. Cindy chose to interpret her silence as permission. She went to the door, opened it, and said, "Have a pleasant evening, everyone. Do enjoy yourselves."

She shut the door behind her, walked to the end of the yard, and lay down in the grass. Her solitude didn't last long, but at least the intruder wasn't her mother.

"That. Was. Epic."

She sat up and looked behind her. A boy about her age stood a few feet away. He wore a dark striped suit, but his shirt's top button was undone. His tie was stuffed in his pants pocket.

"Thanks," she said. "Who dragged you here?"

"My dad. His company wants to merge with your mom's company, so he's here discussing amortization or something else I'm supposed to find riveting. At least he was. When I left, everybody was talking about you."

"And you didn't want to stay? Whatever they're saying, it must be scintillating."

The boy snorted. "Like all my dad's friends, they were proving Kierkegaard's axiom: 'People demand freedom of speech to make up for freedom of thought, which they avoid.'"

Cindy was astounded. "You read Kierkegaard?"

"Yeah. He's the one person who speaks most clearly to me. Except maybe for Spinoza."

She closed the distance between them with a few strides. "I'm Cindy."

"I know," he said, shaking her outstretched hand. "Your mom's got a lot to say about you. I'm Darren."

They stayed outside and talked for hours. No one else came out to get either of them, and after a while people stopped looking at them through the window. Cindy knew her mother would go no further than bemoaning her disgraceful stunt while her guests were present, but once everyone left, there would be a war such as had never been seen in the Kingdom of Winstonville.

That was okay. Part of her looked forward to it.

Cindy and Darren were looking up at the stars and speculating on how many people would want Copernicus arrested if he were alive today (for having the nerve to say the universe did not revolve around them) when the door opened and Darren's father emerged. He said nothing, but stepped off the porch and stared at them.

Through the open door, they heard the clock chime midnight.

"Larkschmidt," Darren said. That was one of the nonsense oaths he liked to think up in lieu of swearing, which he considered a sign of low intellect. "I gotta bail."

He had shoved his hands in his pockets to warm them. He took off running and his tie fell out of his pocket. Cindy picked it up and shouted, "Wait!" But he was already in his car. He started the engine, rolled down the window, and yelled, "You coming?"

She started to make a joke, but glanced back at the house and saw her mother marching toward her. That was all the incentive she needed. She ran around to the passenger's side and got in. Darren's father had only enough time to exclaim, "What in the...?" before they sped off.

266

"So now what do we do?" Cindy asked. "I'm guessing this isn't your car."

"Nah, it's my dad's. I've got my own, but he insisted I ride with him so I couldn't sneak out early. He does that often enough I finally had my own key made, in case it ever got so bad I wouldn't care if he found out. We can drop this one off at my house and take mine. Your mom was sucking up to him all night. I'm sure she'd love to give him a ride."

"Definitely. There's nothing she likes better than a captive audience."

"I keep a little place my dad doesn't know about," Darren said. "It's where I go to get away from him and generally decompress. You can crash there tonight if you want. It's got all the amenities. You know, walls, a roof, a door. Maybe after your mom's had some time to cool down, she won't rip into you so hard."

"Thanks for the thought, but she doesn't cool down. She keeps the fire stoked. I've seen her do that for weeks."

"So what do you want to do?"

"I know we're gonna have a knock-down drag-out. It's been brewing for years. I think the best thing to do is get it over with. So maybe we could just hang at your place for a while and then go back. We didn't finish our discussion, and it's a pretty safe bet your dad's never going to let you see me again."

"Who says he has to know?"

"What?"

Darren took a deep breath. "Okay, here it is. I've got a trust fund that matures on my next birthday. That's in a few weeks. I'm the only one who can claim the money, and it doesn't matter where I am when I do it. I was planning on taking off the minute I had it, but I figure I might as well go now. I've got some money saved up in a regular account. So if you can tell me honestly you want to go home, I'll take you back and that'll be that. But the deal is, I don't want that to be that."

"That's perfect!" Cindy said. "I've got some money saved up too. Enough to live on for a while. I've been working as much as possible to keep myself out of the house. I just have to ask you one thing."

"And that is?"

"What are your feelings about Ohio? I'm going to college there in the fall."

"Never been there, but that's a point in its favor."

Neither of them ever returned home. However, their disappearance did not overly concern their families. As much as her mother and his father hated to admit it, they both knew their offspring were pretty good at looking after themselves.

And Cindy and Darren lived a while after.

POCKET WATCH

As always, there was a pile of presents under the Christmas tree. As always, most of them were for Gina. As always, she ran down the stairs and went straight for the largest one.

Her parents, Roger and Sharon Walker, trudged blearily into the living room as she ripped off the last of the paper. On her way down the hall to the stairs, she stopped long enough to pound on their door and yell, "Wake up! Wake up! It's Christmas!" They got up, got dressed, and made it down the stairs on autopilot.

They woke up once they got into the living room, since Gina had thoughtfully turned on all the lights in the living room, the dining room, the kitchen, and her brothers' rooms. Her brothers were used to this by now, so the rest of the family was spared their choicer complaints.

Roger squinted at the clock on the opposite wall. "4:17. She let us sleep in this year."

Sharon gave him a backhand slap on the arm, but she knew he was right. She still remembered the year before last, when they finally got her to bed sometime after eleven. They even sang her to sleep in a two-part melody, and were themselves serenaded by the sound of her tiny fists pounding on their door at 3:23, a record they hoped would never be broken. They had actually thought being awakened in the middle of the night would be a thing of the past once she was out of diapers. How wonderfully foolish they had been.

But they saw Gina light up like the tree and forgot how tired they were. Her brothers had staggered into the room just in time to see it.

"A Polly Pocket dollhouse!" Gina squealed. "You found it, you found it! Who found it?"

"It was a relay," Sharon replied. "None of us had any idea where to find it, so we switched off until one of us got lucky."

"That would be me," said one of the brothers.

"Thanks, Hans," she beamed.

He smiled back. "Anytime."

His real name was Theodore. He and Bruce both played college football, and when they were dressed in what they slept in, identical gray sweatshirts and sweatpants, they reminded Gina of the Saturday Night Live characters Hans and Franz.

"Why did you want a Polly Pocket dollhouse, anyway?" Bruce asked. "They haven't advertised those on TV since I was your age."

"That's why I wanted it. The stuff they have now is all dumb. One time I was talking to Aunt Margaret and she told me she had one of these and she said how cool it was and she's my favoritest aunt and I wanted it."

That sounded reasonable if you lived with a nine-year-old. "I see," he said.

"Can I take it up to my room?" she asked.

"Of course, sweetie," Sharon said, "but don't you want to open your other presents?"

"I'll do it later."

She ran up the stairs, clutching the box to her.

None of them expected that. She said "I'll do it later" on a daily basis, always in response to a request to clean her room or do her homework or wash the dishes. But a child *never* turned down an invitation to open presents. That broke one of the Cardinal Rules of Childhood.

Their confused looks followed her up the stairs. When she was in her room, Roger glanced at the clock and said, "Well, I guess I should get ready."

"And just where do you think you're going?" Sharon said.

"I have to get to the lab. You know we're at a critical phase of the work."

"You're *always* at a critical phase. How many critical phases can there be?"

"When you're trying to prove conclusively the existence of gravitons? A great many, thank you very much."

Gina heard the latest round of fighting start up and softly closed her door. Hans and Franz also made a discreet exit. Their parents were getting pumped up, but not in a good way.

"Roger, if these particles exist, they're not going anywhere. It's *Christmas*. Surely you can wait until tomorrow to probe the mysteries of the universe."

"Sharon, we've been all through this—"

"And you still don't get it! Roger, the Superconducting Supercollider is not your home. Your home is here, with your family. But that thing sees more of you than we do."

"Honey, the research will be completed soon. And when it is—"

"And when it is, you'll find another problem you absolutely have to solve. And then another, and then another, and then another. It's always the same."

"Not this time. After this I'll take some time off. I promise."

"You always promise. But you never do."

"Sharon, you just don't understand how important this work is."

"You're right. I don't. I don't understand how a collection of subatomic particles can be more important to you than your wife and your sons and your daughter. But there's one thing you'd better understand. Go ahead, discover that gravitons are out there. But if you keep this up, one day you're going to discover that we won't be here."

She marched to the bathroom and slammed the door behind her. That always made him wince, even though he had lost count of the number of times they'd had this argument, or one very much like it, and it always ended the same way.

He had to make her understand. It would be different this time, really it would. The completion of this project would make his reputation and his career. In the meantime he couldn't afford to let up for a moment.

Roger had recently been named director of the facility. That had been the happiest day of his life, but his new title came with a price. Being a researcher was a lot like being a gunslinger. When you were at the top, everyone else was always looking for an opportunity to take you down. He could not let that happen. He had to hold on to his position. He owed it to his family. Yes! He was doing all this for them. One day they would understand that. One day everyone would understand. One day he would be vindicated for all the work he had done, all the long nights alone at the lab. All the times Sharon sat up waiting for him so she could scold him yet again. All the times he broke a promise he made to Gina...

He snapped out of his reverie and hurried up the stairs for his coat and keys. Now was not the time for recriminations. There was work to be done.

He ran out of the house, jumped in his car, and drove as fast as he dared. At this hour on Christmas morning, the odds were remote that there would be any police along his route, and time was critically short. The Atlas Project waited.

Thinking up names for projects was a tricky business. It couldn't be anything obvious, either to the public, most of whom believed all this theoretical stuff was a waste of their tax dollars, or to the legions of competing researchers, who fought like piranhas for a piece of the shrinking grant pie. The slightest edge would be exploited without hesitation.

At the same time, the name couldn't have any kind of military implication. That was why grandiose names suggested half-jokingly, such as Project Valhalla or Project Liberation, were rejected. The close relationship between scientists and the military made the average person uneasy. Not without reason, Roger had to admit. At the moment, names from classical mythology were in vogue, and naming a gravity project for the god condemned to carry the world on his shoulders for all time was appealing.

Ten minutes later, Roger pulled up to the gate. The guard was not in the booth (*because he's at home with his family*, Sharon piped up in his head), so he swiped his keycard through a slot just under the window and the gate slid back on its tracks. He parked in his designated space, walked through a deserted office building, used his keycard again to activate a restricted elevator, and rode down. A long way down. It had been constructed a kilometer underground, to minimize interference from cosmic radiation and everything the people on the surface were doing.

The doors slid open. There, in its immensity, was the Supercollider.

Roger never got tired of looking at it. The outermost part, the circumference collider ring, was nearly ninety kilometers around.

The whole thing had been built under sixteen thousand acres of land in central Texas.

Congress cut off funding for the project after construction had already begun. It sat unfinished for twenty years, having to wait for a president who understood and appreciated the value and beauty of science to revive the project and authorize its completion. Who knew what could have been accomplished in all that time? It made him angry whenever he thought of it.

No one else was here. Perfect. He would get a jump on everyone.

He had no idea how long he'd been working—he always lost track of time when he was here, as Sharon never tired of reminding him—when something odd happened.

As usual, he accelerated a stream of protons around the track of the cyclotron until their velocity was close to the speed of light, and slammed them into the target. The usual batch of superheavy particles was created, only to wink out of existence within a few millionths of a second.

This time, not all the energy released by the initial impact could be accounted for in this way. There was a tiny bit extra, not even enough for a few stray electrons. But...

What had he heard at that symposium on dark matter? It had been discovered that there was far more mass in the universe than what could be seen, but nobody knew where all that extra mass could be hiding. The prevailing theory was that neutrinos were not completely massless, as had always been believed.

The people who launched the Atlas Project had thought of that, so apparatus were set up to detect neutrinos. There was not a peep out of them.

But if neutrinos were not massless, then the other nonhadrons (the family of particles to which neutrinos belonged) would not be massless either.

That included gravitons, if they existed.

And it now seemed they did.

He recorded everything in exacting detail. It was not conclusive evidence, but there was no other explanation. Until somebody came up with one, that was good enough, especially because in many cases no one ever did.

The discovery of the method of promulgation of gravity was a fair day's work, he decided. He put everything back the way it was, locked up, and went home.

For once he was leaving work and couldn't wait to see Sharon. He could just imagine the look on her face when he told her he had solved the mystery of the most elemental force in the universe. He had secured his place at the top of the facility's pecking order for all time, and he would probably be in contention for a Nobel Prize.

All things considered, he thought, there were worse ways to spend Christmas.

"And *you* didn't want me to go to work today." After he recounted the day's events, he would tack that on at the end for good measure. He said it out loud in the car, just to see how it sounded. He liked how it sounded.

He walked in the front door. Sharon was not in the living room, which meant she had cooled off a bit. He was almost disappointed; he had wanted her to be in a perfect fury when he made his announcement. That would make his victory all the sweeter.

On his way to the dining room, he heard a commotion upstairs. From the sound of it, everyone was in Gina's room. He went up to see what was up.

They were clustered around Gina's dollhouse. It was on the floor, and they were staring down at it.

"What's going on?" he asked, and they all jumped.

"Daddy," Gina said in a terrified whisper, "it's being weird."

"What do you mean, weird?"

"Go ahead, honey," encouraged Sharon. She was stroking Gina's hair but glaring at him. "Tell Daddy what you mean."

He glared back at her. He had seen that look in her eyes before, and there was no mistaking its meaning. Whatever was going on, she was saying it was his fault. How that was possible, he had no clue. He hadn't even been here. But he had to hear Gina out.

"I was playing with my dollhouse," Gina said. "I had it on my table. The table broke under it."

"Well...it was an old table, honey. We'll get you—"

"Hans and Franz heard the noise," Gina went on. "I was trying to pick up the dollhouse but I couldn't move it. It was too heavy."

Roger's stomach contracted into a knot. "Too...heavy?"

"Uh-huh. So they tried to pick it up."

"The thing felt like it weighed four hundred pounds," Theodore said. "It took both of us just to set it upright. And it's getting heavier by the minute. We tried to pick it up a little while ago and we couldn't budge it."

"Okay, all right, very funny," Roger said and forced a chuckle from a mouth full of cotton. "You're playing a trick on old Dad, that's it. You had me going for a while, but you couldn't—"

As he said this, he walked to the dollhouse and tried to lift it. It might as well have been nailed to the floor. He even looked for nails, still hoping this was an early April Fool's joke but knowing it wasn't.

"Bruce," Sharon said, still staring at Roger, "tell your father what you said when you tried to pick it up."

The color drained out of Roger's face. He knew what was coming.

"I was saying it was like that episode in *Star Trek*," said Bruce, "or whatever show it was, where everything got super-heavy because the gravity was different."

Because the gravity was different.

Roger went numb and had to sit on Gina's bed. Sharon stood over him and leaned down until their noses were almost touching.

"Roger?" she said in an artificially sweet voice. That did not last long. "What...did...you...*do?*"

What did I do? Nothing much. I opened a pocket of supergravity in our nine-year-old daughter's Polly Pocket dollhouse, that's all. By the way, did you change your hairstyle? It looks great.

"I...I...I..." Was this really the moment Roger had been anticipating a few minutes earlier? He swallowed, and in a defeated, mechanical voice he told her everything that had happened.

"And these escaped gravitons," she said when he finished. "I don't suppose you know where they could have gone?"

"Uh...well...neutrinos and other such particles...they don't interact much with normal matter, so they can pass through miles of solid rock."

"Do they just keep going? Or do they stop somewhere?"

"Well...once they've passed through a certain number of molecules, eventually they will collide with something, and then they stop."

"And then they stop," she repeated. "And you said that gravitons, if they're real, would behave in much the same way, did you not?"

He looked at the floor and nodded weakly.

Sharon lifted his face to hers, forcing him to meet her eyes. "So is it possible that you let loose some of these gravitons, and they traveled up through the ground and into our house—the house you insisted we buy because it's so close to the Supercollider—got as far as Gina's dollhouse, and stopped?"

Roger heard his own voice as though it came from another room. "That is theoretically possible, yes."

"And now, theoretically, they're trapped in there. Increasing its gravity. How long are they going to keep that up?"

That he didn't know. He opened his mouth to say as much when he was interrupted by a loud cracking noise. The dollhouse was beginning to collapse in on itself, and the floor was collapsing under its weight.

Roger knew what was next. It would break through to the first floor, and keep going. By now the house must have weighed tons. So much mass in such a small object would be too much for the floor and the ground. It would keep falling until it reached the center of the Earth.

What would it do then?

There were several possibilities, none of which boded well for this little planet. As hard and solid as it seemed to the humans that walked its surface, the Earth was held together by the force of its own gravity, which was barely strong enough to do the job.

If its gravity were disrupted...

All these thoughts went through his head in a fraction of a second. He flung himself onto the dollhouse just before the floor gave way, in a desperate attempt to stop what he had started.

It fell through the second and first floors. Roger Walker, physicist, would-be gunslinger, and belated family man, fell with it.

Keeping a safe distance, his wife and children looked down into the tunnel that was bored through the earth, and knew they were looking at the way Roger had chosen to write his epitaph.

For the latter half of his life, he had ignored them because he couldn't give up his work. As a consequence of his work, he gave up his life to save them.

All things considered, he might have thought, there were worse ways to go.

END OF THE ROAD

Jason Rimsdale was ending his night in the usual way: swallowing the last bite of a deep-dish everything-on-it pizza, chasing it down with the last swallow of his second bottle of beer, watching the last few minutes of *Star Trek Voyager*, and wondering how much time he would have to spend doing Klingon calisthenics before he looked good enough to have a shot at the gorgeous crew member who was known as Seven of Nine. She was human but had spent almost her entire life as a member of the Borg, a cybernetic species that had designations instead of names. He caught a glimpse of himself in the mirror and saw the answer to his question. *In your dreams, petaQ.*

At the ripe old age of twenty-seven he was already going to seed. The only part of his body with any definition was his sizeable gut. This was no surprise to him, since pizza and beer were pretty much what he lived on. Still, it wasn't the best sight to be confronted with every day.

It took half a bottle of Pepto Bismol, but he finally managed to get to sleep. When he woke, he felt surprisingly good.

He switched on his bedside lamp, got up, and trudged to the bathroom. He was almost there when he noticed it was still dark outside.

There were occasions when he woke up in the middle of the night, but it was always because he had rented a little too much beer and it was now past due. This time, his bladder was empty.

It was an unusual occurrence, but not one he needed to obsess over, so he went back to bed and turned off the lamp. He wondered what time it was, but his clock's display was dark.

He nudged the nightstand out from the wall and felt behind it for the clock's cord. Still plugged in.

The power must have gone out sometime during the night. No big deal. Except his clock would be blinking, and his lamp still worked, and his air conditioner was still humming. Good thing. Otherwise the Dallas heat would have woken him.

Okay, a circuit in the clock burned out or something, he thought. *I'll run out in the morning and get a new one. Problem solved.*

He lay back down, but an hour later he was still awake.

He had never had a problem with insomnia, especially not since he'd begun his nightly drinking ritual. He had found that if he was still sober when he went to bed, he would think only about how much he didn't want to go to work the next day, but if he was buzzed (or better yet, plastered) then his thoughts were much more interesting. Especially the ones that involved the college girls in the apartment down the hall. But now he was awake, it was nighttime, and he was stone sober.

That problem was also easily solved...no, it wasn't. He had finished off the last of his sleeping aid.

He decided to go for a drive. Since there wouldn't be any traffic to speak of, he figured that would calm him. He dug out a t-shirt and jeans from his hamper, shoved his feet into a pair of ancient Nikes, grabbed his keys, and left. He lingered for a moment, as he often did, at the apartment across the hall and four doors down, where the coeds lived. But this was not the thing to do if he wanted to relax, so he continued out to the parking lot.

Soon he was on Interstate 45, heading south. More than once he had seriously considered getting on this road and not stopping until he got to Houston, where his ex-girlfriend had moved after she dumped him. True, it was a five-hour drive, but it wasn't as if he had many other places to go. That, he now remembered Rachel telling him, was a big part of the problem. His life was going nowhere, and that was exactly where he seemed to want to be. If that worked for him, fine. It didn't work for her.

He wondered idly how far he could get before he would have to turn around, go back home and get ready for work.

Then it hit him: *Why?*

He worked as a stocker at a Home Depot three miles from his apartment. A dead-end job to go with his dead-end life. Everything was the same now as it had been five years ago, when he graduated from college. Boy, was that money well spent.

The fact was that he was deluding himself if he thought anyone would care if he didn't show up. They could hire a monkey to do what he did. The manager would probably think the monkey did a better job.

Jason had once looked Rachel up in yellowpages.com and gotten her address and home number. He never worked up the nerve to write or call, but he thought that for once he should take responsibility for his own fate. Now was as good a time as any.

Maybe he should start waking up in the middle of the night more often. He felt like a whole new person. Maybe it was the night air, or the fact that he was actually able to drive, unimpeded by Dallas' near-constant gridlock. Whatever the reason, he intended to savor it. He set out with a full tank, which by his estimate should get him as far as Conroe, thirty miles or so out of Houston.

Was this it? After all the time he'd spent fantasizing about it, was he really going to go down there and try to win her back?

Yes, he was. He was unclear for the moment as to exactly *how* he was going to do this, but he was going to all the same. And five hours should be enough time to come up with a workable plan.

The problem would be her parents. Her goodbye speech included the information that she had gotten a job as an investment counselor at Morgan Stanley and would live at home until she saved up enough to put a down payment on a house. He knew her parents would have been delighted to take her in, and he had no trouble imagining them repeatedly telling her that leaving that no-account bum was one of the smartest things she had ever done.

He was in no position to disagree. If he pulled up in their driveway, his Chevy Impala would take one look at her father's BMW Roadster and die of shame.

Obviously he needed a supplemental plan. But what?

Stability was the way to go here. He would have to get a job and find a place to live. But where would he stay while he was job hunting? He didn't know anyone else in Houston.

Okay, maybe I should have thought this through better. But something will come together. I know it will.

He decided the best thing to do was wait until he got there and do a little recon. It shouldn't be too hard to find an apartment complex with vacancies, and as long as he wasn't too picky about what part of town it was in (as if he ever had been), he probably had enough in the bank for two or three months' rent. As for a job, there had to be lots of places that could use a college-educated monkey. He would just leave out the part about having gone to college, for all the good that had ever done him.

After a few months with a home and gainful employment, he would go and see Rachel. During that time he would select and perfect his approach.

Maybe, if she's still single. What if she's found someone else by then? What if she's got someone else now?

He rapped his knuckles against his right temple, hoping his brain would get the message and lay off the negative thinking. That wouldn't help anything.

One step at a time. Think happy thoughts. That's the ticket.

Satisfied that he had at least the beginnings of a Master Plan, he settled back and emptied his mind of everything except the road unfurling beneath him. There was nothing else that required his attention, not even any other cars.

He saw no road signs either, apart from the ones marking Exit 265 or whichever number the exit was. There was nothing around, anywhere. No cars, no houses, no buildings. If he had only this highway for evidence, he could easily believe he was the last person on Earth.

Which meant that hot cheerleader who was a year ahead of him in high school would have to go out with him. Or would he have to wait for hell to freeze over too? Ahh, forget it.

Everything was harder to see at night, but why was it still night? He had gone to bed at one o'clock and had to have been asleep at least an hour before he woke up. He tried for another hour to get back to sleep before he gave up. His gas tank had been full, and the needle now flirted with the E. That meant he had driven about two hundred fifty miles. He was in no hurry and he wanted to maximize his gas mileage, so he kept his speed around sixty, meaning he'd been driving for four hours. By now he should at least be seeing the first tendrils of dawn creeping over the horizon. But it was still pitch dark. No sun—and no stars.

The sight of stars was a rarity in Dallas. Out here, with no towns of any size for miles around, the sky should have been liberally sprinkled with stars. It was not.

It was time to get his bearings as well as gas, so he got off at the next exit. The pump had no card reader, and no sign that said "Please pay before filling." Weird, but it made no difference. After he filled his tank, he went inside to pay and to ask the clerk where he was. This last part turned out not to be as easy as one would assume.

The man behind the counter was laboriously restocking the cigarette display. He was tall and lanky, with leathery skin, a wisp of white hair, and arms so long that when they were at his sides, his fingertips brushed his knees. He wore a faded chambray shirt and dark blue overalls.

Straight out of Rubesville, Jason thought. Still, those arms must come in handy for reaching the high shelves. He stood at the counter, waiting for the man to notice he had a customer. He did not.

"Excuse me?"

"You know," the man said without turning around, "I get more customers with these babies than with anything else." He was apparently referring to the cigarettes, which might have explained why he had so many that they took up almost the entire back wall.

"Good for you. Listen—"

"Good for me? I suppose so. Depends on your point of view. 'Course, the customers might tell you differently, if they could."

The cackle that followed indicated that the man found this very funny. Jason found it a bit unnerving. He found this man unnerving. He had to get what he came for and get out, so he asked his question before the man could say anything else.

"Can you tell me where I am?"

"You're on the highway."

Great. A wiseguy. "Yes, I know that. But I haven't seen any signs for a long time, so I was wondering—"

"Don't need any signs. Everyone comes by here, sooner or later."

"Huh? Look, all I want to know is what city is near here. Is it Conroe?"

"Nope."

"Huntsville?"

"Nope."

"Centerville?"

"Nope."

There was a lilt in the man's voice; he seemed to be enjoying this. Jason was not so amused. He gripped the counter tightly and spoke in a low voice, trying to keep his cool. "Okay, I'm not near Conroe, and I'm not near Huntsville. Where am I?"

"You're at my station."

Gad! "How far is Houston? I'm on my way there."

"Not anymore."

"What do you mean, not anymore? I know for a fact Houston is on Highway 45."

"Maybe. But this ain't Highway 45."

"That's impossible. I—"

"Don't tell me what's impossible, sonny." The man turned from the cigarettes and stared at Jason with startlingly bright hazel eyes. "I been at this here station a long time, and this station's always been on this here highway. And this highway ain't no 45."

Jason opened his mouth to argue, but stopped himself. The man could be right. If nothing else, that would explain why he hadn't seen any signs. He did have a tendency to zone out while he was driving, and on the outskirts of Dallas there were half a dozen highways curving every which way. It was possible he had gotten on the wrong one.

Wonderful. Absolutely freaking wonderful. I've been on the wrong freaking highway for two hundred and fifty freaking miles. There's no telling where I am now. This freak isn't going to tell me anyhow. I'm not sure he even knows. From the look of him, he comes from one of those especially close families.

Only one thing for it. He had to go back the way he came. Retrace his route. All two hundred fifty miles of it. And when he got back to Dallas, he would just go home and go to bed. Sweeping Rachel off her feet could wait.

Frustrated and shaken, he walked out of the station without paying. The man watched him go and went back to his stacking.

Jason got in his car, started the engine, and studied the feeder road for a moment. A hundred yards up from the station was an intersection. He could make a U-turn there, so he did. There was no light at the intersection, probably because there was never enough traffic to necessitate one. Just a stop sign. He paused long enough to make sure no one else was coming, then turned left under the overpass, left again on the other side, and was soon back on the highway.

In the absence of any other markers, he would know he was going the right way because the exit numbers would increase instead of decrease. The last one had been 217. The next one would be 218. Simple. He felt better already.

After about five minutes, the next exit sign came into his field of vision.

Exit 216.

It wasn't possible! He was going north now! Or whichever direction was the opposite of the way he'd been going!

He had to wait almost ten minutes before he saw another exit.

It was exit 215.

He was still going the same direction. He had no idea how, but he was.

Whatever had happened, he had to fix it. He veered off onto the exit and found himself on a road that ended a short distance ahead, with one of those brightly-colored signs informing him that he could only go left. Right or straight ahead was out.

That was fine. He most definitely wanted to go left, which he did. The road made a graceful curve to the left. Even though he had no choice but to follow it, and it seemed to be taking him the way he wanted to go, he inched along, watching his surroundings with the utmost care. Whatever happened the last time was *not* going to happen again.

He got back on the highway and stayed in the right lane, never taking his eyes off the shoulder. There was no way he would miss the sign. He kept his speed at sixty, knowing that at this rate he would see it in about ten minutes.

Ten minutes passed. No exit.

Fifteen. Still no exit.

Was he going faster than this when he came to the last exit? Probably. He had been so anxious to get off that road that he hadn't watched his speed. But now, with the first gnawings of real fear eating their way up and down his spine, his eyes darted between the speedometer and the shoulder.

After another ten minutes, a sign appeared at the edge of his headlight beam. His foot eased off the accelerator and he leaned over to get a good look. This had to be the right way. *Had* to be. There were no other roads on that feeder. There was no possible way he could have gotten confused.

The signpost did not agree.

Exit 214.

He pulled off onto the shoulder. Swept along in rolling tides of confusion, frustration, rage, and despair, he gripped the steering wheel, squeezed his eyes shut, and prayed for a break. Something. Anything.

Later he opened his eyes, his mood still as dark as the sky. Perhaps one would change with the other.

Unable to think of any other course of action, he turned off the engine, put the seat back, and settled in to wait for the sunrise that should have come already but couldn't possibly be much longer.

A nap was what he needed. He hadn't slept much tonight and he was exhausted, emotionally and physically. By the time he woke up, the sun would be high in the sky. Then he'd go somewhere and get exact directions. A gas station, a supermarket, a police station. He would even call a cab if he had to. Hang the cost. And he would just leave his car here. If it got towed, so what? He couldn't believe anyone would want to steal it, but if they did they were welcome to it.

That was the plan. It seemed serviceable enough. Of course, that was probably only because he had most likely lost his mind, but he'd been drowning his brain cells in alcohol for years. How many could he have left?

He needed a nap. He didn't get it.

It was rare that he ever got as tired as he was now, and when he did, he was out three seconds after his head hit the pillow. Maybe he was overtired and couldn't sleep because his nerves were frayed. That was reasonable, but it didn't help him. And he was long past reasonable—by now, about three hundred miles past it.

After what seemed like two hours but was only about forty minutes, he sat up and raised his seat. Not going anywhere wasn't getting him anywhere. He had to keep driving. There was the possibility, however slight, that he would get lucky and come across a highway he knew.

He started off again and sped up until he was doing eighty, actually hoping to get pulled over. He would have gone even faster, but his car would not.

Every so often he checked his rearview mirror, looking for flashing lights, but there were none. *Just my freaking luck. The one time I want a cop and there's none in sight. I can't catch a break.*

Most of these exits had no gas stations or much of anything else, and the exits themselves were getting farther and farther apart. At his present speed it still took fifteen minutes to reach the next one. Nothing. Twenty-two minutes later he reached Exit 212. Thirty-one minutes after that, Exit 211.

Exit 210 had a station. Maybe he could use their phone and call AAA.

He pulled in, jumped out, and ran into the store. What he saw brought him to a screeching halt just inside the door.

It can't be.

It was.

The man behind the counter was reading a newspaper. Unnaturally long arms held the pages scanned by the bright hazel eyes. A page was flipped, and the displaced air played with a wisp of white hair. When the man shifted in his chair, dark blue overalls revealed a bit more of a faded chambray shirt.

An identical twin of the man at the other gas station would have been bad enough. But—the fact that it was blatantly impossible notwithstanding—it was the *same man.*

The man looked up from his paper. What he said was just ordinary enough to be terrifying.

"Wondered when I'd see you again."

A thousand questions formed in Jason's screaming mind, queueing up in his dry throat. He asked none of them. He backed out of the store, ran back to his car, revved it up, and peeled out of the station, nearly taking out one of the pumps.

As before, he could make a U-turn a little way up. He did, knowing what he would do if it didn't work.

An hour later he had his answer, in the form of the sign reading Exit 209.

All right. If that was how it was going to be, he was done playing by the rules.

He drove onto the shoulder, made sure no one was coming, then turned the wheel to the left as hard as he could. One good thing about his car was its small turning radius. A moment later he was driving the wrong way, but for him it was the right way.

He flipped on his brights so that if he did see another car, he would have plenty of time to get out of the way.

When all else fails, cheat.

Those were generally not the best words to live by, but one way or another he was getting off this highway.

Before he saw the back of the previous exit sign, he was able to figure out the reason for the absence of stars. They were hidden behind clouds that had gotten weary of holding up their million tons of rain and finally let loose.

He had to slow to thirty and turn his wipers on full blast, but it did little good. If he stayed on the road he might not see an oncoming car until it was too late, so he eased onto the shoulder to wait. Blinding downpours like this were a regular feature of Texas summers, but they seldom lasted long. Not five minutes later, this one stopped as quickly as it started. He waited another couple of minutes to be sure it wasn't just taking a breather, then resumed his course in a considerably better mood.

The sun still hadn't made its appearance, but this no longer bothered him. It would even be all right if it was still dark when he got back home. He could crawl back into bed and forget this night ever happened.

No cars were in sight. Feeling cheery and a little reckless, he sped up to sixty. When he slammed on the brakes it wasn't because of an oncoming car. It was because of the signpost he was about to pass.

The one reading Exit 208.

It was on the right side of the road, as though he were going the same direction as before.

Could he have gotten turned around in the rain? Impossible. But how much of what had happened tonight was possible? Not a whole heck of a lot.

What should he do now? Even if he seemed to have an unaccountable surplus of time, he was running out of options. All he could do was drive. But for how much longer?

Quite a while longer, it seemed. Not all the weirdness was outside his car. He had driven more than four hundred miles since he filled his gas tank, but it was still half full.

A long-buried memory leaped to the front of his mind. Something his physics professor had said one day in class. That he remembered anything about his physics class was incredible enough, but this one thing had a macabre relevance to his present situation.

Relativistic dilation, the professor had called it. Einstein had shown that the closer you get to the speed of light, the more time slows down. It doesn't really slow down, of course, it just does for you. If you took a near-lightspeed jaunt to Mars and back, and there was a clock on your spaceship, it would tell you the voyage had only taken a few minutes. But anyone waiting for you back on Earth would say you had been gone for decades.

He supposed a science nerd would find that interesting, but why was he thinking of it at all? The professor might as well have been speaking Martian then, and the concept didn't make any more sense now.

But the key word seemed to be *dilation*. He happened to know that word because it was what his pupils had done once after a potent party cocktail. It meant something was getting stretched.

He had noticed almost from the beginning that there were longer and longer stretches between the exits. And this night was stretching on forever—it had now been twelve hours since he left his apartment for what was supposed to have been an uneventful five-hour drive to Houston.

His gas mileage was also stretching out. Four hundred miles on half a tank? Not even the hybrid fuel-cell cars he'd heard about could do that.

He was never going to figure any of this out, and he was past caring, so he simply drove on. Another two hours and twenty minutes brought him to Exit 206.

According to his odometer he'd gone six hundred miles. Only a handful of highways in the world were that long. How had he never heard about this one?

The road must be dilated too. Everything about this place is dilated. So why not me? How come I'm not seven feet tall? And why didn't my car turn into a Cadillac?

It was a good sign that he could laugh at the unfairness of finding himself on an endless highway and getting almost infinite gas mileage, but still having to be the same old person and drive the same old clunker.

A bit more than three hours later he came to Exit 205. This one had a gas station. He still had more than a quarter-tank, but there was no telling how far the next exit was. He had abandoned all hope of getting off this highway, but moving was better than stranded.

Something about that last thought grabbed whatever was left of his attention.

Abandon all hope.

In college he had taken a class in medieval literature with the idea of impressing Rachel. He didn't make it halfway through the course, but he remembered that phrase from Dante's *Inferno*. It was part of the sign posted over the doorway to Hell.

Was that where he was? Fire and brimstone or not, it would make sense. Or maybe he wasn't there yet, but was on the highway that went there. Had he been so inclined, he might have told AC/DC to eat their hearts out.

That made him remember something else his physics professor had said. Stay gone long enough in a dilated frame of reference, and as far as the people you left behind knew, you would be gone forever.

Was he going to be on this highway forever? It was starting to look that way.

That would mean he was...

Whatever and wherever he was, he had a feeling the guy at the station would know.

It was the same man behind the counter. He looked up from his newspaper when Jason entered, but said nothing.

The last time, there were a thousand questions Jason had wanted to ask the man. Now there was only one worth asking. He asked it.

"Where does this highway go?"

The man gave him a slight smile. Apparently he got all kinds of questions and that was one of the few sensible ones.

"Can't tell you that, son. Route's different for everybody. For all I know, the end is too."

Jason nodded. He hadn't really expected a direct answer. And the answer he got reminded him that there was one other question he had to ask. It was unavoidable now.

"I'm dead, aren't I?"

"Yep." Just like that. No explanation, no dramatic scene. It was probably better that way. "Always a shame when I see young fellas like you. Really shoulda taken better care of yourself."

He couldn't argue with that, although he had tried at least a few of the hundreds of times Rachel had told him the same thing.

"So I guess I don't have to pay for my gas?"

"What'd be the sense of that?"

"And I guess I'll see you again, huh?"

"Yep. Whenever you're ready."

Jason walked out. There was nothing else to say.

Back on the highway, he wondered what finally did him in. Heart attack, most likely. That last bout of heartburn had been one too many.

Oh well. It wasn't as if he'd had much to look forward to.

Then he thought of Rachel. The one bit of good fortune in his worthless life. Her father had once said that to him, probably in those exact words, and Jason couldn't help but think how right he had been. How right everyone had been. Especially Rachel, who had tried so hard to see the man he could have been but had still loved the man he was. His darling Rachel.

Except she wasn't his anymore. She hadn't been for a long time. And he was officially and forever out of chances.

But the next man will be better. He'll treat her the way she deserves to be treated. He'll give her everything she should have gotten from me.

His own life was over, but he could hope for the best things for hers. He could wish for her to live as the princess she was. If he had never done anything else for her, at least now, at the end, he could do that.

He passed Exit 199 about seven hours after Exit 200. After that, he chucked his watch out the window. No point keeping time anymore. The good thing was that he didn't really have to watch his gas gauge anymore either.

He looked at the woman in his passenger seat. He couldn't have said exactly when she appeared there, but it didn't matter. All that mattered was that after so many lonely nights watching her on *Voyager*, here she was: Seven of Nine, Tertiary Adjunct of Unimatrix Zero-One, in the Borg-implant-enhanced flesh.

"Where do you think we'll end up?" he asked her. "What happens when we get to Exit 1? Or wherever it is we're going?"

"Speculation is futile," she said. He had always loved the coolly efficient way she had of putting things. "We will see for ourselves when we arrive."

"Yeah, I suppose we will."

They drove another few minutes before he spoke again.

"You know, I never imagined it would end this way."

In reply, she said the only thing a former drone could have said.

"Imagination is irrelevant."

"Yeah. At the end of the road, I guess it is."

He looked at her and smiled. She smiled back.

And they drove on.

THE CRINKLING CURSE

The events of that holiday season occurred long ago, but to this day it is all I can do not to cringe in fear when I see anyone dressed as Santa or—far worse—one of his elves.

I had never been a fan of Christmas to begin with. For most of December there is almost nothing to watch on television except saccharine holiday specials, and it had been the one time of year when it bothered me that I had no family to spend the most important of all family holidays with. By December 26th I reverted to the grateful bachelor.

I had no use for the symbols of the season, so mine was one of only two houses on the block that never sported Christmas decorations. The other was that of my next door neighbor, who was a Jehovah's Witness and did not acknowledge Christmas.

The children on the block regarded me as something of an oddball. They also knew that at the time I was a professor of theoretical physics, so it was great sport for them to besiege me with questions about how Santa was able to make his famous round-the-world flight. If I could crack the secret of his reindeer games, the older ones would tell me, I might be the one to end America's dependence on foreign oil. Maybe I would even win the Dumbbell Prize.

Of course I never gave them the satisfaction of responding to such foolishness. So it happened that one December 23rd, when I went out for a walk, a group of these urchins lay in wait for me. When I rounded the corner they began pelting me with idiotic questions, vulgar parodies of Christmas carols, and hard-packed snowballs.

I was a short distance from my house, so I sprinted from this onslaught. Fortunately I had my garage door opener in my pocket, so as I ran I fished it out of my pocket and stabbed the button.

However, my haste had overridden my powers of observation. The garage door had not fully risen, I did not think to duck under it, and my head collided with its metal base. The force of the impact was sufficient to knock me unconscious. But it did not.

The next instant—by what means I know not—I was transported to a barren Arctic landscape. All about me was snow and ice, but I was not affected by the elements. I was only dimly conscious of the cold, and I did not have to shield my eyes from the glare of the ice reflecting the light of the sun.

But I was acutely conscious of the desolation of my surroundings. My senses detected not a sign of human or animal. Intuition told me this would not change while I stood where I was, so I set off in search of whomever might be hardy enough to call this land home. There was nothing to indicate any direction would be more promising than any other, so I walked in the direction I happened to be facing.

After some little time I began to hear the sounds of industry. There was a hill, roughly ten meters in height, directly in front of me. When I gained its summit I saw all.

Sprawled out before me was a valley. Nestled within it was a small cluster of houses, and I did not doubt this was the only settlement to be found in this remote place.

I cursed my slowness of thought—how could I not instantly have known where I was? There were no colored lights, pine-needle trees, or any other Western symbols of Christmas, but the truth was literally staring me in the face.

Even as a child I had never believed in Santa Claus. But here, in the stark light of the far northern sun, my ignorance was revealed. *For I was standing not more than two hundred meters from his fabled workshop.*

My legs began to carry me down to the wondrous house, even as my mind struggled to absorb the immensity of what I had discovered. But as I drew near, my amazement was supplanted by uncertainty, then fear. I knew the houses to be occupied; I could hear faint scurryings within, but the windows were dark. Now of all times of the year, the community ought to be bubbling with activity. I should have been able to sense the good cheer even from the hilltop. Instead I sensed

293

the opposite. The atmosphere of this place was not one of happiness, but one of menace.

I marshaled my nerve and marched with a bravery I did not feel to the front door of Santa's workshop. The closer I got to the low-arched doorway, the greater my unease became. Even the faint noises I had heard a moment ago had ceased, and no matter how carefully I trod, each step I took seemed to reverberate in the preternatural quiet. Each meter I crossed increased my belief—my *certainty*—that something was waiting for me inside the darkened cottage, and that that something was neither rotund, jolly man nor cheery, industrious assistant, but some malign, unnameable blasphemy that had escaped from some Stygian abyss and conquered this purest and most magical of realms...that it was this thing which had summoned me here, by some unimaginable method and for some unspeakable purpose...

Quickly I bent over, grabbed two handfuls of snow, and slapped them on my cheeks, hoping the shock would restore my reason. Giving in to atavistic fears would achieve nothing.

I felt the pressure of the crumbling snow against my skin, but that was all. It was similar to what I would have felt if I had a mouth full of Novocaine, but otherwise I did not feel numb. I willed myself forward the last few steps, gripped the iron handle, and pulled without hesitation.

The room within was flooded with light and brimming with activity. A score of men with the physical dimensions of children but the facial characteristics of adults, festively dressed and hard at work, manufacturing, wrapping, labeling, and cataloging toys and other small items. They were slender and small, their mien and appearance more Oriental than elvish, and it all combined to create a scene not greatly different from the legendry. And there, seated on a plush chair against the back wall, overseeing all with a seasoned eye, was the great man himself.

When he saw me, he stood. Everyone else paused a fraction of a second to register my presence and went back to their tasks. They forgot about me at once—or so I then believed.

I knew I was to go inside, though no one had said a word to that effect or any other. As I did so, I noticed all the windows were draped with some kind of heavy black paper. I marveled at the opaqueness of the substance; it permitted not a photon of ambient light to penetrate it in either direction. Everyone running to and fro, flowing effortlessly around me as I traversed the room, stirred up faint currents of air, which caused the paper to rustle. That could have been the source of the noises I had heard and mistaken for furtive human movements.

Mr. Claus was regarding me with the utmost seriousness. He did not seem surprised that a stranger was standing in his workshop. Indeed, his expression told me—I would swear to it—that he had *expected* me.

He turned away and walked toward a darkened recess in a far corner of the room, crooking a finger at me. I followed him into the alcove. Two things happened the instant I was inside. The room was flooded with light—I saw now that a room it was, large and sparsely furnished, instead of the hallway it had appeared to be—and the egress through which I had entered the room vanished, so that behind me was a brick wall *where none had been a second earlier.* I even pushed against it, and confirmed that it was as solid as any wall ever constructed in the world of men.

There was no longer any doubt that I had been transposed to some other world entirely. Some alternate dimension, or parallel plane of existence, or some other term I recalled from the pulp science fiction magazines I had read as a child. Whatever the details, I could see clearly that the laws of physics that were unbreakable in my own reality were mere suggestions here, to be observed or ignored according to one's whim.

"How..." I started to ask the obvious question. He held up a black-gloved hand to forestall it.

"You want to know how you came to be here. You believe I can tell you. And you are correct, I can. But be very sure you want to know. I can show you the way back to your home now, and you will be free to continue as before. In the world you know, no time will have passed. You have realized that the power of Santa Claus—the power that children have believed in and sustained for centuries—is real. But it was never intended to bring joy to those who wield it. We who dwell here know the secret of the power because we are cursed. And to know the secret is to know the curse. Therefore choose wisely. I can satisfy your curiosity, but you will never have a restful night's sleep again. Why not simply return to the place you came from, secure in the knowledge that you will never feel the need to lie to your own children, should you choose to have any, about the existence of Santa Claus?"

"You know so much about me," said I, "that surely you know I would spend the rest of my life trying to find this place again, even if it can't be accessed by human means. I would become consumed with it and I would never have another restful night anyway. So I must have the answers only you can give, whatever those answers bring with them."

Mr. Claus nodded soberly. He had hoped I could be persuaded, but had known I could not. He motioned me to a chair with a wave of his arm, and began his tale.

He was born at the end of the third century A.D. in Smyrna, a region of what is now Turkey. While still a young man, he decided to dedicate his life to serving the Church. After taking his holy orders, he was assigned to the parish of a bishop named Nicholas.

Yes, he said when he saw my eyes widen. *That* Nicholas. The shy, humble man who went out by night to leave presents and gold coins at the homes of the poor children of his village, and thus had been the origin of the legend of Santa Claus. He was canonized after his death and forever after had been known as Saint Nicholas, or more colloquially, Saint Nick.

Despite his wealth, Nicholas' lifestyle was modest, even ascetic. He denied himself every luxury in order that he might never lose his empathy for the poverty-stricken masses to whom he ministered. Mr. Claus, inspired by his example, served his own office well—at first— and performed many good deeds.

Though he tried valiantly to maintain the proper focus for his thoughts, he saw himself slowly succumbing to envy, then jealousy, and finally the blackest, most venomous hatred of Nicholas, who seemed until his death to be piously unaffected by the praise continually heaped upon him. But Mr. Claus knew he had to keep a tight rein on his tongue and to permit only humility to be seen in his own visage. Otherwise he risked censure, even excommunication.

The years passed, and day by day he saw himself splitting in half: the man the outside world saw toiling in contented obscurity, disdainful of worldly honor and glory, and the *other* man—his inner self, his true essence. The man who coveted the power of Nicholas' office and the gold in his purse. The man who craved for himself the adulation showered upon the bishop. The man who, one night, lying on his mat in his room while everyone else slept the sleep of the righteous or the ignorant, made a solemn oath that he would do anything that was necessary—*anything*—to obtain what he had come to believe was his by right.

His eyes were closed and his hands clasped, but not in prayer. That activity had long since ceased to be anything more to him than a performance, one to be given only if the audience was important enough.

He opened his eyes a moment later and sat up, aware of a presence standing at his bedside. There was no light, so he could see nothing, but he knew.

"I have heard the desires of your heart," said a soft but resonant voice, "and I have come to help you."

"God?" He no longer even believed in a Supreme Being, by that or any other name, but the word was out before he could stop himself.

"Oh, come now," said the visitor, in a tone that mixed amusement with ageless malice. "Do you truly believe he would bother with one such as you, after all the maledictions you have spoken in your heart against him?"

Mr. Claus sank into his mat, too terrified to speak or move, knowing now that he was in the presence of...the other. (For all his boasting to himself of how composed he would be should he ever actually find himself face to face with...him, he found he could not say his name aloud. He was reluctant even to think it.)

"Do not be afraid," said the being. "Your thoughts are as plain to me as the writings of your holy scriptures are to you. I am not the one whom you rightly fear. I am only his emissary. And you are fortunate indeed, for he has decided to bestow his favor upon you."

"What...what must I do?" asked Mr. Claus in a frightened whisper. He knew the dark one's gifts were never given without a price.

"Anything that is required, of course," said the emissary. "You did say that, did you not?"

"Yes, yes, anything!" exclaimed Mr. Claus, glancing anxiously at his door and the faint light beyond. He had not been overheard.

"The bishop will die in seven days. At that time, the wish that lurks in the deepest recesses of your soul, your so-called 'forbidden desire', shall be granted."

Mr. Claus had not heard that Nicholas was ill. As far as anyone knew, the bishop was in excellent health. But he dared not question the word of his visitor.

He briefly allowed himself to dwell upon that which he did want above all else but had not permitted himself even to think of outside his cell, lest one of these accursedly perceptive monks see it reflected in his face and report him to the abbot, who harbored an unexplained but extreme dislike of him.

Then, though he heard no sound of departure, he knew he was alone once more.

He lay awake for a long time, half of him trying to convince himself that he had been in the grip of a delusion created by his conscience in a final attempt to turn his soul from the path to destruction, the other half counting himself blessed above all others. It was the latter half that emerged triumphant when he was roused for morning vespers.

Basking in the great fortune that would soon be his, he seemed to be a changed man. He carried out his duties with a conscientiousness and ardor he had not been capable of for years. Even Nicholas took him aside and commended him for his reborn industry.

Seven days after the appearance of the emissary, Nicholas took to his bed at the usual hour and died in his sleep.

The next morning, the abbot called a meeting of all the village clergy. By immediate and unanimous consent, they decided Nicholas would have the grandest funeral their cash-strapped parish could manage. Throughout the day, Mr. Claus threw himself with almost maniacal intensity into his work to distract from the considerable effort required to mask his glee.

The herald returned during the first watch of the night, but only long enough to deliver a cryptic message. "Your new existence will soon begin, and will never end. Be watchful."

Mr. Claus tried to figure out what that might mean, but his lack of sleep the night before, combined with the activity of the day, made coherent thought impossible. The next thing he knew, he was being roused from a troubled sleep by two monks standing by his bed. He had not appeared for vespers or for breakfast, so they had entered his cell and spent several minutes trying to wake him before they finally succeeded.

He tried to assure them he was fine, but he had difficulty speaking and he did not feel fine at all. The monks looked him over with worried expressions and told him they would petition the abbot to permit him to remain in bed for the rest of the day.

That was where he remained for the rest of the week. He was afflicted with a strange malady, one that drained him to such an extent he had to have his meals brought to him. The brothers assigned to do this would rush in, drop his tray near his pallet, and hurry out again. They collected it in the same fashion when he was finished. Whatever his sickness was, they were understandably anxious to avoid contracting it, especially now.

Nicholas' funeral service and burial had to be taken care of quickly. The parish was not equipped to handle the crush of mourners that would descend upon it once news of the beloved bishop's passing got out. Also, they had to get the sad duty out of the way so that they could focus on dissuading their parishioners from taking part in Saturnalia, the pagan festival celebrated throughout the Roman Empire at the end of every year.

This was a losing battle. Pagan converts to Christianity brought many of their traditions with them. Saturnalia with its unabashed revelry was among the most popular, and few there were among the general populace who saw any harm in it. The Church fathers were already regarded as a mirthless bunch who did not see why anyone should be permitted to indulge in festivities when they themselves were not, and so their thunderous denunciations of Saturnalia, and just about everything else, were to no avail.

Mr. Claus had been indifferent to the controversy before and was oblivious to it now. His strength slowly returned, but whatever relief this would have brought him was sharply tempered by his alarming increase in appetite. Unable to help himself, he stole into the kitchen one night and consumed enough food to sustain the order for four days. Even then he had to force himself to stop, though his hunger pangs were still acute.

Because his order never kept an excess of food, the depletion of the larder was noticed at once the following morning, and a search was made of all the rooms. His own room was saved for last, because his infirmity placed him above suspicion. When they got to it, they found no food inside.

Nor did they find any man inside. He was not there.

No one had seen him anywhere else on the grounds, and the sight of him up and about would have been remarked upon at once. A second, more thorough search was made, which only confirmed the incredible truth: the wayward priest had vanished without a trace.

He had sneaked back to his cell from the kitchen, crawled into bed, fallen asleep instantly, and awakened elsewhere.

His eyes opened to show him a large room devoid of furnishings. From the amount of light spilling through the windows, he judged that it was midmorning. He sat up, completely disoriented, and looked around. There was a long table on the other side of the room, covered with food—breads, fruits, cheeses, fish, meats, and pastries of every kind, including delicacies he had never seen before. At the sight of the banquet, he ceased to wonder where he was or how he had gotten there. His growling stomach silenced inquiry. He got up and gorged himself.

After an undetermined period of time, the door opened. A few flakes of snow wafted in, and a pile of clothing was tossed in. Whoever it was did not enter, but said, "Put those on and come outside after you have eaten your fill. However long that takes is irrelevant. Time is of no consequence here." Then the door shut.

If he knew nothing else just then, he knew he had no choice but to heed the directive. He resumed eating, scarcely less hungry than when he started. It was as though his body had been hollowed out and his stomach had expanded to fill the void.

When at last he was sated, little more than crumbs were left of the feast. He went over and picked up the clothing that had been left for him: black gloves, black boots, a red cap, and a curious red and black costume with white trim, not very different in appearance from what bishops had been known to wear to observe certain sacraments during the winter months.

He changed as quickly as he could and fearfully stepped out into a howling snowstorm. He stopped just beyond the door and saw, twenty paces away, an imposing figure in a white robe, whose face was hidden beneath a voluminous hood. It was difficult to see in the swirling white tempest, but when it spoke, Mr. Claus heard it clearly. He could not determine whether it was the same messenger that had appeared to him in the monastery, but all things considered, it hardly mattered.

"You will do what the bishop did, and far more," intoned the cloaked figure. "You shall be greater than he ever was. His name was known only in your obscure little corner of Europe, but yours shall be known the world over. His memory will soon fade, but yours shall endure even unto the end of the world."

"How can this be?" he asked.

"Three days hence, as you measure time, will be December twenty-fifth. This shall be your time. In the place you came from, you know it as the Winter Solstice, the apex of the bacchanal you call Saturnalia. You will deliver gifts to the children of the world every year, on the eve of this date. You will enter their homes during the night. You will permit no one to see you."

Mr. Claus understood none of this. Not what he was to do, nor how he was to do it, nor why he was to do it. "How can this be?" he asked again.

"I told you that time is of no consequence here. It is more correctly said that it does not exist here, not as you know it. This is the place of time beyond time, the space between spaces. You were brought here because only here will it be possible for you to do the great work you have been chosen to do."

This was obviously a being of great power, so Mr. Claus feared to tell it that nothing it was saying made any sense. He was perfectly willing to do whatever might be required of him, but he knew he would have to ask forgiveness for his ignorance and plead for an explanation simple enough for his feeble intellect.

"Go back inside," the specter ordered, before he could say anything else, "and you will be shown what you must do."

It was clear he was being dismissed, and he had no wish to tax this being's patience. Fortunately, his years of service to the Church had long habituated him to obedience without comprehension. He hastily backed through the door and shut it in front of him.

He had only been outside a few minutes and had stood only a few inches past the threshold. Yet where he had left silence, he returned to cacophony. The room was now piled floor to ceiling with thousands of objects, none of which he could identify. Two dozen men or more, working at such a blistering pace that his eyes could not track them, were assembling these objects and wrapping them in brightly colored paper of a kind he had never seen.

The men were the size of children, but were clearly not children. They glanced up at him as he entered, but otherwise did not acknowledge his presence for many minutes. He could only stand there, eyes glazed, jaw slack, grasping for the tiniest thing in any of this monstrously weird business that he could wrap his mind around. But the effort was worse than futile. The more he tried, the more lost he became. The only thing he understood was that he had been made an inextricable part of something hopelessly beyond his understanding.

So dazed and overwhelmed was he that he did not immediately notice a rough tugging at his pant leg. Finally he looked down and saw one of the small, silent men holding something up to him. It was a comically thick white beard and mustache with no visible means of fastening. The little man did not speak, but the expression on his face expressed quite plainly that Mr. Claus was to put the thing on, without question and without delay. So he took the beard and pressed it to his face, where it stuck fast. The little man stalked away. Mr. Claus tugged at the beard, gingerly at first, but he soon found that no matter how hard he pulled, he could not remove it.

Another man approached with a large red sack slung over his shoulder, which he dropped on the floor. Mr. Claus bent down to pick it up, noticing that it contained several boxes wrapped in more of the peculiar colored paper. When he stood up again, burden in hand, the wall before him was no longer unbroken. A rectangular hole had been cut out of it, forming a doorway.

Beyond was a darkened room dominated by a coniferous tree two meters high, festooned with green, red, and blue lights; small, vaguely humanoid figurines; and a long, silvery, feathery coil wound around it.

Mr. Claus stood mesmerized by the sight, as beautiful as it was bizarre, until the man kicked him in the shin and pointed impatiently at the aperture. He took an uncertain step in that direction, and the man made shooing gestures with his hands, urging him on. He walked up to the hole, hesitated briefly, and stepped through.

At the instant of transition he felt a flash of searing pain, as if he were being crushed in a giant's hand, and he crumpled to the floor. The agony subsided at once, but like a piece of paper that had been so treated, he felt smaller, weaker, *wadded*.

If he took any time to rest, he might incur the wrath of his inhuman taskmaster. He struggled to his feet and looked behind him, but the place he had just left was gone as if it had never been. He was now in a large house, whose windows showed him it was night here… wherever "here" was. With no idea what to do next, he started to call out, but clamped his mouth shut. For all he knew, he would rouse a demon instead of a man.

Then he remembered the sack he held. He set it down and took out one of the packages. After a moment's thought it occurred to him that since he had been directed to bring these things here, and he had no way to return while they were in his possession, perhaps he was to leave them here. Therefore, because it was the most convenient place, he arranged the boxes around the base of the beautiful tree.

No sooner had he put the last of them under the tree than he became aware of bright light behind him. The doorway had reappeared, with the snowswept cottage beyond. After taking several deep breaths, steeling himself for the pain, he snatched up the empty sack and hurried back through it, looking back only long enough to confirm that the portal, no longer needed, had vanished.

No one here would praise him for a job well done or even tell him what he had done. Another man was there, and another large sack was on the floor in front of him. Mr. Claus picked it up and saw another doorway to another house, with a similarly decorated tree. What he had to do was now obvious.

He hoisted the bundle and stepped through.

"And that," he said to me, "is what I have been doing ever since."

Such a mode of travel made more sense to me than flying reindeer ever had. The reindeer and sleigh were nineteenth-century poetic constructs, but I recognized the "doorway" he had described as the creation of an Eigenspace "warp" or "fold" in the fabric of four-dimensional space-time—like folding a gigantic sheet in half, poking a hole through it near the edge, unfolding the sheet, and seeing the two widely separated holes that, while the sheet is folded, can be traversed instantaneously. Perhaps the sensation of being crushed was a time-independent four-dimensional voyage interpreted by a time-dependent three-dimensional body. The science of quantum mechanics is so weird to the twenty-first-century layperson that a fourth-century priest could scarcely be blamed for ascribing such things to diabolical magic.

"The reason you were always so hungry," I theorized, "is that your body had been transformed. Otherwise, the physical stress of crossing Eigenspace would be fatal. But it still takes so much out of you that you have to consume huge amounts of food to replenish your strength."

"Just so," he said. "It has distended my stomach to these grotesque proportions, but it has sustained me. Do you know the story of Persephone?"

I answered that I did not.

"In Greek mythology, she was the daughter of Demeter, the goddess of plants. She was abducted by Hades and taken to live with him under the earth. A feast had been prepared in her honor, but she refused to eat it. She knew that anyone who ate anything in the kingdom of Hades could never leave it. A nice bit of symmetry, is it not?"

I could see the connection, tenuous as it was. I even thought of suggesting that this might have been Cocytus, which was supposed to be a domain of ice rather than the traditional fire, but the reference would be meaningless. Mr. Claus had lived nine hundred years before Dante wrote his *Inferno*, and he would not believe this place to be the Ninth Circle of Hell any more than I did.

"We can also infer," I said instead, "that the time you pass in each house—in the world we know—doesn't pass here. So you return here from one house, collect more presents, and take them back through the portal to the next house. It seems to you that time passes normally. But if someone had been awake in each house while you were there, and had seen you, and if they had all compared notes, they would say that you had visited all of them *at the same time*. That you were everywhere at once."

"How else could I be expected to deliver presents to all the children of the world in one night?"

How else indeed? The primary reason my parents were never able to persuade me of the existence of the man in the white-trimmed red suit was the absurdity of the method by which he displayed his generosity. I was likewise unimpressed by the requisite appeals to the innocent, eager credulity that only young children can possess, and to that cheap catchall, "magic."

"Are you still visited by the emissary?" I lowered my voice in reflex on the last word, fearing it might appear if it heard me speak of it.

"It remained outside on that first day when it set me to work, and I have not seen it since. I would pray to God never to see it again, if I had the right. I have often wished I could pray for some means by which to escape the fate I have earned."

"An obvious answer occurs to me," I said, "but no doubt it's obvious because it's wrong. Parents are quite capable of giving presents to their own children, and every shopping center in the Western hemisphere boasts its own Santa Claus or Father Christmas or Père Noël. In order to be the true Claus, you've been given great powers. Couldn't you use them to leave this place for good, make a new life for yourself in some far corner of the mortal world?"

"Fool!" he cried. "Can you truly believe I have not tried? That which I do as Santa Claus, I do with the aid of that foul doorway and those mute creatures. I have been given no powers, great or small, and the power to die has been taken from me.

"The door of this cottage is never locked, and the sun never sets here. So one day, who can say how long ago, while those creatures were occupied with their own tasks, I crept outside. I was not concerned that I would freeze to death. I would have welcomed it. So I walked long and long, until I saw a dark speck on the horizon. I drew closer, and I saw that it was another house. Closer still, and I saw it was not another house. It was *this* house.

"There were no landmarks, nothing to tell me that for all my walking I had not succeeded only in tracing out a circle. I turned and ran before anyone who might be looking out the window could sound an alarm. I must have run for kilometers, but I did not tire, and finally I came upon another house. This house.

"I could not escape the truth. I could not escape this house, at least not that way. When I walked in the door a little man handed me another sackful of presents, as if I had not gone anywhere. Which I suppose I had not.

"It was at the moment I lifted the sack that inspiration struck. I knew the portal would open behind me the instant the last present was delivered, so once I had stepped through and the portal had closed, I opened the front door of the house and went outside. But at once I felt myself begin to...*crinkle.* I can think of no other word to describe it. Imagine being a parchment thrown into the fire, charring, blackening, curling, crinkling. There was no fire, but I felt all these sensations, felt them exquisitely. And I was glad of them. Glad, do you hear? Surely it was the Angel of Death, come to claim me at last, now that I was out of that nameless place where he holds no dominion.

"I even wanted to invoke the name of Jesu, that he might watch over me for what little span I had left and thwart the will of the other, who meant to keep me alive, if such you can call it, and in his thrall for all time. But I did not. I could not. I had forfeited all hope of pardon. I knew that and was resigned to it.

"So I closed my eyes, awaiting the end...and opened them here. I was sprawled on the floor, deathly ill, yet not dead. I was alone, and remained so. I lacked the strength or the will to stand, but I felt so near to death that I knew I must be. I waited, waited, but it was no use. In this place beyond time, I was beyond the reach of death.

"Then I saw a table, just like the one I had seen when I first came here, laid with as great a quantity and variety of food. I had no wish to remain so ill and weak if there was to be no hope of release, so I crawled to the table, pulled myself upright, and ate, and ate, and ate. I could no longer even taste it, but I was no less ravenous for it.

"When I had eaten my fill I turned, saw the same portal was again open, and knew there was no alternative. I stepped through and it closed behind me. I set out the presents, it opened again, and I returned.

"Now at last I understand what he meant when he came to me in my cell that first night. In my pride and vanity I believed I deserved everything Nicholas had and more, to be greater than he was in every measure. Now I am cursed to have everything I so foolishly believed I wanted, and to have it forever, in exchange for my soul and my eternal servitude."

While he described his first attempt to leave this cottage, I thought of something that would explain what had happened. A cosmological model of four-dimensional space-time describes it as curving in upon itself. That is, if you travel far enough in any one direction, you will end up back where you started.

According to one class of solutions for Einstein's equations of special relativity, the universe is comprised of twenty-six dimensions, most of them collapsed in upon themselves. Could this be one such dimension? A collapsed (one might even say crinkled) plane of existence, unobservable and undetectable from the vantage point of the one we know, but every bit as real to anyone inside it?

As to what happened the second time he tried to escape, there was an answer for that also, but it was not found in physics.

"You mean to say that you sold your soul to Lu—"

"Do not speak his name!" he shrieked.

"I...I'm sorry," I stammered, recoiling from the force of his terror. "But...but is that what you did? He drew up a contract and—"

He laughed, a rasping, hideous cackle. "How little you know of his ways! But I suppose that is by his design. No, there was no legal transaction. I renounced Christ while I was still a priest in His church. Any soul that has not been given freely to Christ remains the property of the other. Why should he purchase what is already his?"

I was in no mood for theological disputation, so I dropped the subject and said, "I'm sorry for you."

He waved aside my pity. "Being sorry for my lot will not change it."

"This is your curse, then," I said. I needed to understand fully. "You must stay in this place and do his bidding until the end of the world, or you'll crinkle up like burning paper, and yet not die."

"No doubt that is why I am also called Kris Kringle."

I stifled the pedantic urge to point out that the name is an anglicized form of the German word for *Christ-child*. It was possible he had meant the remark as a joke, but I saw little point in asking.

"But can you now tell me," I asked, "how I came to be in this place?"

"Thank you for not assuming I had anything to do with that. But despite what I said to you before, I have no idea. Unless *he* has taken an interest in you."

I felt myself turn as white as Mr. Claus's beard. I had never had any more faith in religion, or in the existence of any of its central characters, than I had had in the existence of the gentleman (or whatever he now was) standing in front of me. But having been proved so thoroughly wrong about the one left me uneasy, to say the least, about the prospect of the other.

"Why would..." My voice came out as a terrified squeak. I cleared my throat and asked, in a slightly less terrified squeak, "Why would he want me?"

"How could I possibly know that?" he shouted.

"Whatever it is, or might be, I don't want to be here when it comes. Send me back now so I can face him on my own ground. I'll even speak a word to him on your behalf." I was babbling, and I knew it.

"I cannot do that," he said.

I was sure I hadn't heard him correctly. "Wh...wh...wha-what do you mean, you can't do that?"

"Were you not listening, fool? I can go only where I am directed, when I am directed. Those little men are the ones who control the gateway. It opens only when they bring me more gifts to deliver."

"Then what if I ask them for help?" That was the one thing I had hoped I would not have to do. I had feared them from the moment I first saw them. They looked mostly human, but that meant nothing. They were not "elves," but I believed them to be something far worse, something that had no name in any human tongue.

"Go ahead, for all the good it will do. What is the year now, by your measure?"

I told him, and he laughed again.

"So I have been here, existing as the embodiment of Christmas, for roughly 1700 years. How time speeds when you are damned! But here, not so. Not only does this sun never set, it has moved not one finger-span in all those centuries. It requires no effort to believe that it will be hanging there, as it is now, when the world has ceased to exist. And when there are no more children, and there is no more use for me, then will I at last be released. As for you, my young seeker," he went on, looking at me in a way that made my every nerve twitch, "there may be a way you can persuade them to help you. Is that what you want?"

In truth it was the last thing I wanted, but I now knew I had no choice. "Yes," I whispered.

"Then face the wall behind you, and name your desire!"

I turned and faced the brick wall, having to beat down the insane but thankfully brief impulse to click my heels together and say "There's no place like home." In a trembling but loud voice I said, "I want to return to my own world!"

No sooner did I speak the last word than a rectangular hole appeared in the wall. On the other side was the workroom, but it was deserted. Empty boxes and miscellaneous things lay scattered about the floor. The machines were idle and silent.

The front door stood open.

I walked through the hole and turned to ask Mr. Claus how I should proceed, but the wall was a wall again. He had not followed me through. I remained in the room for some minutes, unable to retreat, unwilling to advance, unaware of other options.

I realized I was actually waiting for one or more of the dreaded little creatures to come and find me here, and…what? Would they provide door-to-door service, just because I asked them nicely? Would they ignore me, which was more likely? Dispose of me quickly and quietly, likelier still?

Or, likeliest of all, would my gall in assuming I could ask anything of them secure me an eternal place in this timeless space, neither alive nor dead, just here, condemned to be the puppet of those silent demons, my only other company fading memories of life and futile dreams of death, for all time and no time?

That must not be. It would never be. I had one other option. It was really no option at all, since it violated even the laws of the strange physics that held sway here, but it required action, and for every action there is an equal lack of inaction. That is my First Law of Sanity, which Newton is not around to correct.

If I was to meet my death this day, I would not stand here cowering, waiting for it to find me. I would march into its arena and stare it in the face.

I started to walk outside.

An elf-thing was there.

He was standing in the doorway. He had not walked there; he had just appeared there, and was staring at me in much the same way Mr. Claus had. His almost-human face was without expression, yet I had to force myself to look into his onyx-black, unblinking, vaguely serpentine eyes.

He was the one I had to ask, so I tried to do so, but every drop of moisture in my mouth had evaporated. My tongue could form no words, only idiot sounds.

But as if he had plucked the very thought from my brain, he jabbed a finger, not at me, but at the wall behind me.

The portal was there, but beyond it was not the room where I had held palaver with Mr. Claus. I saw, with an encroaching sense of hopeless terror, that it was an unlit room of a house, near the center of which was an artificial Christmas tree.

On the floor in front of me were the familiar costume and bulging red sack.

This, I saw in an instant of horrific clarity, was the reason the priest had not followed me back through the wall. The elf-things were willing to allow me to go back to my world, but only on their terms. Similarly, they were willing to release Mr. Claus, whatever his given name had been, from his bondage in this frozen neverwhere...

But only if I took his place.

That was why I was brought here. Had Mr. Claus known that? Was that why he seemed to have been expecting me?

But why me? Why had the loathsome little creatures chosen me?

Why they had was immaterial. That they had was plain. I was now to be the incarnation of Christmas.

Santa Claus is dead. Long live Santa Claus!

Abandoning all reason—for what was reason in this place of nightmare?—I took off running at the elf-thing. I was three times his size; surely I could overpower him and escape.

But who was to say that he was alone? Or that there was any place to escape to? Or that my greater size conferred any advantage? The story told for generations had it backward. These small, silent creatures were the masters of this realm. I had already seen what they could do, and I could not doubt that what I had seen was only a sampling of the powers they possessed.

I could not stop to think about any of this, or all was lost.

Just before I would have reached him, the elf-thing stepped aside faster than any human could have. I had expected to collide with him, and the effort of compensating for the fact that he was no longer in my way nearly sent me sprawling, but I kept my footing and ran past him.

Out of the corner of my eye I saw...I did not dare look straight at him to be sure, but he seemed to be smirking. He was letting me go because he knew I could not get away, but it would entertain him to watch me try.

The landscape was stark and forbidding as ever, but no one waited to ambush me. Getting what I could of my bearings, remembering the direction from which I had approached the cottage, I headed back that way.

I ran to the hill I remembered as the one from the top of which I had first seen the house. At the base of the hill was a tunnel, large enough for me to enter without having to stoop, which meant it was not a tunnel for *their* use. Was I meant to find and enter it? A rat in a maze?

I saw nothing past the mouth of the tunnel. If I went inside, what would I find? Would it be my salvation, or my doom?

Whichever it was, there was no other way. Mr. Claus had only been transported once from the open air, and that had been from

311

my world to this. His experience on that occasion was not one I was anxious to duplicate. I had likewise been brought from there to here. Other roads did exist, but they all seemed to be one-way. It was the tunnel or nothing.

As I neared the mouth of the tunnel, I felt again what I had felt when I first walked to the door of the workshop: a *presence*, as of no creature I could describe or imagine, an evil and indescribably ancient thing. For an instant I was certain that if I walked into the mouth of the tunnel, it would close behind me as the brick wall had, and I would feel myself being rent and shredded by gargantuan teeth, washed down an immense throat, and digested in a Cyclopean stomach.

If I could be grateful for one small favor, it was that no stalactites or stalagmites ringed the mouth of the cave. The sight would have given substance to the illusion, made it stronger than my desperate resolve. In its absence, I just managed to force myself to go inside.

I was soon smothered by impenetrable darkness. I put out my hands far enough that they could warn me of any obstacles that would pose an immediate threat, but not far enough, I hoped, that either any elf-things that might be lying in wait, or anything that might live in this Plutonian night, could lunge out and grab them.

Soon I felt the ground slope downward, but I could not turn back. The horrors I could see were no better than those I could not, and the sunlight outside, though strong and bright, was as devoid of comfort as it was of warmth.

The walls began to curve this way and that, following the twists and turns in the path, which continued always downward. But I had chosen this course and had to see it through to the end, whatever form that end took.

Then something did happen. It was not what I had feared. It was worse.

The tunnel was getting smaller. I struck my head on an unseen protrusion of the ceiling and fell back. I got up, carefully, and crouched down. My head scraped the ceiling again, so I had to crouch down further. Soon I could no longer walk, but was forced to crawl. And still the distance between ceiling and ground continued to shrink, so that I had to slither.

Obviously if the tunnel became so small that further progress was impossible, I would have to back out until I could stand, then make my way up and out. My only remaining choices would then be to return to the cottage, to wander the tundra, or to stand where I was. Doing any of those things entailed doing the one thing I was determined not to do: admit my fate was unavoidable and meekly await my demise.

As long as I could move forward, there was a thin, frail hope. I held fast to that hope, knowing it might crumble to dust at any instant, and propelled myself onward.

The path was straight for a while, then it curved again to the right. When it straightened, I could see a pinprick of light directly ahead. Whatever it could be, whatever it might mean, I had no choice but to go on, toward it.

The tunnel did not get any smaller, so I could continue to slither. However, neither did it get any larger, so I could do nothing else. The ground beneath me continued its downward trajectory. The light shone there, unflickering and unmoving, so I knew at least that it was not merely some bioluminescent insect. It seemed to beckon and mock me at the same time.

It was unlikely that it was an exit from the tunnel, since by this time I might have been as much as half a kilometer underground. That was a terrestrial measurement and of no use here, but what else could it be?

I refused to consider possible answers to that question. Through a continual effort of my fading will, my focus was as narrow as that point of light. I permitted nothing else to intrude upon my thoughts, so that I might retain my sanity.

Retain it for what?

That was another question not worth considering.

I closed my mind to whatever arbitrary sense of the passage of time I had left. The physical effort required to keep moving and that point of light were now the sum of my consciousness. Nothing else existed.

In the absolute silence of the cavern I was able to hear the beating of my heart. I noted the fact but did not dwell upon it. Only the light... the unchanging light...

No. Not unchanging. It was...

Pulsing? Yes. Perhaps I had been too far away to notice it before, but the light was brightening in rhythmic pulses. A regular beat, almost like the beating of a heart.

That was precisely what it was. This eldritch light was pulsing *to the rhythm of my own heart!*

This observation, too, I tried to store away—it meant nothing to me now—but I could not. Having long since reached the limits of what I could process, I had now reached the limits of what I could ignore. My heart began to beat faster and stronger, and the light in identical sympathy pulsed faster and brighter.

My breathing came faster and shallower. I felt myself going lightheaded…I could not start hyperventilating…I had to get control of myself…

I felt the thudding of my heart throughout my body. I pushed myself to the light. Only the light…the light was there…the light was all…so bright…hurting my eyes…had to close them…could not… heart pounding…would soon burst…tried to look away…could not… no room to turn…had to reach the light…stop it…before it blinded me…before the end…before everything was…

Darkness.

The light was gone. I could see nothing. Had I been blinded?

As awareness returned to me piece by piece, I became aware that I was still prone, but on my back, not on my stomach. And I was not lying on cold rock, but on…a mattress? I pressed down with my right hand. The surface gave a little. Yes, it did feel like a mattress.

Then I realized my eyes were closed. Slowly, uneasily, I opened them.

White ceiling. Fluorescent lights.

I moved my head from side to side. Small room. Single door. Bare white walls. Small bed, white sheets, thin white blanket.

I tried to sit up. Couldn't. I tried to call out. Only a hoarse croak escaped my parched throat.

And I was tired. So very tired. Wanted to sleep, but was afraid to. Might not wake up. Couldn't keep my eyes open. Had to stay awake. Find out where I was. How I'd gotten here. If I was alone.

Eyes closed anyway. Forced them open. Heard the door open.

Someone came in. Dressed in white. A woman. Normal-sized. Not an elf-thing. Looked human. Did that mean she was?

Saw her look at me. Heard her say something. Didn't understand it.

Had to stay awake. Had to talk to her. Had to get answers.

But so sleepy…so sleepy…so…

"So you're finally awake. You had us a little worried for a while."

I was fatigued, but no longer sleepy. My mind was clearer. I had opened my eyes and seen the same woman at my bedside, a woman I now recognized as a nurse.

"Where am I?" I asked, though I could see I was in a hospital.

"Your next-door neighbor saw you lying unconscious in your driveway and called an ambulance. They brought you here with a nasty bruise on your forehead. You've suffered a mild concussion, but you don't seem to have any other injuries. You might have hit your head on your garage door. My brother-in-law did that once. Do you remember what happened?"

"Yes," I said, "but maybe I should wait for the doctor."

"Why is that?"

"Because I have a story to tell, but it'll take a while, and I don't want to keep you from your other patients."

"Oh, don't worry about that. My shift is almost over. I could use a good story."

"I did warn you," I said, and told her everything, from colliding with the garage door to seeing the blinding light at the end. My adventures in that other place had imprinted themselves upon my memory in exacting detail, but I made a concerted effort to relate them in a detached and clinical manner. I had known how insane it would sound, and I knew that any extraneous emotion, any attempt to describe how it had *felt*, would further undermine my credibility.

I was grateful for the glass of water at my bedside. It was empty when I had finished.

She listened in silence while I talked, and went on looking at me for a few seconds after I stopped. Abruptly she stood up and said, "You're right, I should get the doctor. Now that you're awake, he should examine you."

"Nurse, believe me, I know how it sounds. But I don't have the imagination it would take to make up a story like that. I'm not a creative person. I'm dull as dishwater, really. Any of my students, anyone who's ever known me, would tell you that. And as incredible as they were, the things I experienced do conform to established theories of physics."

"I'm in no position to agree or disagree with you," she said. "The doctor has a much stronger background in science than I do. In fact, I think he either majored or minored in physics. He'd be the one to judge the merits of your story."

She was gone before I could say another word.

I did not have long to wait before a man came in, introduced himself as Dr. Salinger, and said, "I understand you've had an interesting experience."

As I repeated my story, he took notes and asked me questions that illuminated both his knowledge of science and his willingness to consider the plausibility of what I had seen and done. However, since he would not answer this question until I asked it, and because I needed to know, I said, "You don't believe me, do you?"

He stopped writing, stared me in the face, and said, "I'm going to be candid with you. I believe that *you* believe these events happened as you say they did. But I do not, and cannot, lend any credence to your belief. I'm not a psychologist, but if I were, my professional opinion might be that your training in physics and the proximity of the Christmas holiday have combined to create an intense desire to recapture some of the innocence of childhood, along with some of its myths. The concussion you suffered was the catalyst to bring these desires, repressed in your subconscious mind, to the surface in the form of a vivid dream, which your mind expressed in terms of principles of quantum mechanics as a way of making the experience more comfortable to you. To protect itself, the mind will often try to blunt the more frightening aspects of an extended dream by integrating mundane real-life details. It was possibly also an attempt to redefine your life in more agreeable terms."

He had hesitated for the briefest instant before saying "dream" the first time. I knew why. He had almost said "delusion."

"Physically, you seem to be fine. We'll keep you overnight for observation, and in the morning I'll refer you to a colleague who can more fully analyze your experience."

He started toward the door, but turned back and said, "By the way, don't worry about your costume. The paramedics brought it in with you."

My mouth went dry, but I managed to say, "My costume?"

"Yes. Your Santa Claus costume. It was lying next to you on your driveway. It's in that bag there."

He pointed at the corner, then left me alone with it.

I turned to look. There it was, a trash bag on the floor with the telltale red and white spilling out of it. I snapped my head away, but which was worse? Not seeing it or seeing it? And if I started screaming for someone to take it away and incinerate it, that would do little to convince anyone of my mental stability.

For an instant I seized on the possibility that my neighbor had left the costume as some sort of joke, but I knew it was nothing of the sort. If he had left anything next to me, it would have been a copy of "The Watchtower," not a Santa suit.

The elves.

That was the only explanation left. They had let me go, for now, for their own reasons. But they had marked me.

It was ludicrous to think I could explain the suit to Dr. Salinger or anyone else. No one would ever believe me. Why should they? If someone had told me a story like that, would I have believed it? But this had not been *someone*, it had been *me*! It was not a question of belief. I knew what had happened! I knew what I saw, what I heard, where I was! Those were *memories*, not "redefinitions" or "integrations"!

Not that it would make any difference if someone did believe. No one could stop the elves from taking me whenever they wished.

The elf-creatures would have had thousands of years, by our reckoning, to construct innumerable apertures—back doors—into our world, in addition to the portal they used strictly for entering living rooms in the dead of night. Their reasons were unguessable, but it was enough to know they possessed the skill to do whatever they wished to do. The base of my garage door must have been one such aperture, and by striking it I had opened it and fallen through, like Alice down the rabbit hole—no! Wrong analogy! That was a fantasy concocted for children, and science had nothing to do with Alice's adventures!

I hit my head hard enough on that protrusion of rock in the tunnel to give myself the bruise and the concussion the doctors and nurses had seen. As I contemplated the nature of the tunnel, I began to understand, to a small degree, what it really was. The path itself had sloped neither down nor up, but I was going from that higher dimension down to this one, and my limited form had interpreted the metaphysical descent as a physical one. In the same way, the dimensions of the tunnel constricted as I got closer to my own plane of existence, so tightly bound in four-dimensional space-time, that has no room for the magic (well, why *not* call it that?) that is as natural to the elf-creatures as walking is to us.

Even the materialization of the costume and bag on the floor of the cottage could be explained. I had gotten an idea of how fast the creatures could move. They live in a place where time is meaningless. It follows that they could easily manipulate my perception of time, with the result that they could move from one room to another and back again before my eyes could register that anything had happened. Isn't that essentially how the portals work, just on a smaller scale? Hasn't relativity proved that time is not absolute? Isn't time as we know it just an extension of reality as we know it?

I had come back through the portal at the base of my garage door and collapsed unconscious, exhausted from the physical and emotional rigors of the journey. My neighbor had not seen me reappear, but had seen me lying there and made the natural assumption from the available facts. Even if he had also seen the costume, he would have said nothing about it.

Dr. Salinger had said he was not a psychologist. There was little doubt that his colleague was. Nor was there any doubt that if I repeated the unvarnished truth to him, he would filter it through the prism of his own experience and training and draw the only conclusion he could: that I was delusional, and my insistence on believing my delusions to be real was a dangerous sign and had to be undone, with confinement, with therapy, with antipsychotic drugs if necessary.

My lucidity, my lack of anxiety or of any undue emotion, would not persuade him. It would probably do more harm than good. One of the oldest tenets of psychology is that only a madman is convinced of his sanity. Thus, powerful medications and other extreme measures were needed to undermine his belief, which was as unshakeable as... well, as a child's belief in Santa Claus.

The colleague would come to see me in the morning. I had to use the rest of this day to determine exactly what I would say to him and how I would say it. The wrong answers would send me to a psychiatric hospital, a purgatory as bad in its way as that to which the ancient priest had been consigned.

I would work out how to tell the psychologist what he wanted to hear, in such a way that he would not recognize that he was being told what he wanted to hear. I would even raise one of the points he surely would, before he did. The priest had been taken to that other place from fourth-century Turkey, and his only company since then has been creatures that never speak, at least not to him. His forays back into this world are brief and always without interaction. How then could he have learned modern English?

The elf-beings are probably telepathic. That is not so difficult to believe, given the other things they can do. And it explains why they never talk, and how they always know the instant he is finished leaving the presents. There is no factual basis for telepathy among humans, but science has a fairly good understanding of how it would work in theory. A given word in a given person's native language stimulates a synaptic response in the person's brain, cultural connotations aside. Telepathy would enable any two people to speak without the aid of a translator, because each person's brainwaves could be altered to interpret the words he hears in his own language.

I would say none of this, but would attribute whatever I had told Dr. Salinger to weariness, or a headache, or whatever. I would play on the psychologist's sympathy.

Then I would sleep—I would ask for a sleeping pill if necessary—so that I would be refreshed, alert, and in full possession of my faculties. My mind had to be operating at peak efficiency if I hoped to joust successfully with a psychologist, and that was the least of what awaited.

Permitting myself any sleep the following night was not to be considered. That was Christmas Eve, and so I would keep a fearful watch.

Santa Claus was coming to town.

THE BEAST IN THE WALLS

The horror began, as it so often does, with a series of mundane events. Marlene Finster was making supper when her husband Christopher stalked into the kitchen and demanded to know why it wasn't on the table already.

Without looking at him, which she could not stand to do anymore, she explained that the price of potatoes at the local farmer's market had been raised beyond what they could afford, and the ones she was peeling had come from the supermarket across town. The extra time spent in getting them was the reason for the delay.

He grunted in reply and went away, leaving her to enjoy the last few minutes of peace she would know in this life.

The meal passed in the complete silence that made shared company almost bearable in the Finster household. Andrew, the seventeen-year-old son, wolfed down his food as he always did. He didn't care how it tasted, only about minimizing his time at the table. Christopher chewed with exaggerated care, examining each bite with what he believed was his refined palate so he could criticize something afterward. Marlene was the balance of their extremes, simply eating, neither too quickly nor too slowly.

Andrew was the first one finished, and was already out of his chair when his father said, "Park it, Andrew," surprising the son and the wife. He often shouted at Andrew but never addressed him evenly as he had just done, and Marlene could not remember the last time he had addressed him by name.

Andrew parked it but stared with undisguised hatred at the man who was his father through no choice or fault of his own, as he often reminded his mother. She was watching Christopher also, the remainder of her own meal forgotten, and they both waited for him to swallow what he had in his mouth.

It was only after he had taken a long pull of his beer and wiped his mouth in the dainty manner so incongruous with his brutal nature that he announced he had sold the house. They were moving to a town at the other end of the state.

Marlene was too stunned to make a sound, but she didn't have to. Andrew admirably filled the gap her silence left. He screamed his disbelief and outrage. He pounded the table, rattling the silver and toppling the glasses, and cursed Christopher in every way he could think of. His tirade was nerve-jangling but not out of character; he had inherited his father's volcanic temper along with his heavy, sullen features.

Marlene was baffled by Christopher's reaction. She had assumed he would scream right back, but he only sat there looking at Andrew, the ghost of a smile playing at the corners of his mouth, as if he expected this torrent of abuse and enjoyed it.

When Andrew finally wound down, Christopher said, "Decision's made. Go to your room and start packing."

"I'm not going."

"Oh yes you are. Believe it. And you're not going to say another word about it, or I'll put you in the wall."

Marlene convulsively gripped the underside of the table and prayed that just this once, Christopher's threat would prove to be an idle one.

Andrew got up, slamming the table with the flat of his hand, and stormed out of the room. He left his dishes on the table, but this time Marlene didn't tell him to put them in the sink. Christopher watched him leave, then went right on smacking his food and picking his teeth as if nothing had happened.

Marlene pushed her food around for several minutes, trying to work up the nerve to ask how he had managed to sell the house. What she really wanted to ask was how much he got for it, but she knew the answer she would get: *That's not your business, so don't ask again.* She could only hope the buyer had at least a passing acquaintance with Christopher and thus knew not to give him anything up front. Whatever money was in his hand by sundown would be poured down his gullet by midnight.

When not staring down at her plate, she cast apprehensive glances at the far corner, and at the wall behind it.

Back when Christopher's hands knew how to hold something other than a shot glass, he had helped to build this house. Thinking of the day when he would have a child, he left a hollow space in one of the walls. It would be a boy, of course, and boys got out of line now and then. But all they needed was a firm hand to slap them down. For Andrew, beginning when he was two and had learned the word "No," that firm hand came in the form of a few minutes shut up in this space, behind the removable panel, alone in the suffocating dark.

Well, not quite alone. There was a beast back there too.

Oh yes, Christopher had told his terrified son. A real live *thing*, from twenty thousand fathoms, from the black lagoon, or maybe from outer space—wherever it had come from, it was here now. It stayed in the dark because it was so horrible that anyone who saw it would go stark raving mad. It stayed in the dark, in *their* dark, roaming the spaces behind the walls, always happy to keep company with little boys who misbehaved.

Christopher told this story and Andrew listened, trembling and whimpering, on the verge of wetting his pants. He looked at his mother, pleading with his eyes for her to say *It's all right, Andrew. There's no monster back there. Your father's just teasing you.* But she never said a word, and the expression on her face never gave any sign that she would, because a warning look from Christopher made it clear that this was his little secret. Her face was too familiar with the back of his calloused hand to betray his secrets.

Christopher soon found, as he had known he would, that it only took a well-timed glance at the wall to do wonders for Andrew's attitude. Specifically, he held his tongue and did as he was told when Christopher was around, and what did he care what the boy did when he wasn't? Boys would be boys, after all. Just not on his watch.

But as Andrew grew, and as Christopher went from picking him up and putting him behind the wall to dragging him behind it to manhandling him behind it, this method of discipline became less frequent. It stopped altogether when Andrew got strong enough that it was no longer a foregone conclusion which of them would end up back there. One such wrestling match ended with his father trying to save face by saying, "Fine, do what you want, you'll probably end up in jail anyway in spite of everything I've done for you, you spoiled ungrateful punk."

That had been three years ago, not long after Andrew's fourteenth birthday. Since then there had been no threat of the wall. Until now.

In the end, Marlene did not ask Christopher about the house or anything else. She finished eating, put their dishes in the sink, then retreated to her room and left him alone with his bottle of Guinness. That was fine with him.

Two hours later he burst into Andrew's room. Andrew was sprawled on his bed leafing through a *Rolling Stone*, stereo blasting, and chose not to acknowledge his guest.

Christopher shut off the stereo. No reaction. Andrew could ignore him as easily at zero decibels as he could at a hundred.

"I told you to get packed."

"And I told you to get bent."

"You don't lip off to me, boy. Not ever. You know what I think? I think some time in the wall would teach you some respect."

Andrew tossed the magazine aside and moved in on Christopher until he was nose to nose with him. The look on his face almost, though not quite, made Christopher take a step back.

"Go on and try it, old man. I'll feed you to that beast, and he'll have indigestion for a week."

The days when he could be cowed by the threat of the wall were obviously long past. Christopher supposed he knew this and decided to switch gears. Looking around the room, he saw how to do it.

"Nice laptop," he said casually.

Andrew shrugged.

"What's something like that set you back?"

"Enough."

"At least," he said with a crooked smile. "Not the kind of thing you can swing on a waiter's tips, though, is it?"

Andrew's eyes narrowed. "What are you getting at?"

"Cut the innocent act, boy. You were born and raised in this town, and I never heard you say one good thing about it. I would've thought you'd be breaking down the door to get out, but you want to stay. Why?"

"I got my reasons," he said, and started for the door. Christopher did a quick sidestep and cut him off.

"Yeah, I know you got your reasons. And they come in little baggies, don't they?"

Andrew's mouth twitched. That was all the answer Christopher needed.

"You think I don't know why you want to stay? Huh? You think I don't know where you get your spending cash? You think I don't know what you're really doing when your mother thinks you're reading to sick kids or whatever line of guff you feed her?"

"So what are you gonna do, rat me out?" There was no fear in Andrew's question, only scorn.

"Nah. The cops'd need evidence, and I don't think you're that stupid. Of course," Christopher went on, rubbing his chin, "if they happened to get an anonymous call one day, say while you were at school or work, and they came over and happened to find something…"

"Something you planted, maybe?"

"Stranger things have happened."

"Unless I 'choose' to join you on this little trip. That's where this is going, isn't it?"

"Bull's eye. And it's where you're going."

"I don't think so, old man. You wouldn't have a leg to stand on. All I'd have to do is say the stuff was yours and you were hiding it in my room. Who do you think they'd believe? It's not like you're an upstanding member of the community."

Christopher grimaced. That was true, and he knew it. "Look, never mind all that. You're doing this and that's the end of it."

"Who's gonna make me? You?"

Whether it was the question itself or the disdainful way in which it was asked, a valve opened in Christopher's head and the last of his restraint poured out through it. He clamped one hand on Andrew's arm and the other around his neck. "Yeah! I am!" he shouted. "You better believe I am!"

Taken by surprise, Andrew was pushed back almost to the wall before he got his leverage. A vicious struggle followed, until Andrew slipped on a pizza box and banged his head on the wall hard enough to daze him. That gave Christopher just enough time to open the panel, shove Andrew inside, and close it again.

"You don't want to pack up your stuff?" he yelled at the wall. "Then your mother will! And she'll throw out all this junk while she's at it!"

"You're dead when I get out of here, old man!" Andrew roared, pounding on the panel. "I'm gonna ram my fist down your throat and yank out your rotten stinking guts! And then I'll shove 'em up your—"

But Christopher had turned Andrew's stereo back on, lowered the volume to a level that wouldn't make the windows vibrate, and left the room.

Marlene heard all this from the illusory safety of her room. She heard, and against all desire and will, she remembered.

Remembered the sound of Andrew's tiny fists on the wall, drumming a frantic staccato like the pounding of a terror-stricken heart, his blubbering voice, muffled by the paneling and the drywall but every frightened syllable still clear. *Please let me out of here! I promise I'll never be bad again! Please don't let the beast get me!* Marlene, half-mad with anxiety, would beg Christopher to let him out, appealing to his mercy, knowing he had none, and when he finally did, Andrew would run sobbing into her arms. Christopher always watched this with a satisfied smirk and then left to reward himself with another bottle or ten of Ireland's finest.

She would hold Andrew, rocking him and cooing in his ear. She listened to his garbled, half-intelligible monologue as he told her how he'd seen the yellow eyes of the beast, had felt its breath on his little neck. As often as not, that night would find her scrunched up in his bed, plotting how she would make Christopher pay, or at least take Andrew and get away.

There were nights when she lay there, slipping off into sleep, and she heard sounds on the other side of the wall, sounds that had nothing to do with Andrew because he was sound asleep beside her. Part of her almost hoped it really was some nameless batrachian horror but knew it was only Christopher, fresh from a bender, dropped off by a cab or by his drinking buddies. Sometimes he had to work his way around the house before he found the door.

Some nights she felt hot, fetid breath on her neck and clamped her eyes shut, knowing that if she opened them she would be staring into inhuman eyes, yellow and curdled with ancient madness. She knew this with the certainty that comes on the leathery wings of the darkest hours of the night. Or if not with certainty, at least with a twisted hope, thinking that whatever might live its unnatural life beyond human sight couldn't possibly be any worse than the man responsible for her own unlivable life.

She remembered all this, listening to Andrew's pounding. She knew that what drove him now was not terror but rage, but she still pleaded his forgiveness in a voice he couldn't hear...

And then the pounding stopped.

She sat up, straining to hear.

"Andrew?" she called. "Andrew?"

"He's fine," Christopher called from the other room.

But he was not fine. She knew that even before the wall shuddered with a blow that did not come from any human fist.

"*Andrew?*" she shrieked.

Then Andrew yelled something, and now even Christopher stood up, not because of the words but because there was primal fear in them. Anything that could scare Andrew that badly had to be very bad indeed. He ran into the room with Marlene on his heels, flung open the panel, and shot out his arms to keep Andrew from falling to the floor.

Christopher called the paramedics, and a few minutes after they got there, they told the Finsters what the Finsters had already known.

Andrew was dead.

Marlene sat on the floor, cradling his head in her lap. She stroked a cooling, hardening face, looked earnestly into unseeing eyes, and whispered apologies over and over into ears that heard only the siren song of the infinite beyond. Meanwhile, Christopher talked to the paramedics, answering their questions, accepting their sympathies, feeding them the right doses of confusion and despair at just the right times. He played them like a concert pianist, and soon the paramedics bore their son away. After that there were no more visits, from the police or anyone else.

There were no visits because Christopher hadn't told them what Andrew yelled from behind the wall. Marlene, her tongue now fettered as much by her inexpressible grief as by years of old-fashioned spousal training, told them nothing. But she would be haunted to her own grave by his last words, which were:

"There's something in here!"

Later that night she asked Christopher, "How can you just…" but could not finish the question. He knew what it was, and answered it without looking up from his packing.

"Well, there's sure no reason to stay here now, is there? The boy should've been more careful, that's all. There's all kinds of holes in the outside walls. Maybe a spider or snake got in and bit him. Got their own special poison out here, they do."

"That was no spider I heard," she snapped. "I know you heard it too. That…that *sound*, like something huge was pounding on—"

He slammed his suitcase shut and stared at her. "So what are you telling me? What? That there really *is* a beast in the walls? The boy was wise to that—"

"His name was Andrew. You do remember his name, don't you?"

He ignored the remark and went on. "He was wise to that story by the time he was six. But he still had to be put back there. You know that. Now, what happened was a tragedy and all, but the thing to do is put it behind us. You'll see. By the time we get to the new house—"

"No."

That stopped him. She hadn't dared to say no to him about anything for so long that he needed a moment to process the strange sound.

"What did you say?"

"I said no, Christopher. You do what you want. I'm staying here."

She was prepared for him to start yelling or slapping her into line, but not for what he did do. He started laughing.

"Oh, that's rich. You sound just like the boy. He thought he was staying too. But at least he would've had an outside chance of doing all right. He—well, never mind. You don't need to know what his second job was."

Marlene already knew what Andrew's second job had been. The main reason she was able to tolerate living with his father for so long was that she was one of his best customers. But if Christopher believed he alone knew about that part of Andrew's life, she saw no reason to disabuse him of the notion.

"Anyway," he was saying, "there's a perfectly rational explanation. You just can't see it because you're a woman and women don't know the first thing about rational. But what most likely happened was, this whatever-it-was bit him, and he jerked up out of reflex and slammed his body against the wall because he had nowhere to go. He was a good-sized kid, and if his body hit hard enough, there's no reason it wouldn't have made a sound like that. See? Doesn't that make sense?"

She said nothing, just stared at him. She knew from long experience that it would be pointless to try to reason with him.

"Glad you think so." Whether he was being sarcastic or took her silence for agreement, Marlene neither knew nor cared. "So like I was saying, we got no reason to stay here, and every reason to go. What I was going to say at dinner before the boy started shouting his fool head off was, the reason we're moving is I got a new job. A *good* job. Twice what I'm making here. I got a buddy that works at the company and he put in a good word for me with the people upstairs. Thing is, they can only hold the job open for another week and then they gotta fill it, they don't care who with. That's why I have to be there, so I can be the one doing the filling.

"Come on, Marlene," he continued in the gentle voice he still knew how to use when it suited him. "You know there's nothing here for you. There never was. But there, in a bigger city…well, who knows? But you'll never know if you don't try, right?"

"Right," she said tonelessly.

"Good. Glad we got that straight. Now go and get me a beer like a good girl, willya?"

She went and got him a beer, like a good girl.

She never told a soul what happened after that—except Andrew, of course, the first time she put flowers on his grave.

Christopher wasn't the one to do the filling after all. He was never seen in either town again. Nobody knew what became of him. Nobody cared enough to ask. It was generally assumed he had run off with whatever floozy was dumb enough to have him, and it was generally agreed that it was the best thing he could have done for Marlene. Maybe after a decent waiting period, some of the men would drop by, see how she was doing. Why not? Even after everything she'd been through with him, there was nothing wrong with her looks.

For once, she was grateful he had been such a dedicated drinker. It was easy to pour the baking soda into one of the widenecked bottles he liked. He had gulped it down, his taste buds already dulled in his intoxicated stupor and past noticing the oddly grainy texture. When the gas filled his stomach, stretched it out, and finally burst it open, she found it in herself to spare one pitying look at his bloated corpse— after giving it a good swift kick. Or two, or three, or fourteen, or fifty. Just to make sure he was really dead.

She never went in Andrew's room again after that night. She almost convinced herself it was only her extreme physical and emotional fatigue that allowed her mind to play such a funny trick on her. Being in the dark long enough...why, you could see just about anything. Who had known that better than Andrew? She had only looked into the back of the hollow space for a moment and she'd been preoccupied. So what if she thought she had seen, suspended six and a half or seven feet above the floor, a pair of pale yellow dots that might have looked like glowing eyes? Did that have to mean anything? If snakes and spiders could find their way back there, why not fireflies? She asked Andrew these questions and they had a good laugh.

Because now her house really did have a beast in the walls.

A dead and moldering beast, but a beast nonetheless.